THE OTHER WITHIN

"This book is a well, a portal, a very carefully tended path into the mysteries of myth. It is also a map, a worthwhile one for learning how to transcend the complexities and challenges faced by individuals on entering this Earth. It is a must-read for those wanting to understand boldness of heart in the face of adversity."

MIGUEL RIVERA, MUSICIAN, MENTOR, TRANSLATOR, AND TEACHER

"*The Other Within* is liberating. Deardorff frees us from the oppressive weight of the ideal, the perfect, and draws our gaze toward the borderlands where we catch glimpses of what has been outcast. The trail that Deardorff invites us to follow through the brambles of the psyche is not easy or comforting. His is a work of descent, an invitation into the depths of soul. It is here that we discover the medicine needed by our struggling world. We enter the hive of vulnerability, sorrow, uncertainty, and shame and recover our shared humanity. This book is a blessing to anyone who ever felt estranged from the shimmering world."

FRANCIS WELLER, MFT, AUTHOR OF *THE WILD EDGE OF SORROW*

"Deardorff's masterpiece weaves a tempestuous spell that tosses us into shadowy depths where we might encounter that strange and strangely familiar one within who is, blessedly, an outcast from the life-destroying, conformist-consumer culture precisely because they understand their destined role in shaping the mysterious new world calling to us in the night. *The Other Within* is one of the few books I recommend to those learning to guide others on the descent to soul."

BILL PLOTKIN, PH.D., AUTHOR OF *SOULCRAFT* AND *WILD MIND*

"I read the first sentence and was stopped in my tracks: 'Denial is contagious and facts are an addictive substitute for truth.' I told Daniel that I could spend my whole life on just this sentence. When Deardorff writes about walking among the ashes, it reminds us that there is a cost to the wisdom journey; there is a cost to freedom. This true and crooked path has gifts for us no matter the wound. With Trickster Wisdom through myths, he shows us the way deeper into ourselves and, by doing so, connects us more to each other."

QUANITA ROBERSON, COAUTHOR OF *THE INNERGROUND RAILROAD*

"Daniel Deardorff searches through our mythic inheritance for the radical otherness that allows the human soul to find and handle the contradictions and oppositions inherent in all of life. With insight and wit, he finds the beauty within disfigurement, the worthiness of crooked things, and the essential genius hidden in the outcast. He offers an imagination of the transgressive, an inventive trickster intelligence that revalues the necessary otherness found both in the margins of culture and in the depths of the individual soul."

MICHAEL MEADE, AUTHOR OF *AWAKENING THE SOUL*

"As I said to fellow wordsmith Michael Ventura just before I went on stage to play drums with Danny, 'maybe Deardorff should be Jim Morrison's replacement. He won't be wearing leather pants, but his depth of soul is a match.'"

JOHN DENSMORE, AUTHOR OF *THE SEEKERS, THE DOORS: UNHINGED,* AND *RIDERS ON THE STORM*

"The storyteller casts spells. The spells that Daniel Deardorff wove spell out the dark myths of othering that rule the world we have created and that warps our relationship to one another and to the Earth. It is most often from the margin or from exile, from the othered, the deviant (physical, racial, ethnic, religious, sexual) that enlightenment and the prophet comes. Never have we more needed to hear the voices of our healer storytellers such as Danny tell and elucidate for us the healing myths."

RAFAEL JESÚS GONZÁLEZ, POET LAUREATE OF BERKELEY, CALIFORNIA

"The boundlessness of Daniel Deardorff's soul, the ferocity and tenderness of his heart rang like a struck bell within each person who came upon his path. In him the divine was constantly working on itself, puzzling its favorite koan: In what sort of body, in what kind of creature, can I most exuberantly dance? This lucid book masquerades as a work of scholarship. Watch it waltz you over the cliff."

DAVID ABRAM, AUTHOR OF *THE SPELL OF THE SENSUOUS* AND *BECOMING ANIMAL*

"Because the important figure of the Trickster has eluded many in our modern culture, I urge you to read Daniel Deardorff on the subject. In this amazing study of the real and imagined 'other,' he has given a valuable roadmap to the profound regions of Story."

GIOIA TIMPANELLI, AUTHOR OF *SOMETIMES THE SOUL*

"At any moment when it seems like we have squandered the spiritual journey and feel like an outcast, we might just stumble into unexpected illumination. Deardorff's *The Other Within* is a unique contribution to our understanding of the inner quest. It shows us how to see the extraordinary beauty in our brokenness."

JONATHAN YOUNG, PH.D., PSYCHOLOGIST,
FOUNDING CURATOR OF THE JOSEPH CAMPBELL ARCHIVES

"*The Other Within* challenges our understanding to grasp not only the conundrum of our mutually destructive impulses but the very roots of the human imagination. Deardorff's book will reward the seeker with its kaleidoscopic range of knowledge to explain that the fearsome stranger approaching is our own visage in the mirror."

PAUL KLEYMAN, NATIONAL COORDINATOR OF THE
JOURNALISTS NETWORK ON GENERATIONS

"Unflinching, sometimes uncomfortable, always brave and provocative, this is a book like no other."

ELLEN DISSANAYAKE, AUTHOR OF *HOMO AESTHETICUS*

"Daniel's polio made him crooked; his heart made him true. We all can be true if we listen to Daniel, not only with our ears but also with our hearts."

DR. RICHARD L. BRUNO, DIRECTOR OF THE
INTERNATIONAL CENTRE FOR POLIO EDUCATION

"The telling of myths is medicine for the soul. Danny is, thanks to his brilliant work in *The Other Within,* just an amazing medicine man the likes of whom will never be seen in this world again. If you had the opportunity to see and hear him, you know how blessed of a man he was and how he blessed all of us who had the privilege and honor to be in his presence. What a remarkable story weaver."

JOHN LEE, AUTHOR OF *ODD ONE OUT*
AND *THE FLYING BOY*

THE OTHER WITHIN

The Genius of Deformity
in Myth, Culture, and Psyche

Daniel Deardorff

Inner Traditions
Rochester, Vermont

Inner Traditions
One Park Street
Rochester, Vermont 05767
www.InnerTraditions.com

Text stock is SFI certified

First edition published in 2004 by White Cloud Press
Second edition published in 2009 by North Atlantic Books

Cataloging-in-Publication Data for this title is available from the Library of Congress

ISBN 978-1-64411-568-8 (print)
ISBN 978-1-64411-569-5 (ebook)

Printed and bound in the United States by Lake Book Manufacturing, Inc.
The text stock is SFI certified. The Sustainable Forestry Initiative® program
promotes sustainable forest management.

10 9 8 7 6 5 4 3 2 1

Text design and layout by Priscilla Harris Baker
This book was typeset in Garamond Premier Pro with Gill Sans, Nobel, and
Salden used as display typefaces

To send correspondence to the author of this book, mail a first-class letter to the
author c/o Inner Traditions • Bear & Company, One Park Street, Rochester, VT
05767, and we will forward the communication, or contact the author directly at
mythsingerlegacy.org.

For Robert Bly

December 23, 1926–November 21, 2021

Robert Bly and Daniel Deardorff, at Bly's conference on
the Great Mother and the New Father, cf. 2003

Note to the Reader Regarding a
Glossary of Terms in *The Other Within*

In this work, the author has coined several new words and definitions. He also uses lesser-known words and terms. A glossary is provided at the back of this book. The first time these words or terms appear they are marked with an asterisk.

◄○►

Songs written and performed by Daniel Deardorff
are accessible for readers at this URL.

https://mythsingerlegacy.org/the-other-within-songs

Contents

Thrown Out the Window

By Robert Simmons

IT WAS A WOUND that brought me to meet Daniel Deardorff. And I will always be grateful for it.

I was attending Robert Bly's Great Mother Conference in 2003 and had been thrilled by the beauty of the poetry, the music, and the amazing talks being presented. Among the early highlights were Daniel's singing, and his elucidation of his upcoming book, *The Other Within*. But my joy soon had a hole in it. A few derisive words, offhandedly spoken as a "joke" to the group, went into my heart like a sword. Suddenly I felt like an Outsider—excluded from the flock—among them but not one of them. Walking alone that afternoon, I caught sight of Daniel, sitting in his wheelchair, by himself in an open field. I went over to him, and soon we were talking. I told him about the hurt I was feeling.

Daniel grinned wryly and said, "Oh! Congratulations! You've been thrown out the window. All the most interesting people are out here."

That conversation led to a lifelong friendship between us, and much learning for me.

—◄o►—

Daniel was no stranger to woundedness. As a young child, he was one of the last people in America to be stricken by polio. The illness was bad, and it led to a series of disastrous experimental surgeries that left his body twisted and scarred. Yet this was not the only injury. The fact of his physical wounds triggered weird reactions in people, which kept them from actually seeing him. Hence, he was frequently, if unconsciously, consigned by them to Outsiderhood, to Otherness.

As we talked, Daniel spoke of offering one's wound up as a sacrificial gift. The wound/gift was to be envisioned as a barter with the divine, for we know not what. And what comes to us, whatever it is, must be viewed as the gift in return. This, he made clear, is the way to renounce victimhood.

Later during the conference, when Daniel played his guitar and sang one of his songs, "Burning Windows," I found myself weeping.

> *I understand the Angels now*
> *Who envy our lives here*
> *And all the great mistakes we make*
> *And all the things we fear*
> *For we are guided by our wounds*
> *As surely as the stars*
> *If you want to read your destiny*
> *It is written in your scars . . .*

These scars are what Deardorff calls "dire gifts." In reading this book, you will have the precious, daunting opportunity to reflect upon your own, and to see how they indeed shape your destiny. This journey requires a descent into life's contradictions, and the examination of one's wounds. If you find your courage, deep in what Daniel called "the nest of your loneliness," you may realize what it is to be fully alive.

—◄○►—

The Other Within is a dire gift of a book. It is difficult, in direct proportion to the truth it conveys. One's ego may squirm, but the soul will find deep nourishment. I will not try to summarize what Daniel says, for I can't match his eloquence. Nor would I want to spoil your epiphanies by warning you about what's coming. Dive in.

ROBERT SIMMONS

Acknowledgments

FIRST AND FOREMOST, to that great shifter of shapes, the many named and nameless one, maestro of the interval, initiator, implicator, most mythic of the mythworld dwellers: the terrible and majestic Genius of Deformity; for the Ravens in the daytime and Coyotes in the night who haunt the meadows and woods around my home, crying and calling and marking-out the passionate folly, the hidden wisdom, of our lives.

After the Divine come the Ancestors: for myth, Joseph Campbell, Mircea Eliade, and Robert Graves; for poetry, Patchen, Blake, Rilke, and Jimenez.

Third come the Teachers: for the mud-colored crow who showed the way, and his shrewd brother the rat, and for so many clues along the pathless way on how to survive the solitary leap of the "whole Divine night," Robert Bly. For the way of living story and staying true to the story-told, Michael Meade. For the thinking of the Heart and the poetic foundations of consciousness, James Hillman.

Then come colleagues and advocates: for attentive reading of the first version and for his publishing my essays, William Doty. For encouragement along the way, and memorable conversation over mussels and beer, David L. Miller. For challenging criticism that made the book grow, Christine Downing. And last, but not least, to Steven Scholl for bravely envisioning a path through which the Other Within might slip quietly back into the village.

Now come the true compañeros: for walking by my side and

watching my back, through so many canyons, over so many peaks, for weathering all my changes, the wrecking storms and the good times too, and for unflagging support, Dan Webster and Lou Pollack; for the bow of taking life and the cup of giving life, my cynocephalic brethren Jeffery Bodony, Benjamin Dennis, Juha Keranen, and all the Spirit Horse nephews.

Now, for my children, of the spirit and the flesh: you for whom, and before all others, this work is made, my beautiful daughters: Suni, Piper, Reszi, and Kaimi.

Lastly, my mother and father, brothers and sisters: for the grace you gave to believe in myself and for the sureness of my belonging in this world with you.

FOR THE SECOND EDITION I thank the readers, for your insights, questions, and complaints; you have helped strengthen the work. Robert Simmons and Kathy Warner of Heaven and Earth Publishing for their profound friendship and untrammeled advocacy. My daughter Piper Deardorff, for her devoted reading and understanding, and for her generous preparation of the glossary. And finally Judith-Kate Friedman, for the magic and music of "proximity," and for the thrilling realization that "it's never too late."

To all the above few, and others unnamed, I render my wholehearted thanks and beg forbearance of my betrayals, the endless correct and incorrect mistakes made herein and all along The Way.

D.D.
MOSSY ROCK, PORT TOWNSEND, WA
JULY 30, 2008

Acknowledgments and Notes
for the Third Edition

To Daniel Deardorff's words, above, I add:

Gratitude to all who carried these stories from ancient times to the present; to all who encouraged the author to take up his physical and digital pens and keyboard along with his drawing and music-making tools and story-telling instruments, and to all who have published his essays and editions of this book, most especially Inner Traditions • Bear & Company for their respectful rendering and expansion of this third edition.

My deepest gratitude to my compadres—Daniel Deardorff's brothers in myth and manifestation—Martin Shaw and Robert Simmons for adding their words to this edition; to them and to my elders, teachers, and colleagues in myth, story, and song with whose trust and guidance, in Deardorff's lineage, I steward his legacy: Robert and Ruth Bly, Gioia Timpanelli, Edie Hartshorne, Birch Gerke, Kathy Helen Warner, Pam McWethy, Brian and Sarah Rohr, and those above-mentioned by Daniel himself; and, deeply, my sisters in courage and creative reciprocity Suzan Goodman, Sasha Soreff, Wendy Botwin, Ann Holmes Redding, Quanita Roberson, Shawna Hett, Audrey di Mola, and Jackie Luna Levin. I give ongoing thanks to my kin of the Living World, especially those family and species who held vigil so fully upon Daniel's passing and now inform me in this stewardship; and to all involved with growing the Mythsinger Legacy Project and helping this book reach everyone who can use it.

Thirteen years of immense planetary and social change have taken place between editions two and three of *The Other Within*. Global connectivity and deepening awareness of "otherness," "othering," and the honoring of self-identity have grown exponentially. Were he here today, Daniel Deardorff would no doubt add material to this new edition. He would expand his references beyond the nearly one hundred authors now included, to further widen its range of scholarly, cultural, and gender perspectives. He would add his voice and presence even more strongly to ever-amplifying calls for justice, democracy, and the healing of "colonizer mindsets."

Although I cannot say how, I believe he would more directly acknowledge his own experience as a scholar, artist, and survivor of paralytic polio and resulting paraplegia, multiple life-saving and life-impairing surgeries, social exclusion, and at times exile, as well as the debilitating bodily landscape of post-polio syndrome (*poliomyelitis sequelae*). *And* he would acknowledge himself as being of white European heritage, and a heterosexual male of mixed class background, traits of privilege which most of his first teachers in myth share.

This said, all these awarenesses on the part of the author are implicate, if not explicit, in his current text. It is my hope that readers of all kinds will find value in the timelessness—and timeliness—of the book's subject, rather than any particulars of its author. Inner Traditions and I have sought to expand cultural inclusion in this edition by inviting a wide range of twenty-first-century authors, many not personally known to Deardorff, to add their voices in the endorsements.

This book, and the stories it contains, is full of instruction on how to hold paradox. As Martin Shaw notes in his afterword to this edition, Deardorff's approach to mythology is *associative,* rather than comparative. As such, it is holistic and revelatory, upholding a plurality of worldviews. Deardorff would encourage readers to proceed with a dedicated but not swift pace; to chew on what is offered; to talk with loved ones and communities in contemplative conversation, and to carry ideas sparked into "feeding the story," including at events hosted by the Mythsinger Legacy Project (mythsingerlegacy.org).

In the second edition, Daniel acknowledges me. (We met through his teaching as the first edition came out and joined our lives between editions one and two.) Now, from the beauty of the Pacific Northwest US where his work is still centered, on this anniversary date of his flight "out of this story and into the next," I have the paradoxical honor of thanking him.

Thank you Daniel Duane "3D" Deardorff for this book and for all the love you gave and continue to give us all through your devotion and the enduring, timeless gift of your arts.

WITH LOVE,
JUDITH-KATE FRIEDMAN

MOSSY ROCK, PORT TOWNSEND / QATÁY, WA
TRADITIONAL LANDS OF THE S'KLALLAM AND
CHEMAKUM AND GATHERING PLACE OF
COAST SALISH PEOPLES
SEPTEMBER 19, 2021

The City and the Forest

By Robert Bly

THIS BOOK CONCENTRATES with a fierce vision on two opposing or contrary forces, civilization with its fixed structures on the one hand, and the authentic life of dream, darkness, and genius on the other. On the side of civilization, we have domestic comforts, the steady life, the fixed order of the intellect, securities of various sorts, and the promise of good things to those who obey. As opposites, we have "the whole divine night," the mysteries of the forest, the madness of the underworld, the lunacy of the moon, the weird road, the wildness of the deer and the whale, the descent, the dive of the genius away from rationality, the ecstasy of art.

Having been brought down by polio in his earliest years, Deardorff finds himself a natural spokesman for the wounded emotional body, the deer pierced by darts, the man or woman on the weird road.

Deardorff is a true inheritor of Joseph Campbell. He is persistent about the intelligence inside the myth. And he gives weight to the wounded emotional body which people on the road of descent possess. He notices that the man or woman who is crippled or fiercely outcast or deformed has an honorary place in the house of mysteries.

Deardorff presents dozens of powerful examples from myth and literature of the contrary states of civilization and weirdness. The civilized king, Gilgamesh, stands for the socialized self, and the wild man, Enkidu, for the second self, the spiritual twin, the daimon. Deardorff discusses how the socialized Gilgamesh is opposite to Enkidu, and he shows how the two "I's" they represent take many forms in our daily lives. He mentions that the King in Iron John contrasts in a similar way with the hairy man who lives at the bottom of the pond.

These are huge subjects for a short book, but Deardorff has done well, even brilliantly. No one else writing today is able to follow these associative roads to the unconscious.

Literally, he has kept his standards high in his language and style as well, so that the book is a pleasure to read. Reading this book, we hear better what Juan Ramon Jiménez was talking of when he declares "I am not I" in his poem that begins:

> *I am not I. I am this one*
> *walking beside me whom I do not see.*

OVERTURE

Raven Whispers &
Forbidden Doors

DENIAL IS CONTAGIOUS and facts are an addictive substitute for truth. All the fact-finding missions in the world cannot convince humankind to face this one troublesome secret. If only we gave credence to those half-heard whispers of the twin ravens who perch on our shoulders each morning. Imagine the difference in our world: contrary mysteries chattered in opposite ears—life and death, sun and moon, future and past, self and other—confusing the rational mind but reaching and informing a wholehearted wisdom. A different world indeed.

The fluent associativity of such thought and memory, whispered to the heart by the voice of myth, has gone unheeded far too long. Neither dogma, nor ethics, nor rule-of-law can speak precisely to the unique depths of the individual person. Only myth, in its sweeping ability to constellate an array of contradictory meanings, has the power to awaken, within the private and particular moment, an immediate sense of what matters most.

There is the "Other" who stands at the margin within society and at once at the edge of consciousness within each individual. The orphaned part of us thrills to every story of the child lost to lowly circumstance; while unbeknownst to the false parents, the child is really the great wizard, the true king or queen, the secret champion waiting to rise from ignominy to a just and rightful destiny. Yet many a noble soul does not rise—they live in "permanent outsiderhood"—the undesirable misfit, tolerated but never truly welcome. As *The Other Within* wanders through the forest of myth and the alleyways of empire, we may catch a sense of meaning and value—discovering that which matters most— hidden in the perennial human circumstance of Otherness.

From the perspective of civil-society, that which is not proper, or normal, or accepted is deemed to evince a social or moral "disfigurement, ugliness, or crookedness."[1] Plants become *weeds,* animals become *vermin,* ideas become *heresy* and *treason,* and people become *infidel, outcast, misbegotten.* This deeming and damning perspective seems immoveable, yet many of the old stories speak to a magical shift: the loathsome beastly shape transformed by a "blessing kiss"—an act of fidelity, love, and valor—as in the strange predicament of "The Dame Ragnelle":

> Her stepmother had by necromancy enchanted her; and she was condemned to remain under that loathsome shape until the best knight of England should wed her and yield to her the sovereignty of all his body and goods. "Thus was I deformed," she said.[2]

When Sir Gawain grants her the "blessing kiss" and the "sovereignty," Ragnelle becomes a radiant beauty. Yet, one must ask, is this magical shift a transformation of form or of perception? And is it possible that perception alone can alter form?

THERE IS THE "GENIUS" who stands beside, before, and beyond us: "The tutelary god or attendant spirit allotted to every person at his birth, to govern his fortunes and determine his character, and finally to conduct him out of the world."[3] The power of this Genius is to *deform*: "de" meaning *to remove,* and "form" meaning *the visible aspect.* To remove the visible aspect is to disclose the interior shape in an aesthetic rupture, or gnostic flood of luminous interiority. The old tribal initiators used this rupture to divert ordinary perception and awaken the imagination to the Mystery of life. In the context of the present work, imagination is understood to be the sum total of all one's capacities.[4] Moreover, "Imagination," as defined by Gaston Bachelard, is "the faculty of *deforming* the images offered by perception."[5]

While my personal life has been immeasurably shaped and informed by a literal deformity of body, the reader should not confuse the author's deformity with the deforming powers of imagination. To be clear, the Genius of Deformity is much more than a vantage afforded by alterity, nor is it a mere capacity of human intelligence—it is the extra-human agent of imagination. It is our lost and longed for twin: the not-I,* the wild-one, the paraclete,* the wounded-healer, the daimon,* the vengeful-guardian-angel, whom we forgot the day we were born, and from whom the walls of social order have kept us divided. Otherness of any kind—cultural, racial, religious, sexual, physiognomic—presents a de-formation which effaces the veil of social, ideological, and physical "structure." Thus, it is offering or threatening the ultimate disclosure—deeper than "appearance"—that totality of reality which can be understood, not by explication, but only by the artful subtlety of what is implied.[6] The "implicate" is the deep-song, the Ghost River, the complex and ever-shifting imagery of myth that has, for a few, revealed and revised the isolating wounds of Otherness to be the common ground of human understanding, compassion, and meaning.

Facing the Other within us presents a terrifying difficulty. The trouble is vividly portrayed in a crucial moment of the tale "Maria Morevna": handing us the keys to the palace she, the great warrior queen, declares, "I must go to battle. In my absence you have the run of things, anything you desire, all is open to you save one small room in the deepest dungeon; that door you must, on no account, seek to prise open." If we obey her interdiction the status quo remains undisturbed—nothing happens—and we live a cheerful mediocrity. Yet in quiet moments we may feel a distressing call to the dark rooms hidden in

---

*When specialized glossary terms are presented without immediate definition in the text, an asterisk will alert you that the definition can be found in this book's glossary.

the dungeons of the psyche; the doors are locked, bolted, chained, and long rusted shut. Tacitly forbidden, they are kept out of mind. Thus, the people at the center of things are buoyantly ignorant, while those at the edge are burdened with a bewildering gravity. In the unknown darkness behind the door something nameless longs for the arrival of one with the cunning and grace to grasp the key. The initiatory journey of ordeals, awe, and thunderbolts will begin the moment we open that door. On the other reluctant hand, the requisite cost of denial is the endless task of finding some person, group, or nation to scapegoat—the great civilizing strategy—foisting our defects onto Others.

The prohibitive cost of denying Otherness could not be more crucial to the survival of the human race. Our mass refusal to face the "Other within" has engendered a regimen of sociopolitical atrocities, genocidal horrors, and environmental devastations—a virulent storm of global proportions. Contrary to the tenets of foreign policy and social activism, a remedy for this aggressive pandemic cannot be mediated, legislated, or enforced at a global, regional, or municipal level; it can only begin at the root, within each individual (*intra*-personally*), and within our nearest and most intimate relations (*inter*-personally*). It is therefore in this small and most private of territories that the potential for a truly humane society begins.

ODIN, THE RAVEN GOD, often came masked as a wanderer; an unexpected guest, appearing on the doorstep at twilight to test our trust and generosity. The wisdom to shield Glory in a cloak of shame is the oldest mercy of the gods. Only thus can it come amongst us. As to how he knew when and whom to visit, they say that Odin had two ravens who left his side only in the half-light of dawn. Returning to his shoulders in the full-light of morning they whispered the whole world condition to his heart; an irrational but imaginal means of gathering information, and a mythic lesson we can only hope to emulate.

Like a door slammed in the Wanderer's face the social and psychological rejection of Otherness constitutes a clear attack on the imaginal intelligence of the soul. Suffering the violations of perceived and projected deformity one's "identity" is split: divided into insider and outsider, worthy and worthless, above and below. That which is above we adore and aspire to personify, that which is beneath us we disdain and hold in contempt. This deeming duality of superior/inferior is the core of civilization's method (i.e., conquest, oppression, and exploitation). The discourse of human rights seeks to challenge the inaccuracy of the imposed category "inferior." Nevertheless, just as Jerome Rothenberg asserts that "primitive means complex,"[7] the assertion herein entails an equally contrary inversion: "inferior means powerful." If rational thought is superior to myth, then it will be in myth's inferiority that the greater efficacy and power reside.

A myth is a story that tells a sacred truth without the use of facts. Myth discloses value: *not* "values" in the moralistic or politically-correct sense, but intrinsic "value" as *valor,* valent, re-valuation, revelation, insight to essence and meaning. The illogical and transgressive manner by which myth works to reverse, revise, and deform our typical ideas and beliefs resembles the Mythic Trickster, the many named, shape-shifting, gender-bending, ambi-valent adventurer—Coyote, Raven, Legba, Loki, Tokwaj, et al. The Trickster comes as harbinger and exemplar of Deformity's Genius and mythopoeic* intelligence, embodying and articulating the *powerful inferiority* employed to leap the split between one's exterior and interior life.

In my writing I generally refuse the use of personal anecdote: the following paragraph, then, stands as an uncharacteristic departure. The summer this book was completed, no longer writing, I felt a strange disquiet, my heart echoed with a clear imperative: "Don't just say it, make it real." I didn't want to, and I'd sworn I never would. Not by happenstance, but by intention—not the stage of the elite performer, but downtown on a crowded corner—for the first time in my life, I took my archetypally appointed place, in my wheelchair, guitar in hand: I sang the blues for loose change. In some eyes I saw the "piteous cripple," in others the "courageous angel." Singing in the tension between the masks, I tested my actions against my words:

> To grasp the significance of the mask, it must be recalled that the mask itself *is* a story. It is crucial to objectify the imposed identity as "the masked persona," which "is then deployed to tell stories," and most importantly, stories told subjectively, *personally,* from a "very specific vantage point"—from the deeper standpoint of identity prior to identification.[8]

If I mistakenly identify my "Self" with the state of piteousness or courageousness, I assume the limits and privileges of that state (social status), consequently losing touch with my innate and implicit value— my "story"—identity prior to identification.

Given the prevalent confusion between perceived-status and inner-being, William Blake says we must: "Distinguish therefore States from Individuals in those States. / States Change: but Individual Identities never change nor cease."[9] Polarized identifications, such as piteous/courageous, ugly/beautiful, inferior/superior, are masks which *obscure* identity. Lao Tzu says: "In my obscurity is my value. That's why the wise wear their jade under common clothes."[10] In other words, as Blake has it: "Shame is Pride's cloke."[11] In order to distinguish the external status—the shameful common clothes—from the interior identity one must remain connected to the value of "jade" and "Pride" obscured and cloaked within. And yet, no matter how grand or degrading the mask may be, it is never just a facade, it has a life of its own, it *is* a story. If we refuse to learn the stories of whatever masks life bequeaths to us, we will never understand what people see when they look our way.

The challenge to accept the imposed identity as a useful cloak while upholding interiority requires a kind of ambi-dexterous, ambi-valent juggling of inner and outer truths—*juglito ergo sum.*[12] The Trickster's mythopoeic ambivalence (*ambi* = both + *valent* = of worth) teaches us to hold contraries in creative tension—*coincidentia oppositorum**—

without dropping, devaluing, or denying one over the other. As in Lao Tzu, "being and nonbeing arise together; hard and easy complete each other; high and low depend on each other,"[13] so in Blake, "Without Contraries is no progression."[14] Thus, we escape the cut of duality's one-sided blade. To deny inferiority, in a half-hearted (mono-valent) effort to "claim a just and rightful destiny," is to abdicate and forfeit imagination—turning our backs on the shadowy roots of wisdom—whereupon a full half the heart is exiled.

Lacking imagination, the "value" of human-life—and of all life—is reckoned as a mere commodity. Even "Love" as Blake said, "becomes a State, when divided from Imagination."[15] There is a slippery correlation between the obscurity of Lao Tzu's "value" and the imaginal life of Blake's "love": in a world where love and value have become the favored *tools* of exploitation, the fidelious authenticity which bears the "blessing kiss" goes underground; out of sight, out of mind, abiding in the cold black dungeon. Meanwhile, the best chance of remembering our inner value, in the face of such overwhelming avarice, ignorance, and prejudice, is Trickster-wisdom: obscurity, eccentricity, lunacy, wildness, deformity—such is the "subversive virtue"[16] of William Blake and Lao Tzu: twin ravens flown from opposites ends of space and time, they are paragons of Deformity's Genius, far ahead of us on the path. Now and then, a black feather drifts down at our feet, showing us the way.

IN THE GREAT STORMS of life the rose and thistle blossoms of status wither and blow away, revealing that which we cared for least to be constant and faithful to self and soul—*to that which matters most.* Reinterpreting *inferiority* as an opening to the real and vital *interiority* will not put an end to castigation and oppression, yet perhaps it can inform the "style" with which one walks this difficult road.

It would appear the better course to steer clear of such a hard path; many will avoid it, others have no choice, and a few will make their way by a blend of compulsion and free will. Blake says: "Improvement makes strait roads, but the crooked roads without Improvement are roads of Genius"[17]; standing at the crossroads of the "crooked" and the "straight," the "formal" and the "de-formed," Lao Tzu proclaims: "True straightness looks crooked."[18] *The Other Within* takes that crooked and precipitous way which Robert Bly has called "the Road of Ashes."[19] Walking among ashes one may feel the grief of loss and resentment. If one walks far enough, the ashes are no longer personal; we feel the grief of sacrifice and fidelity. These are the ashes of the bison, of the Black Forest, of Hiroshima, Auschwitz, Tulsa, and Wounded Knee. It is not an inviting or desirable road; it is the left-hand path of departure from the ordinary life. True *and* crooked, the path descends before us offering a chance, a priceless and devastating hope—in the words of poet Roque Dalton:

> *Love becomes a diamond because it had the chance to become ashes.*[20]

PRELUDE

Songs of the Dog-Man

EVERY HUMAN BEING, in the infinite variety of body and soul, comes
into this world, so unique and so alike, with so much promise; each
one prepared and appointed for the best . . . It's not going to happen.
The promise of life will break—early or late, far and away from the life
that might have been—we fall, and thus, we are betrayed. Crushed and
broken, this anomalous, aberrant, unimaginable shape of life, strange to
the eyes of the pack, if not concealed, means a life of exile. Although,
as will be shown, this betrayed condition is ultimately the condition of
everyone, there is the considerable matter of degree. Not to establish
a comparative hierarchy or heroics of "woundedness," but simply to
make the case herein by reference to its most conspicuous exemplar: the
Outsider amongst us—the one with no escape from

> *That defiling and disfigured shape*
> *The mirror of malicious eyes*
> *Casts upon his eye until at last*
> *He thinks that shape must be his shape . . .*[1]

"Wisdom"—the vision of doom or being doomed to vision—
begins in the unforeseen catastrophe which strips away life's promise,
reduces hope to ashes, and leaves one castaway in the original darkness. Consciousness is stripped down to nothing; what remains is
what we are.

What remains is the "hierophany* of betrayal"; here is the violent strike of a Thunderbolt—the irrevocable summons to a deeper life—and for a few, the hard-won discovery that the very instrument of betrayal, the Thunderbolt which afflicts them, is *also* the soul's invincible core.

The ground of betrayal opens the senses to something ineffable. The "hierophany" (*hier* = sacred, *phany* = manifestation) according to Mircea Eliade, "designate[s] the act of manifestation of the sacred." In addition, he remarks, "It is a fitting term, because it does not imply anything further; it expresses no more than is implicit in its etymological content, i.e., that something sacred shows itself to us."[2] The hierophany, in terms of the present work, is the personal experience of undifferentiated sacrality:* the gnostic influx—in-formance*—of "divine energies" which shape and orient the whole being to accord with an ever shifting cosmos. Again, in Eliade's words: "the hierophany reveals an absolute fixed point, a center."[3] However, this coming to center is not the beatific "silver lining," the dawn after the night, the light at the end of the tunnel—it is the lightning-bolt-trident of Shiva, by which life is destroyed and created at once. Moreover, for those thus stricken, the hierophany perpetuates and redoubles the circumstance of betrayal; if our society marked us as undesirable before, now wielding the de-structuring, de-forming, visionary Thunderbolt, we shall be *anathema*.

"Betrayal"—to be traded, delivered, handed over, no longer held, dropped—is the crisis of a rupture in the veil of the ordinary-life. A violation in which we are in-formed by assault: dis-possession, dis-appointment, dis-ease; every indignity, every wound, every curse, every tragic fall brings us to this crossroads.

The contrary roads of this exterior/interior intersection seem to represent a choice; but the power of the crossroads will not be found in dualities: in either/or, black or white decisions; where choosing one denies the other. The potency of the crossroads lies in Novalis's "seat": where the inner-world and the outer-world meet and overlap. Here is the dialectic betwixt-and-between, the both-and,* the neither-nor.

And this must not be confused with the middle way of compromise and reconciliation, rather, it is the emergent Third-way of holding the tension while participating fully in both extremes of the contradiction. To "choose one way" or "hold the tension" presents the vast but subtle difference between being robbed or making a sacrifice.

The crux of this disjunction lies in the dissonance between the image-of-self as reflected, *inter*-personally, in the mirror of society's "malicious eyes," and the other image-of-self, *intra*-personally, in the mirror of one's soul. When the tension between these disparate reflections cannot be endured, the attendant crisis results in *exile* from one sphere or the other—i.e., either *society* or *the heart*. This crisis is definitively portrayed by Morris Berman:

> The shock is not that an Other exists, but that you realize that *you are an Other for other Others.* What now opens up, and deepens until age eight, and is something you are condemned to deal with for the rest of your life, is that an interpretation can be put upon you that is antagonistic to what you feel about yourself.[4]

This disjunction is the consequence of an *imposed* "shape," an external "status" assigned to an exotic deformity, weakness, or poverty (and sometimes, ironically, assigned to exotic beauty, wealth, or strength) where the imposed inter-personal status is experienced as a *violation*— a disfigurement and disqualification of the intra-personal *implicate* interior-shape:

> All deformities are signs of mysteries which may be either benign or malign. Like all anomalies, the first emotion they arouse may be one of repugnance, but this is a ground or a sign of being favoured, by the concealment of something very precious which requires great pains if it is to be acquired. This explains the mingled fear and respect in which African society holds the feeble-minded, the halt and, especially, the blind, the latter being judged able to see beyond

the outward appearance of things. . . . To understand the anomaly, one must overstep the normal bounds of judgment. In so doing one gains a deeper knowledge of the mysteries of being and of life. . . . It is a commonplace that the blind are often regarded as "seers" in the sense of being "second-sighted" or clairvoyant. In the same way, deaf people may be regarded as being "clair-audiant." . . . Deformity makes its victim the benign or malign intercessor between the known and the unknown, the dark and the bright side of nature, this world and the beyond.[5]

The deformed, limbless and handicapped have this in common, that they are marginalized by human or "daylight" society, since their "evenness" is affected, and must perforce now belong to the other order, that of darkness, be it celestial or infernal, divine or satanic . . . the odd man out can carry the meaning of someone who has offended the social code, either criminally or heroically. Both criminal and hero derive from the sacred.[6]

Any oddness then—in visage, action, or thought—can mark the odd-man-out. Deformity, or lack of "evenness," is not limited to physiognomy. And yet the stricken one is "favoured, by the concealment of something very precious which requires great pains if it is to be acquired."

This concealed and precious "something" cannot be seen or known in any ordinary sense: "To understand the anomaly, one must overstep the normal bounds of judgment"; that is to say, beyond right and wrong, the fall into oddness is a "step" toward the *wyrd*-doom* of destiny—toward the expression of one's apportioned cup of Mystery and sacrality. Rilke says:

> *Those in need have to step forward,*
> *have to say: I am blind,*
> *or: I'm about to go blind,*
> *or: nothing is going well with me,*

or: I have a sick child,
or: right there I'm sort of glued together . . .

They have to sing; if they didn't sing, everyone
would walk past, as if they were fences or trees . . .

But God himself comes and stays a long time
when the world of half-people start to bore him.

In this, his title poem of "The Voices,"[7] Rilke articulates each voice in the choir of the *shunned*—"The Beggar," "The Blind Man," "The Drunkard," "The Suicide," "The Widow," "The Idiot," "The Orphan," "The Dwarf," and "The Leper"—*nine companions* who are in fact members of our communities, our families, and ourselves.[8]

Here are the mysterious songs of the dog-man; the blessing born of the curse, the genius that is in the wound, the hierophany—the sacred song which attracts the gods—hidden and bequeathed within life's utter betrayal:

Mmmmm, standin' at the crossroad, I tried to flag a ride
Standin' at the crossroad, I tried to flag a ride
Didn't nobody seem to know me, everybody pass me by.[9]

Only primitives, fairytales, madmen, and poets sing of such dire gifts. But, "they have to sing; if they didn't sing, everyone would walk past, as if they were fences or trees." There was a time when these songs were not simply dismissed as eccentricities or entertainments—i.e., non-essential, non-productive, self-indulgent fantasies—rather they were valorized as the most potent and embodied enactments of mystery and truth. Perhaps, in the era of mass-civilization, when the "divine energies" have withdrawn, as Hölderlin foresaw, "we arrived too late"; and so with him one may well ask: "in the lean years—when the divine energies are isolated in the archetypal world—who needs poets?"[10]

The betrayal of the promised life throws the broken and oppressed one down to the crossroads into the abyss: the famous "dark night of the soul"; as if to spend in misty Wales, a night alone, in the cold stone chair, high atop the mountain peak of "Cader Idris, 'the Chair of Idris' [Arthur] where . . . whoever spends the night is found in the morning either dead, mad, or a poet."[11] These three alternatives—none of which seem quite socially promising—bring us to the guiding inquiry of this prelude: what if I was *born* in such a chair? By what standard shall I— the initiand and victim/beneficiary of the Thunderbolt—confirm my shape and the value thereof? What if I alone cannot measure whether I am dead, mad, or a poet? What if I am a little of each? If those who find me—having no use for the mad-poetics of wisdom—deem me useless and malignant, what will be their disposition toward me? If I am unwanted and unwelcome, betrayed by the inter-personal human world, what shall I do? And how shall I live?

Scapegoat
A Stricken Deer

I was a stricken deer, that left the herd
Long since; with many an arrow deep infixt
My panting side was charg'd, when I withdrew
To seek a tranquil death in distant shades.

WILLIAM COWPER,
"I WAS A STRICKEN DEER"[1]

WITH THESE WORDS William Cowper renders the precipitous fall from the promised life. Here is the one *driven* to interiority marked by the wound, and wounded for bearing the mark. There is no renunciation; the deep piercing arrows are the cause of departure. Leaving "the herd," in this sense, is to break away from the imposed-identity of the social structure. Those who *drop out* of "position" in this parade drop *down and out*—and out of sight.

In the words of Robert Bly the stricken one is on "The Road of Ashes, Descent, and Grief"; it is, he says, "the whirlpool, the sinking through the floor, the Drop, what the ancient Greeks called *katabasis*."* And there is a stigma to *katabasis*: "People know immediately when you are falling or have fallen: doormen turn their backs, waiters sneer, no one holds the subway door for you."[2] A myriad slight but countless degradations invite one to dwell on the victim's road. A few of the stricken, however, once removed and hidden from ordinary perception, will find—*or be found by*—something miraculous:

> *There was I found by one who had himself*
> *Been hurt by th'archers. In his side he bore,*
> *And in his hands and feet, the cruel scars.*
> *With gentle force soliciting the darts,*
> *He drew them forth, and heal'd, and bade me live.*

As wonderful and marvelous as is this "apparition," the event can be quite tricky. In a certain way, once we have fallen, we have a right to expect such a *paraclete*—"divine mediator" or intercessor—to arrive. But if expected only in the perspective of concrete literality, the arrival of the Wounded Healer—the one who's side, hands, and feet bear the cruel scars—will pass unmarked and unavailed of.

The arrows and darts of malice and misfortune, that leave such identifying scars, are equally the Thunderbolt shafts of divine election; to mistake the hierophanous-touch for the mundane is to miss the star of destiny—the "wyrd road" of the initiand. One must bring to bear a much wider imagination than accommodated within the ratio of reasonable daylight thought. For who or what is *appointed* to heal and mediate the "stricken" may just as well be a gust of wind, a ghost, a book, an animal, a leaf, or a gesture. Whatever it may be, the feeling touch of the paraclete will move or remove us to an extra-ordinary vantage, a different kind of vision:

> *Since then, with few associates, in remote*
> *And silent woods I wander, far from those*
> *My former partners of the peopled scene;*
> *With few associates, and not wishing more.*
> *Here much I ruminate, as much I may,*
> *With other views of men and manners now*
> *Than once.*

The extra-ordinary vantage of "other views" begins in the isolation of the "silent woods"; and thus begins the way of The Wanderer: the long exilic path of the nomad, gypsy, mendicant, homeless, pilgrim—who haunts the edges of civilization's uneasy sleep. This isolation is both cause *and* result of the singular, private, impossible-to-report hierophanic apparition:

> [Henry] Corbin, who has commented on these and similar apparitions in Islam, calls them theophanic visions. Their perception, he says, is "an *event of the soul,* taking place *in* the soul and for the soul. As such its reality is essentially *individuated* for and with each soul: what the soul really sees, it is in each case alone in seeing. The field of its vision, its horizon is in every case defined by the capacity, the dimension of its own being."[3]

"What the soul really sees, it is *alone* in seeing"; a Wanderer "with few associates" guards against the risk of the withering gaze—as Goethe advised: "Tell a wise person, or else keep silent, / Because the massman will mock it right away."[4] Conventional or standard values and "views" will tell us nothing of the hierophanic depths. Wandering back from the crossroads, bereft of all former habits and reliances, one faces the paradox of identity: "am I dead, mad, or a poet?" Whereupon, as Cowper finds: *here much I ruminate, as much I may.*

To "ruminate," as a mode of thought or contemplation, is to chew, swallow, regurgitate, chew again, swallow, and take nutrition—to take *in-formance* alimentally, through the gullet, blood, tissues, and bones. This gnosis is *embodied* and *enacted*—actualized—with an un-common outlook; that is to say, with "other views" that have little or nothing to do with rational/empirical consensus.

Ruminating, upon *what* or *who* "I am," the *plurality* of "other views" emerges as most significant. For it can be taken to imply a multi-perspectival consciousness which is *not* monological, rigid or fixed, but varilogical,* open and kaleidoscopic. Kaleidoscopic consciousness* (which includes the unconscious, instinct, inspiration, and gnosis as essential to wisdom) will be taken up in greater depth further down the road; at this juncture the relevance of *plurality* pertains to the necessity of releasing the former, now shattered, identity. The deeper vision is dependent on a self-image which is a constellation: a dance of many view-points. Groping for this unprecedented identity, it is as if one stands before the gates of the divine, where the common singular position will not satisfy the Gatekeeper—this very crisis, it is said, was once faced by a Celtic god, the many-gifted Lugh:

> When Lug first approaches the citadel at Tara he is refused for having no art. In successive knockings at the gate Lug identifies himself as a wright or builder, a smith, champion, harper, warrior, poet, historian, magician, physician (or leech), cupbearer, and brazier (or craftsman in metal), but is told [each time] that the Tuatha Dé Danann already have one. Then he asks if they have someone who could perform all these skills . . . and when Tara's denizens admit they do not, he is allowed to enter.[5]

Thus the "other views," one could say, are the multiple perspectives which constellate a *pantheon* of the deep identity.

In the "peopled scene" the poet's reinterpretation of "men and manners" involves a looking back at "societal structure"—taking the perspective of a ghost—looking from the outside *in*. Thus, in one sense we die—or the courteous and civil persona dies—to conventional structure and the ordinary life. Abruptly one finds oneself standing in the new-life looking back at the old order—a threshold upon which David Miller clarifies:

> When the body is in the grave, dead and buried, or when there is a death of ego and its perspectives during one's lifetime, then a deeper spirit or soul can come to be. A deepening of historical being occurs by way of an under-the-worldly point of view. The descent

into the underworld of souls (*psychai, animae*) is a descent into a soul-perspective or depth-perspective concerning history. One might say that the descent into hell is actually the ascent of soul. It brings a sense of soul into ascendancy in life, and it gives the human ego a perspective from a soulful point of view. The descent is itself a resurrection.[6]

Each time the god Lugh is denied entry, something dies; it is only with the unprecedented realization *"I am all this"* that entrance is granted. This is not the naïveté of wishing to be free of ego; rather, this "soul-perspective," being plural, is purchased at the expense of the ego's superiority—a dethronement which will be unremittingly resisted—in the egocentric-persona's view a fully constellated identity is seen and understood as certain death; and yet, ironically, it is only the superiority which dies. For just as the celestial constellation moves within the held-tension of gravity, so the plural identity constellates within the field of ego. As stated by Miguel de Unamuno: "That which we call egoism is the principle of psychic gravity."[7]

However we valorize the implicate multiplicity of the "soulful point of view" the practical problems of imposed outsiderhood remain. The former ways of the "peopled scene" no longer lure and beckon; one must find a way to deal with society's judgment as to the benignity or malignancy of this new-found wisdom:

> *I see that all are wand'rers, gone astray*
> *Each in his own delusions; they are lost*
> *In chase of fancied happiness, still woo'd*
> *And never won.*

Again this is tricky, even perilous; to see that "all are wand'rers" lost in their "own delusions" may move one as easily to contempt as to compassion. If, dualistically, one way or the other is chosen, the hard-won jewel of the under-the-worldly-vision is lost. Too much contempt will prevent us from entrusting this multifaceted jewel to anyone, too much compassion will lead us to squander it on the massman—on those who will mock and deny—in either extreme the wisdom gained is not delivered.

In an effort to further delineate the significance of leaving the herd—the socio-psychological departure referred to herein as the hierophany of betrayal—a meeting of David Miller's *descensus ad inferos** (descent into Hell) and Victor Turner's "ritual liminality" (ritual destruction of social status) will prove invaluable. For to understand the "sinking through the floor" of *katabasis* in the terms of *descensus* and liminality* will be to acquire an indispensable appreciation of the ultimacy, ubiquity, and utility of the betrayal—beginning with Miller:

> *In-fero* means "to carry inward," "to gather in." Therefore . . . the *descensus* may be read as referring, not to some actual physical place, but rather to a "journey to the interior." The *descensus* is *ad inferos*. It is a "carrying inward." Hell is a *descensus,* and encountering it is a "deepening."[8]

> Tradition imagines the descent into hell as a descent into "darkness," or into a "hole," or into a "pit," or into "invisibility" (Hades' name means "invisible"), then no matter how a person may feel about such experiences of being in the "dark," in a "hole," in the "pits," or "invisible" to others, that person is encouraged to search such deep moments for their disclosures and expressions of profound "soul."[9]

Compare this now to Victor Turner—speaking specifically of the African *Ndembu* and of the ritual process in general:

> Liminality is frequently likened to death, to being in the womb, to invisibility, to darkness, to bisexuality, to the wilderness, and to an eclipse of the sun or moon.[10]

Liminality, marginality, and structural inferiority are condi-
tions in which are frequently generated myths, symbols, rituals,
philosophical systems, and works of art. These cultural forms
provide men with a set of templates or models which are, at one
level, periodical reclassifications of reality and man's relationship
to society, nature, and culture. But they are more than classifications, since they incite men to action as well as to thought. Each of
these productions has a multivocal* character, having many meanings, and each is capable of moving people at many psychobiologi-
cal levels simultaneously.[11]

Liminality and *descensus ad inferos* are descriptions of the same process
and condition. Miller's work is crucial as it shows the liminal descent to
be implicate in the individual human soul regardless of social context:
to wit, "the motif of the descent into hell is archetypal in nature, fundamental to the human soul, universal in scope, yet dead in the wake of
ecclesiastical literalism and theological rationalism."[12]

Turner's work is equally crucial in portraying the same descent
within the *living structure* of a "ritual community," a context entirely
missing in mass-civilization; that is to say, a context "dead in the wake
of ecclesiastical literalism and theological [as well as secular] rationalism." The grievous lack of a social structure which conscientiously
fosters, confirms, and sanctifies the "divine energies" of the liminal-
descent recalls Hölderlin's conclusion that "we arrived too late." Ergo,
the question: how, given the modern absence of confirmation in "ritual
community," can one alone—betrayed, dropped, and handed over—
cultivate and maintain the experience of hierophany?

How can there be an experience which is both at once? How can a
person's descents be sensed as being in the hole, in the pits, in darkness, in prison, in the midst of a gnashing of teeth, deep in the belly,
among clashing rocks, earthquakes and war, *and*, at the same time,
as an experience of the treasures of soul, a second birth, a moistening

of a dried-out life, the initiation which is a key to the magic of life, a doorway to a deeper perspective?[13]

> The descent into the "middle," into the "between" . . . implies a perspective of both-and. It is not the "place" of death only, or of life (resurrection) only. It is "between" death and resurrection, and it brings with it a perspective that is dialectical (moving back and forth), fundamentally ambivalent, seeing all things historical under the double sign of a *coincidentia oppositorum,* a "coincidence of oppositions," in the richness of imagination.[14]

Miller is clear: the lonely descent of death is also a resurrection. So one answer to the lack of a confirming-community must be the hierophanic vision of the Wounded Healer, the *paraclete*—but what on earth is that? To say that it resides amidst the neither-this-nor-that of the *coincidentia oppositorum,* that it is manifest in the held-tension of the "cross," is to reiterate: the power of the crossroads will not be found in either/or, black or white decisions. To be concise: the potential "hierophany" in the liminal-descent *is* "the soulful point of view," the "perspective of both-and"; not merely to behold the paraclete, but to "see what the soul *really* sees" in the perspective *of* the paraclete: "The seat of the soul is there, where the inner world and the outer world touch. Where they permeate each other, the seat is in every point of the permeation."[15]

It must be interjected at this point that many people are stricken and fallen in this way and yet they fail to find the "richness of imagination" which yields "the treasures of soul, a second birth, a moistening of a dried-out life . . . the magic of life, a doorway to a deeper perspective." Nor are they able to generate: "myths, symbols, rituals, philosophical systems, and works of art." For these desolates all is death, invisibility, darkness, wilderness, being in the hole, in the pits, in prison, in the midst of gnashing teeth, deep in the belly, among clashing rocks, earthquakes and war; something for them is missing—the Wounded Healer, the hierophanous *paraclete,* does not appear.

It would be regrettable indeed if left unsaid that the work in hand is emphatically *not* meant, in any way, to be a "self-help" program. There are no solutions offered here; there is only the impossible expedition, ever deeper, into the contradictions. And even this descent may be blocked: the harsh reality, that some shattered souls are irretrievably damaged, cannot be overlooked. Sometimes the betrayal comes too early, imagination is arrested, and there is no chance, in the aftermath, to intervene in any meaningful way. For these souls the violence in the moment of betrayal becomes the only meaningful and communicable *reality*.

The ultimate scapegoat, the absolute-victim—i.e., ten-thousand-years-of-repressed-desire-incarnate—is not self-determined, but is rather, literally a "pathological symptom" of collective dysfunction. When the god in the "symptom" *becomes* the whole-human-being the individual implicate identity* is displaced, perhaps even erased, without a trace; possessed by generations of accumulated forbidden and unfulfilled desires "until at last he thinks that [imposed] shape must be his [implicate] shape."

Nothing more can be said; and yet, merely saying it does not fulfill our obligation. One cannot simply pay homage and then set aside these irretrievably broken ones; *they are in us,* companions to be carried and expressed in earnest and respect, especially with respect—to look and look again. In this admission is the two-fold task of, perhaps, the most incommensurable *coincidentia oppositorum:* on one hand, I must possess an identity complex enough to incorporate and carry the burden of all these repressed and despised collective energies, while on the other hand and at the same moment, I must retain, protect, and cultivate a separate and personal identity: my unique and unprecedented "shape."

A final point to drive-home in this interjection is that whatever wisdom is to be found in this book, it must not fail to include and account for the abrupt and inarguable logic of those who live by the violence of the promise betrayed—the knife's edge not as a symbol, but as cold-steel persuasion, the endless intrusions of terror, coercion, bare-survival, and death. Facing death at knife-point all our lofty ideals and sublime self-images whither and blow away—stripped down to nothing—*what remains is what we are . . .*

> At certain life crises, such as adolescence, the attainment of elderhood, and death, varying in significance from culture to culture, the passage from one structural status to another may be accompanied by a strong sentiment of "humankindness," a sense of the generic social bond between all members of society—even in some cases transcending tribal or national boundaries—regardless of their subgroup affiliations or incumbency of structural positions. In extreme cases, such as the acceptance of the shaman's vocation . . . this may result in the transformation of what is essentially a liminal or extrastructural phase into a permanent condition of sacred "outsiderhood." The shaman or prophet assumes a statusless status, external to the secular social structure, which gives him the right to criticize all structure-bound personae in terms of a moral order binding on all, and also to mediate between all segments or components of the structured system.[16]

For the initiand (in Turner's above elucidation) what *remains* will be more than the frozen imagination of violence. It is imperative that the liminal "crisis of passage" from one "structural status to another" is understood as death—no death, no transformation.

In this understanding the life-sequence of initiatory passages can be said to delineate the stations of a universal Passion Play—birth, childhood, adolescence, elderhood, death, and resurrection—with the transformative abyss of Death dividing each station. And the whole circle-dance of this initiatory round is distilled down by Robert Graves to "the *single* poetic theme of Life and Death."[17] This point is of the greatest importance: the *poiesis** of myth and ritual can express the whole range of human experience but always in the efficacy of the One Theme—the constant and drastic alterations of Life *and* Death. The crises of "humankindness" which transform mere outsiderhood to the truly poetic and mediating condition of "sacred outsiderhood,"* arrive in the life-giving-kiss of Death which awaits us in the *descensus ad inferos.*

This Mystery of Death, however, in "civil society," will be a most unwelcome messenger. The perfect-shape of life is *immortal;* ergo death and decay are corruption and deformity. As previously cited: "Deformity makes its victim the benign or malign *intercessor* between the known and the unknown, this world and the beyond." And thus even in malignancy, the permanent outsider must still assume the burden "to criticize all structure-bound personae" and "to *mediate* between all segments of the structured system." In this way the wisdom of the *paraclete*—the perspective of the Wounded Healer—arrives as the *particular deformity in the shape of one's life.* Mass-civilization, however, by definition, refuses the "soul-perspective" of the particular poetic/shamanic/deformity, for the massman has no functional category within which to adopt the unprecedented wisdoms carried back from the abyss:

> Aborigines construct ceremonies from what a shaman "sees" either while asleep or alone in the desert. He returns to his people and shares with them what he experienced—a dance, a narrative, a song. The others participate with him in enacting a ceremony that is both new and old. . . . Performances made from vision-quests, drug-induced visions, or dreams are treated by many of the world's peoples with special respect precisely because they hinge two spheres of reality. A shaman is a professional link connecting disparate but interacting reality spheres.[18]

A community woven by connecting the "disparate but interacting reality spheres" of Life and Death presents the antithesis of modern civil society. Again: There was a time when such hierophanous songs—"vision-quests, drug-induced visions, dreams"—were not simply considered eccentricities or entertainments, rather they were *embodied enactments* of Mystery.

It can now be stated with confidence that the common ground of the *descensus ad inferos* and ritual liminality *is* this "intermediate function" of the sacred outsider—who returns from the wilderness of death bearing the gift of the both-and-perspective; without this cultural infusion there can be no confirmation of the deep-life and any so called "community" is merely a swindle.

Insofar as society cannot confirm the sacrality of the intermediate condition, the way to confirmation will have to be found alone. And of a certainty there is a deeper way, however lonely, into community: the "crisis of humankindness"; a pre-structural ontologically* unitive ground—where utterly alone we may find absolute communion—the "soul-perspective" of *communitas:**

> For communitas has an existential quality; it involves the whole man in his relation to other whole men. Structure, on the other hand, has cognitive quality; as Lévi-Strauss has perceived, it is essentially a set of classifications, a model for thinking about culture and nature and ordering one's public life. Communitas has also an aspect of potentiality; it is often in the subjunctive mood. Relations between total beings are generative of symbols and metaphors and comparisons; art and religion are their products rather than legal and political structures. . . . Prophets and artists tend to be liminal and marginal people, "edgemen," who strive with a passionate sincerity to rid themselves of the clichés associated with status incumbency and role-playing and to enter into vital relations with other men in fact or imagination.[19]

Unlike the narcotic oblivion of mass-identity—i.e., nationalist and religious mobocracy*—the devastating in-formance of *communitas* bequeaths a singular individual identity, before names, before categories, before structure. In this view the meaning of *communitas* is refined and narrowed: it is not some inflated self-transposing-identification, but the universal devastation which constitutes the primary human commonality—"in fact *and* imagination." Yes, as Turner has it, the anti-structural products of *communitas* are indeed "religion and art," but only *religion* before dogma and *art* before dollars.

THE CIVILIZED CHOICE is either black *or* white, good *or* bad; but never this-*and*-that—never the crossbred, chymeric,* and monstrous *both*. In this flat, dualistic, and half-hearted view we choose between the bright victorious pose of denying the wound while projecting the defect, or the lackluster victim's pose of shame, violence, and bitter remorse for "the life that might have been." In either posture, victim or victor, one's identity or shape is defined and determined only by *imposition:* by exterior structural circumstance and events, rendering all initiatory suffering meaningless. As Miller puts it: "Lacking the poetry" and lacking "the images and imaginings of the underworld, one takes one's torments literally and personally, being thereby *merely* down, with no way to sense soul's ascendancy in the moment."[20] To lack the "images of the underworld" is to be exiled twice: once from community, and once again from our own interiority. Yet if this disjunction can be entered and endured one may descend all the way down to the hierophany: that deep, kaleidoscopic, shape-shifting wisdom in which—*a stricken deer with many an arrow deep infixt,* joins the vision/doom of the *paraclete,* the daimon, the guiding ghost—*with gentle force soliciting the darts.*

At last the utterly individual *and* the utterly universal embrace in the *plurality* of a mythopoeic consciousness. To sustain the Life and Death tension in the crossroads of identity,* one must avow, along with Juan Ramón Jiménez:

> *I am not I. I am this one*
> *Walking beside me whom I do not see.*[21]

Aporia

Alexander's Iron Gate

STANDING LIKE THE appellant god at the crossroads-gate, the initiand now surveys a puzzle with no solution—an *aporia**: one road for the good citizen, and another for the scum of the earth, the dirty-low-down-dog. In his *Myths of the Dog-Man* David Gordon White situates the dog as an ubiquitous mythological image for the undesirable, exotic, and inferior races. The image presents its loathsome apex in the miscegenic, *cynocephalic**—dog-headed—man. The complexity of just why the dog is given this slanderous distinction will be explored shortly; in the meantime, it is enough to know that the dog-men were originally thought to inhabit the wastelands at the edge or threshold of the world. On civilization's terms this situation is "just fine": so long as the monsters do not transgress the boundary. However, as imperialism expands toward the outlands, and with the occasional invasion of "cynocephalic hordes," protective measures must be taken to ensure the continuous purity of social structure.

Keeping the dog-man separate from civil society is synonymous with keeping one's personal "defects" walled off from consciousness—and especially walled off from the visible public persona. A Great Wall, then, is erected to be the first and last line of defense against all that is "outcast and vagabond." This ideological wall has its most potent precedent in the legendary Iron Gate, built by Alexander, to hold back the barbarian tides:

31

This image, of a hero plugging the sole gap* between the civilized and savage races and worlds, was undoubtedly a very powerful one given the perenniality of this account across a wide array of legends and over several centuries. . . . [T]his episode of the Alexander Romance . . . [appears] in a fourteenth-century Persian miniature entitled *Iskandar Builds the Iron Rampart*. In this miniature, it is the break between civilization and savagery that is most evident. On the near side of the wall are men in brightly colored clothes manning forges, machines, and other tools used in the wall's construction. On the far side of the wall are grey desert mountains with ragged underbrush in which crouching, hairy semi-human creatures may be made out, their bodies quite difficult to distinguish from their natural surroundings.[1]

Of course the world has changed since the time when this portrayal was taken as fact: instead of the finite flat-earth, we now have a round globe with no apparent edge; boundaries shift daily; the great exoteric walls are demolished. Civilization—Alexander's side of the Gate—has now overrun the entire surface of the earth.

The term "civilization" or "mass-civilization" as used throughout this work includes not only all varieties of state and pontifical rule, but also, and more particularly, the tyranny of "civil society." In its devotion to the one-sidedness of structural status and public persona, civil society must be seen as the tool of oppression and exploitation, a tool bent on upholding the ideal of an individuality with no actual association to the depths of the implicate shape. Consider the buoyant contemporary argument: that civil society is "a social sphere of freedom, voluntary association, and plurality of human relationships, identities, differences, and values" and, more grandiosely, "Civil society [is] upheld as the key notion required to conceptualize the potential for freedom and liberation which this arena contains."[2] These assertions are, to be moderate, absurd; yes, in civil society we *are* granted many options— freedoms and liberties—to choose from a thousand kinds of breakfast cereal; unwittingly the good-citizen is kept busy, as Michael Meade says, with "choices that don't count."[3] The half-heartedness of civil society is clearly a contrived seduction to the superficial life of the public persona, the imposition of "structural superiority" as the measure of human value, and, at bottom, an anesthetic to interiority and a conquest of "what the soul *really* sees."

Mass-civilization is *not* community. A mature community valorizes and confirms the initiatory passages/deaths of each individual's personal/cosmic identity by its whole-hearted participation in both structure *and* anti-structure; whereas civilization renders the implicate individual alienated, devalued, and anonymous. Civilization is structure decreed for structure's sake; as the words of anthropologist Stanley Diamond make so profoundly clear: "Civilization originates in conquest abroad and oppression at home."[4]

Something from the Other-side of Alexander's Gate—something of primitive consciousness—has been lost; yet there can be no rallying cry here to idealize primitive or tribal society—obviously the tendency to ostracize abnormality is as old as life itself. Nevertheless, it would be naïve in the extreme to overlook the fact that this inherent predisposition to *exclusion* has reached its pinnacle with the advent of mass-civilization.

Most good citizens have long since decided to let Others carry their strangeness, and so to live half-hearted, to keep the world-gate safely locked and bolted. Upon this it may be inquired: "Well what's so bad about that? Why not live and let live?" But Alexander's side of the Gate has overrun the whole earth and the soul-laden dog-man has nowhere left to go. This fact—that there is no longer any "edge of the world" to which deviants may be exiled—has brought about the ever-increasing implementation of *institutional* wastelands, "structures of exclusion" for incarceration of the dog-man in prison, asylum, or zoo. Thus, for the structurally inferior, the paths of exclusion are laid out and seemingly unavoidable. Seduced down into the bowels, they often simply disappear.

If life is understood to be a seamless progress from one structural status to another, then whatever structure we are living in—whether Pentagon or penitentiary—will be the only reality; and what departs from that reality presents the abysmal death-threat of anti-structure. Now the Evil Empire is personified as the Other Within: the exotic dog-man among us.

BUILT FOR POSTERITY, the monument of the Iron Gate still stands strong. Between the known and the unknown—the locus of Alexander's wall* is precisely where it has *always* been: in the center of the human heart. The cosmic split, "the break between civilization and savagery," between the *village* and the *forest,* denotes the ontological *gap;** a gap that by now the reader will easily recognize as the crossroads of identity: "the seat of the soul." Standing thus divided by the ancient wall, there are amputated parts of us scattered on both sides.

The aporia faced by the *out*-sider stranded on the *in*-side of Alexander's Gate adds another dimension to the plight of the Other Within. One yearns to "leave the herd" and escape structural inferiority by returning through the "sole gap" to some forgotten homeland—however savage and bizarre. And at the same time one wishes for "membership"; yet the Gate confronts incessantly: barring each bright avenue to inclusion the galling sign reads "no admittance." The double-bind of this circumstance throws the wanderer betwixt the clashing rocks of *no-entry-into* and *no-escape-from.* Consequently, the Other Within will need both resistance and resilience, to face the conundrum of Alexander's Iron Gate; for the spell of its damnation will fall when least expected and where most vulnerable. As Clyde W. Ford—a mythologist who is also an African American—recounts:

With a deepened interest in mythology and especially in the hero's journey, I was excited to turn to the contributions Africa has made to world mythology. But what a surprise it was to consult *The Hero with a Thousand Faces* by the late Joseph Campbell, perhaps the most famous modern text on mythology, and read this opening phrase:

"Whether we listen with aloof amusement to the dreamlike mumbo jumbo of some red-eyed witch doctor of the Congo, or read with cultivated rapture thin translations from the sonnets of the mystic Lao-tse."

These words were my Symplegades*—the ominous clashing rocks through which the Greek hero Jason had to pass before reaching the Sea of Wonders en route to recapturing the Golden Fleece. I closed the book with a heavy heart.[5]

To his profound credit Dr. Ford persevered and made passage between the "clashing rocks" of this betrayal going on to give us *The Hero with an African Face.*

DISMISSIVE "ALOOF AMUSEMENT" is just one civil trick, among many, in the massman's unconscious defense against the terror of Otherness. As already indicated, maintaining structural purity by keeping the dog-people separate from "civil society" is synonymous with keeping one's personal defects walled off from the inner-sanctum of ordered consciousness—and especially walled off from the pure and bright public persona.

In self-defense, the egocentric identity, quite rightly, recognizes that the crisis of rapport with Otherness will mean its certain death (it is hard to abandon even the thinnest illusion that we are *normal*). Still, if one hopes to survive as the Other Within, it will be vital to accept and exercise the poetic-power in the deep ambivalence evoked by "the symbol of the dog . . . at one and the same time a guardian and benign spirit *and* the object of God's curse [contraries which] make it the pre-eminent example of the 'fallen angel.'"[6] After all, is it not the "fallen angel" within us and amongst us whom we most fear?

The "Hounds of Herne the Hunter," or the "Dogs of Annwm," which hunt souls across the sky are, in British folklore, also called

"Gabriel ratches" or "Gabriel hounds." . . . Gabriel, whose day was Monday, ran errands for Sheol (the Hebrew Hecate) and was sent to summon souls to Judgement. . . . This was Hermes's task, and Herne, a British oak-god whose memory survived in Windsor Forest until the eighteenth century, is generally identified with Hermes. Gabriel and Herne are equated in the early thirteenth-century carvings around the church door at Stoke Gabriel in South Devon. The angel Gabriel looks down from above, but on the right as one enters are carved the wild hunter, his teeth bared in a grin and a wisp of hair over his face, and a brace of his hounds close by. But Hermes in Egypt . . . was the dog-headed god Anubis.[7]

The dog-man, then, is a Devil inspiring both awe and dread. Herne the Wild Hunter of souls, as Graves shows, is another face of Hermes, the angel Gabriel, *and* the dog-headed god Anubis. Thus, a visitation from this cynocephalic deity confronts the human soul at the cusp of life and death. Just so, the dog-man threatens the structure-bound with the looming corruption of Hell:

> Guardians of the gates of hell, hellhounds, and the souls of the dead themselves are often depicted as canine. In fact, it is not so much that the dog's role extends beyond the world of the living into that of the dead, but rather that the dog's place lies between one world and another. . . . The place of the dog in nearly all that it does in its relationship to man is liminal.[8]

"Guardians of the gates of hell" summoning souls to judgment and damnation! No wonder the structure-bound are so anxious.

Even if "the divine energies *are* isolated in the archetypal world" association with such evocative images must still be handled with caution. Over-identification with the mythic-personage, or archetypal-presence, of Death would be a huge inflation, potentially displacing one's implicate identity. Nevertheless these mytho-logical explanations for the massman's irrational reactions—of awe and dread—instill a sense to the senseless and meaningless suffering of imposed inferiority. In spite of the insult one may understand that there *is* an archetypal "presence" or resonance *in* the imposition, and hence a potential influx of divine energies. Here again, put in different terms, is that same difficult *coincidentia oppositorum:* where comprehension and acceptance of the efficacy and burden of the archetypal-imposition—the mask of the dog-man—provides a *refuge* and a *theater* for the implicate life.

If the use of the term "dog-man" to denote persons, across the gamut of racial, sexual, religious, psychological, and physical "difference," tends to raise the hackles of the reader, perhaps a few words of valorization should be said: (1) knowing friend from foe on the instant, speaks of the deep instinctive/intuitive capacity of the dog; (2) in the hunt the dog leads the way and is therefore associated with both path-finding and providing sustenance to the collective; (3) being liminal, the dog is the guardian of the threshold, and is thereby a protector of hearth and home, of structure and tradition; and, (4) in a world that has forgotten how to "welcome"—as Malidoma Somé remarks: "if you don't know how to welcome, ask someone who has a dog."[9] Finally, and perhaps most importantly, (5) the human emotional-body *is* a dog: no amount of rationalizing, intellectual justification, or explanation can move the grief, shock, and fear of the betrayed emotional-body; only *time* and *care* can heal that instinctual trust. Hence, we must tend our own woundedness—*with gentle force soliciting the darts*—as we would tend a beloved and wounded animal.

Clarissa Pinkola Estés tells us that "in the world of archetypes, the dog nature is both psychopomp—messenger between the topside world and the darklit world—and chthonic—that of the darker or farther back regions of the psyche, the underworld in particular." Thus, the "Dog" represents a deeper, oft forgotten, part of us—as Estés explains: "As in the ancient Babylonian epic 'Gilgamesh,' wherein Inkadu [Enkidu], the hairy animal/man, counterbalances Gilgamesh, the too-rational king, the dog is one entire side of man's dualistic nature. He is the woods nature, the one who can track, who knows by sensing what is what."[10]

Insofar as one may give it this positive twist, the term *dog-man* remains ambivalent: it feels right *and* wrong, insulting *and* confirming. In its ambiguity the image of the dog-man best portrays the Other Within: unlike the demonized rat or serpent, the dog is both angelized as "man's best friend" and demonized as the dirty-low-down, mad, or rabid dog; both attitudes dismiss and alienate the actual, implicate being. Either way it is an insult; anyone who has been socially devalued knows the sideways degradation of being romanticized (read neutered) as innocent, cute, harmless, simple, or childlike.

Angel-*and*-Hellhound, the dog-image—hound, wolf, jackal, hyena, coyote, fox, *Cynocephalus*—resonates and oscillates back and forth, from shadow to light, from wildness to domesticity, from admiration to a deep-rooted fear in the darkest reaches of the collective human soul:

> *The alpha wolf chooses his mate*
> *For life, & the other she-wolves*
> *Stare at the ground. Yellowish*
> *Light drains from notorious eyes*
>
> *Of the males, stealing their first*
> *& last sex. The pact's outcast,*
> *The albino we humans love,*
> *Whimpers, wags his tail,*
>
> *& crawls forward on his belly,*
> *He never sleeps at night.*
> *After pacing down thorny grass*
> *Where the alpha male urinated,*
>
> *A shadow limps off among the trees.*
> *Already sentenced into wilderness,*
> *As if born wounded, he must stand*
> *Between man & what shines.*[11]

Wasters, Rhymers, Minstrels & Other Vagabonds

CLEARLY WHAT HAPPENS to the one *born wounded* in the "dark night of the soul" is that the resulting deformity—of perspective, identity, and presence—is met with the imposition of permanent outsiderhood. Once removed from social standards and structures there arises the problem of just what standard to employ in confirming one's shape and value. This is largely a question of identity: am I dead, mad, a poet—or a little of each? The reply must be the same as voiced by the many-gifted Lugh: *I am all this.* And if the structure-bound deem the individual useless and malignant, what will be the disposition toward her or him? And the answer?—nothing less than Alexander's Iron Gate; any who breach this wall, whether in society or in the heart, will be assigned the inferior status of the dog-man, the dreaded corruption of hell, deformity, Otherness.

Having recollected the account so far of this prelude's guiding inquiry, henceforward, the focus will be the generally unanswered and remaining question: "Thus betrayed by the inter-personal social world, what shall I do? And how shall I live?"

THE "WANDERING MINSTREL"—personified as the Greek Orpheus, the Celtic Taliesin, or the Native American Kokopelli—is a messenger from the unknown. This singer-of-songs, as preserver of the "old ways," comes from the woodlands into villages, towns, and cities to deliver the news and to re-member wisdom. The structure-bound welcome them as "entertainment," and yet structural authority denies them membership; they are encouraged to move on quickly, and take their "efficacious" and trouble-making remembrances with them. The Wanderer—*already sentenced into wilderness, as if born wounded*—must be resourceful indeed to survive.

The scapegoating of deviants is a function of most, if not all, societies. More importantly, it has been a constant and vital mechanism for the maintenance of uncorrupted civilization. Wherever it has been established, whether of the church or of the state, its laws are reassertions and recapitulations of Alexander's Gate, legislated to keep the order, and ensure the peace—as in "the repressive law of Henry IV enacted in 1402," here cited by Robert Graves:

> To eschew many diseases and mischiefs which have happened before this time in the Land of Wales by many wasters, rhymers, minstrels and other vagabonds. It is ordained and stablished that no waster, rhymer, minstrel nor vagabond be in any wise sustained in the Land of Wales to make commorthies [i.e. *kymhorthau*, "neighbourly gatherings"] "or gatherings upon the common people there."[1]

It is important to note that, despite sanctions denying all sustenance, the preservation of the Arthurian myths—and so much lore of the British Isles—is attributed, not to the "Bardic Establishment," but to these ragtag and outlawed minstrels.

Resistance to political and religious oppression emerges now as one of the dog-man's two primary expressive-disciplines. Borrowing terms from Henri Nouwen's book *The Wounded Healer,* this resistance is "the revolutionary way"; while its counterpart—to be explored later on— is "the mystical way." These two ways can be instructively associated, in the words of Arthur Koestler, to "a dual tendency to preserve and assert . . . individuality" on the one hand, "and to function as an integrated part of [a] larger whole"[2] on the other. As Nouwen sees it, one way or the other is taken up in defense of the individual against the alienation and dislocation experienced in modern civilization; where individual meaning is denied and meaningful inclusion is thwarted. This "meaninglessness" characterizes a nihilism which, borrowing from Jerome Rothenberg and Pierre Joris: "not so much *postmodern* [as] post-bomb and post-holocaust."[3] The ability to literally and utterly destroy the world is the ultimate expression of imposed law and order. That is to say, the "revolutionary way" arises in response to the insanity of modern surgical warfare and threat of nuclear holocaust; as Nouwen himself describes, "man becomes aware that the choice is no longer between his world or a better world, but between no world or a new world. It is the way of the man who says: Revolution is better than suicide."[4]

Nouwen's conception of the "revolutionary way" is constrained to fit within the structural frame of his Christian ministry, hence, it is fundamentally "altruistic." In the context of this work, however, revolution must be understood as one pole of an extreme opposition. Contrary to Nouwen, this rebel may not be too concerned with saving the world; in its extremity the revolutionary way is more like Koestler's "self-assertive tendency" run amok; here one would actually *prefer* the mass-suicide of "no world" to the current alternative-world of oppression and degradation.

CONTENTIOUSNESS, CIVIL DISOBEDIENCE, defiance, resistance, and revolt move us from the Confucian program of civility to the Taoist path of the wild man Lao Tzu. In this spirit the break with imposed political order is not mere anarchy and lawlessness, rather, it is to follow the Tao, the *unnamed,* the implicate order,* the deep politics of the "edgepeople" who mediate wildness, chaos, and sacrality back *into* the structure.

The whole revolting array of intermediate material—"vision-quests, drug-induced visions, dreams," "myths, symbols, rituals, philosophical systems, and works of art"—has been designated by James A. Francis (in a book of the same title) as *Subversive Virtue.* According to Francis, in pre-Christian Rome various forms of pagan asceticism arose in critique and protest of structural excess:

> Deviance is a fact of life. In any human community exist those who simply will not conform to prevailing standards. . . . The way in which a society uses its authority to deal with dissenters offers an intimate glimpse into its inner workings—its values, assumptions, and spirit. Confronting dissent not only provides a measure of a society's tolerance, but also of its vitality and creativity in the techniques it chooses for defending its culture and norms. The issue becomes more intriguing when deviance is manifested in behavior that appears innocuous or even laudable, at least when viewed in isolation. Ascetic behavior presents just such a case of subversive virtue.[5]

Whether one *will* not or *can* not conform, deviance is indeed a perpetual element of life. And this is not always seen as a "bad" thing. Setting the question of "society's tolerance" aside, at this point the focus must remain the predicament of the individual deviant; yet it should be at least noted that it is not *impossible* for a society to act with "vitality and creativity in the techniques *it* chooses" in handling the deviations of the unprecedented individual.

David Gordon White offers a fortunate etymology relating "ascetic deviance" to the dog-man by way of associating the *Cynocephalus* (dog-headed-man) to the "Cynics (from *Kunikos* 'little dog')."[6] It seems that early descriptions of the dog-men sometimes portrayed them laudably to live simply, sleep on the ground, express their natural inclinations and appetites openly, and in other words, idyllically, "to live naturally"— Francis's portrayal of the Cynic supports the connection:

> Renunciation opened the path to inner freedom, a freedom manifested in indifference to social mores . . . rigorous freedom of speech especially before authority figures . . . and the overturning of accepted social values manifested in both ascetical minimizing of the requirements of life and

in public acts meant to outrage common sensibilities. . . . Asceticism was less a matter of battling natural instincts than of limiting their satisfaction to simple, visceral acts. The Cynics did not disparage—much less abstain from—food, drink, and sex. Rather, they abstained only from the pursuit of ever more refined and extravagant pleasure to satisfy the desire for them. By gratifying instinct immediately, simply, and naturally, the Cynic ceased to be in thrall to desire and its ever-escalating demands. In reducing the satisfaction of instinct and the requirements of life to natural essentials, the Cynic also reduced his dependence on others, and on the organization and structure of society itself, to satisfy his wants and needs.[7]

The performance of "public acts meant to outrage common sensibilities" show pagan asceticism to embody the self-assertive "revolutionary way." In addition, the characterization of "gratifying instinct immediately, simply, and naturally," echoes White's etymology, connecting the heretic dog-man with the ascetic Cynic. These associations are confirmed yet again in *The Cambridge Dictionary of Philosophy:* referring us to "Diogenes of Sinope (c. 400–c. 325 B.C.)" we are told that "he apparently wanted to replace the debased standards of custom with the genuine standards of nature—but nature in the sense of what was minimally required for human life, which an individual human could achieve, without society. Because of this, he was called a Cynic, from the Greek word *kuon* (dog), because he was as shameless as a dog."[8]

THE OTHER WITHIN embodies anti-structure; hence the obstacles to his or her inclusion in the structures of society and psyche abound. And yet, Joseph Campbell professed that our greatest obstacle will also be our greatest opportunity. Although it is terribly difficult to accept that one's mere presence evokes the looming threat of plague, pestilence, whirlwind, earthquake, war, and Death—it is only by accepting the "opportunity" in that difficult evocation that one may locate the back-door to the revolutionizing delivery of an unprecedented wisdom.

Fire on the Mountain

TURNING NOW to cosmic identity and the "mystical way," we meet the starry-eyed gaze of *the fool on the hill*. The Other Within is like The Fool of the tarot: his number is *zero*—he has no value, no fixed position in the sequential structure (as in Chinese cosmology where *zero* is the unnamed, the pre-existent and immanent Great Way of the Tao). Thus The Fool of the tarot—like Death—is both the beginning *and* the end of the transformative journey—as well as the liminal interval of transition between each station. Depicted as "The Wanderer": knapsack hanging from walking stick, and little dog leading the way, the image is harmless, unprepossessing, unimposing, self-effacing, simple, elusive, transient, and forbearing:

> The mountain . . . stands still; above it fire . . . flames up and does not tarry. Therefore the two trigrams do not stay together. Strange lands and separation are the wanderer's lot. . . .
>
> When a man is a wanderer and stranger, he should not be gruff nor overbearing. He has no large circle of acquaintances, therefore he should not give himself airs. He must be cautious and reserved; in this way he protects himself from evil. If he is obliging toward others, he wins success.
>
> A wanderer has no fixed abode; his home is the road. Therefore he must take care to remain upright and steadfast, so that he sojourns only in the proper places, associating only with good people. Then he has good fortune and can go his way unmolested.[1]

It is not quite right to say that society is *like* a mountain or that the Wanderer is *like* a swift fire; the likeness actually lies in the *relationship*—to be precise, the relationship of "fire to mountain" is *like* the relationship of "Wanderer to society."

The advice of the *I Ching* tells "The Wanderer" to pass swiftly like the hexagram's image—*Fire on the Mountain*—to make few demands, be "obliging," and attain "success through smallness." In other words, if one is to remain on Alexander's side of the Gate, as a lunatic or deviant, society must relate to us with *tolerance* in the same way that the abiding mountain relates with infinite tolerance to the fleeting insignificance of a fire. Furthermore, the Wanderer must relate to society with forbearance just as a fire relates with forbearance to the imposing mountain.

The "mystical way" engenders a manner of grace, gratitude, and graciousness. The Wanderer seeks to be "tolerated" within the structured order just as the incivilities of a dog are tolerated within a household. Again: the suggestion that one should graciously accept the status of a dog may be offensive, repugnant, outrageous—and, of course, it is: "so what." Like it or not the task set before us is to look beyond and deeper than the cursed indignity of the massman's mockery, to hold on to the thread of the implicate identity and so to *actualize* the hierophany hidden in the betrayal; and all this, accomplished covertly, under the protective cloak of society's "indifference."

Tolerance is the product of disinterest and indifference; it is the bearable range of play or torsion, the tree bending in the wind; ergo tolerance affords a refuge for the departure into liminality. Thus the inferior position, role, status, or public-persona inspired and evoked by one's "difference" provides a cloak—as Blake said: "Shame is Prides cloke."[2] That is, among enemies one may employ the shame of "structural inferiority" as a cloak—the mask of radical-politeness—which then safeguards the fiery pride of the implicate shape. To thus remain "unconquered" is the "ritual power of the inferior."[3] More precisely it is the recognition that to cunningly wear the cloak of whatever distasteful imposed shape grants a secret liberty and subliminal efficacy.

Still, it is a trap to go too far with this obsequity; for the gracious way of *propriety* is not entirely available in the extreme case—where one is marked *improper* on first sight. And how naïve to think that one could "only associate with *good* people":

> The mystical way is the inner way. Man tries to find in his inner life a connection with the "reality of the unseen," "the source of being," "the point of silence." There he discovers that what is most personal is most universal. . . . There he feels that he belongs to a story of which he knows neither the beginning nor the end, but in which he has a unique place. . . . There he touches the place where all people are revealed to him as equal and where compassion becomes a human possibility. There he comes to the shocking, but at the same time self-evident, insight that prayer is not a pious decoration of life but the breath of human existence.[4]

If this sounds foolish, sentimental, unsuspecting, and naïve—it is. Without the balance of self-assertive revolt the "mystical way" will accept the beauty and perfection of every indignity. Not to say that these, Nouwen's, sentiments are never authentic, but that in isolation they may be too optimistic, half-hearted, ungrounded.

The strength of the mystical way is that it provides a private antidote to social displacement: *to know one's place in a cosmology*—a fully constellated metaphysical, mytho-logical identity/location. The cosmic-identity accepts, with no candy-coating, the bitter privations and degradations of structural inferiority, because it is wide and deep enough to include *communitas*—the ultimate inferiority of everyone.

> *In a world where no one knows for sure*
> *I hold the blanket for the snow to find:*
> *come winter, then the blizzard, then demand—*

the final strategy of right, the snow like justice over
stones like bread.

WILLIAM STAFFORD offers a more complex view of the Wanderer's life. How can one live on snow and stones? The body needs literal bread, and justice too—but the descent has granted a deeper imagination where the strange likeness of snow to justice impartially blanketing all alike—reveals the poet's life, not as it ought to be, but as it is:

> *"Tell us what you deserve," the whole world said.*
> *My hands belong to cold; my voice to dust,*
> *nobody's brother; and with a gray-eyed stare*
> *the towns I pass return me what I give, or claim:*
> *"Wanderer, swerve: but this is a faint command."*

"Faint" yes, but difficult to miss; "that no waster, rhymer, minstrel nor vagabond be in any wise sustained in the Land," the message arrives a thousand times a day, sideways, backhanded, under-the-breath—the Iron Gate whispers shut with a sickening precision: "Wanderer swerve, no place for you here."

> *Only what winter gives, I claim. As trees*
> *drink dark through roots for their peculiar grain*
> *while meager justice applauds up through the grass,*
> *I calm the private storm within myself.*
> *Men should not claim, nor should they have to ask.*[5]

Winter gives harshness, starkness, scarcity; to "claim only what winter gives," and to admit the "private storm," feels more adult and serious than hoping for "proper places" and "good people"; a more adult ground to stand than "the place where all people are revealed as equal." Stafford's Wanderer seems to claim: "my condition is about my relationship to the earth, to time, to my wyrd, my star, my destiny." This

Wanderer does not need fame or human approval to have an identity—as Rilke said: "If only we would let ourselves be dominated / as things do by some immense storm, / we would become strong too, and not need names."[6]

Finally, there is a quiet but firm contentiousness in Stafford's closing statement: "Men should not claim, nor should they have to ask." The mystic and the revolutionary have now found their mutual orbit:

> *with few associates, in remote*
> *And silent woods I wander, far from those*
> *My former partners of the peopled scene;*
> *With few associates, and not wishing more . . .*[7]

Mandorla
The Bird-Masked Dog-Toothed Dancers

. . . in bird masks, with pig noses, dancing,
teeth like a dog's, sometimes
dancing on one bad leg!
They do what they want, the dog's teeth say that.
ROBERT BLY, "MY FATHER'S WEDDING 1924"[1]

NOW "DANCING ON ONE BAD LEG"—the mystic way of the modest, unimposing, obliging; *not*-claiming, converges with the radical way of the self-assertive, contentiousness, subversive, deformative. The wisdom, sought herein, must weave these two strategies together. The revolutionary will be the way of *cunning;* and the mystical the way of *grace*. Grace and cunning together make a Song-and-Dance of Life and Death—forever leaping from the shadow-steeped edges to bright center stage and then quickly back again to shadow. Reality, in this flux, is never either/or but simultaneously both/and *and* neither/nor; all of creation, never complete, eternally pouring into existence through the *lived poiesis* of the "mandorla":*

Two circles are sometimes used to symbolize the Upper and Lower worlds, that is, heaven and earth. The union of the two worlds, or the zone of intersection and interpenetration (the world of appearances), is represented by the mandorla, an almond shaped figure formed by

49

two intersecting circles [. . . symbolizing] the perpetual sacrifice that regenerates creative force through the dual streams of ascent and descent (appearance and disappearance, life and death, evolution and involution).[2]

The mandorla—the almond/acorn/hazelnut/seed; the *vesica pisci;** the deep diving salmon of wisdom; the aperture of the mouth; and the *yoni,* vulva of sex and birth; *vagina dentata,** the Symplegades, the devouring jaws of hell. The mandorla is the "seat of the soul," the *coincidentia oppositorum,* the crossroads "where disparate reality-spheres are hinged": the bird mask for the all-embracing "above" and the dog's teeth for the self-assertive "below."

THE MANDORLA-DANCE performed *openly* in the daylight-world is a heresy and a sedition. Therefore those who dwell in the permanent outsiderhood of the mandorla-heart must obfuscate; for the Other Within negotiates structure by confounding the light-hearted seductions of civil society, invisibly traveling the Rat's Way:*

> Sometimes farm granaries become especially beautiful when all the oats or wheat are gone, and wind has swept the rough floor clean. Standing inside, we see around us, coming in through the cracks between shrunken wall boards, bands or strips of sunlight. . . . [H]ow many birds have died trapped in these granaries. The bird, seeing the bands of light, flutters up the walls and falls back again and again. The way out is where the rats enter and leave; but the rat's hole is low to the floor.[3]

The poem could not be more apt: there is no food or life left inside the hollow structure, only "bands or strips of sunlight." The sudden wound of *katabasis* has dropped us to the uttermost bottom of structure, and still, amazingly, the initiand must not be tempted upward, but continue down and deeper into shadow.

The Rat's Way is a hard way; in addition to the wounds and despair of one's individual history, this private descent will be made more difficult by the collective failures of humanity at its most malign. Paradoxically such collective failures form an integral part of every individual and of wisdom itself—as Miller noted: "A deepening of *historical* being occurs by way of an under-the-worldly point of view," it is thus impossible to contemplate the *descensus ad inferos* (whether of psyche or society) without attending that "deepening of *historical* being," the darker legacy of "molten cities and scorched earth, of chimneys blowing human ashes through the air, of slaves in labor camps and gulags, of nations enslaved to other nations, of racism and apartheid rampant."[4] This is the darkness that we will have to integrate—eat, take-in, absorb, inspirate. Partaking here is the initiatory alimentation of a *lived poiesis*. The Rat's Way leads where the massman dreads to go:

> [Where] all subjects/themes [are] possible—from the most demeaned to the most exalted, from the most commonplace to the most learned, from myth to history and back, from present into past and future. . . . The results are contradictory and often self-contradictory, yet one senses behind them a commonness of purpose: to throw down and restore. And with this comes a necessary reassertion of the role of the poet as seer and chronicler.[5]

With the "reassertion of the poet as seer and chronicler"—as shaman— the poet assumes the "low to the floor" position of the quintessential Other Within.

It is not that poets must become more shamanic, but rather that those who have died the shamanic death of Otherness must assume the intermediate functions of the sacred outsider, the *quintessential poetic task*—"to throw down and restore." Not to say that we all become professional versifiers, but that "life itself, insofar as it is informed by imagination, is now poiesis—a work of art."[6] The liminal-descent of a *lived poiesis* has always been the furtive Rat's way of deviance, resistance and exception to the over-waxing fixity of dogma and orthodoxy—according to Miller:

> Perhaps—since the motif of the descent into hell is archetypal in nature, fundamental to the human soul, universal in scope, yet dead in the wake of ecclesiastical literalism and theological rationalism—it will come as no surprise to discover that what begins in myth, and then turns into doctrinal belief in institutional religion, reappears in a new form long after the literal belief dies away. Indeed, there occurs a virtual flowering of images and metaphors of the *descensus ad inferos* in secular poetry. . . . When archetypal *mythos* fails as literalism in theology, it is reborn as metaphor in poetry.[7]

What began in myth, and eventually dies in the wake of literalism, now flowers in the images and metaphors of the *descensus ad inferos*—blossoming in *poiesis*! Myth, now dead to science, religion, and politics, descends to the living root in *poiesis*—to re-store the stories, the her-stories and his-stories of our lives. And this is a radical move to bring *poiesis* and *feeling* (as Berman advocates) back from the edge into History.

The dog-man on the Rat's Way, sings the blasphemy of "what the soul *really* sees," singing to "criticize all structure-bound personae" and "mediate between all segments of the structured system"—in a synaesthetic, kaleidoscopic, mythopoeic-praxis:* a story-dance in which there is no single self or fixed shape. A mystic revolution—the plural vision-and-doom needed to escape the barren granary of the collective—reclaiming and returning the ancestral voices of our interior *and* exterior outcast and vagabond—as Rothenberg and Joris state: "the reinvestigation and reconfiguration of the entire poetic past and present . . . a renewed sense of history as personal history . . . a tension, then, between extremes of the personal and communal—the 'unspeakable visions of the individual' . . . and the reconstructed 'tale of the tribe.'"[8]

The Rat's Way is not simply to escape History; rather it is to find and recover what the light-seeking-high-flyers have missed. This inestimably critical point comes clear in the words of William Irwin Thompson: "The edge of history is myth. If we study myth in a scientific way, we miss the experience of moving into a mythopoeic mode of consciousness."⁹ Armed only with "logic" we miss the theo-poeic, psycho-poeic, anthro-poeic, geo-poeic, socio-poeic, *ad infinitum.** In other words, if the many-gifted Lugh stands before the gates of the "mythological realm," *lacking imagination*, and identifying himself only through the eyes of "monological study," then there can be no entry into the soul-making way of myth's poiesis. What is needed is not the merely logical, but, the mytho-logical; a leaping consciousness,* the generative tension *lived in the mandorla,* between the "unspeakable visions of the individual" and "the reconstructed tale of the tribe."

SEEN THROUGH "the mirror of malicious eyes," taking the Rat's Way is to disappear—by accident, calamity, misfortune—down a dreadful hole, whereupon the whole world mocks and laughs. If the fallen one then clings to the feeling of betrayal and to self-judgment according to the massman's measure—*lacking poetry*—the ignominy will be unen-durable, impassible; only the cosmically-anchored-individual can feel the profound correctness of this tragicomic play:

> Imagination in its archetypal capacity is a cosmic power subtilizing all life and making the "impossible," *not possible,* but real and actual. In other words, what is possible for imagination is more real, "higher" and "nobler" than what is actually possible in the so-called real life. In this role imagination is like the court jester who sees through the Emperor's clothes. Jesters are tolerated by the kings for the contrast they provide to a life that otherwise would be intolerable in its sheer and uninterrupted pomposity. The court jester is the "possibility" for the kingliness of the king and in that sense higher and nobler than and ontologically prior to the "actual" king. He is the subtle fellow who knows the secret desires of the king and converts them instantaneously into the reality of his own presence.¹⁰

Correctly mistaken, then, like the foolish "jester," we fall through the Rat's hole and find—*imagination:* what the "structure-bound" would call delusion, hallucination, madness. And yet according to Roberts Avens (the author of the above quotation) imagination "is our whole power, the total functioning interplay of our capacities."[11] For the initiated the devastating Thunderbolt is "real and actual . . . 'higher' and 'nobler' than what is actually possible in the *so-called real life.*"

Within social structure the jester is "tolerated," he is accorded no rank or structural power; yet to remain vital the king/center needs the sideways mediation of the jester/edge. If this is true for the *inter*-personal king, it is equally true for the *intra*-personal:

> The term "herlechin," like "harlequin," is a variation of the word "hellequin," and it designated the leader of a ghostly, ghastly, ghoulish troupe of clowns and comic actors. These actors often employed a trapdoor on the medieval stage, a door through which they dropped out of sight and into the "underworld." The trapdoor was called *la chappe d'Hellequin,* * "the mouth of the comedian" or "the jaws of hell." Presumably, we laugh at the poor clown who drops into these "jaws," not because we are relieved that it did not happen to us, but because it has.[12]

In "the so-called real life" the clown, the jester, (Miller's) hellequin, the mutant-monster, the exotic dog-man—outsiders all—share this thankless task; of facing Death and submitting to display and represent *la chappe d'Hellequin,* the mandorla-jaws of hell, the Rat's Way; and the further task, to recognize and accept the advantage afforded in the consequent "archetypal imposition."

The king/jester polarity is embodied in the contrary person of the Mythic Trickster, who stands outside structure at both ends of the spectrum—and fixing him at either end is a drastic mistake. A full investigation of the Trickster, as a role model for the Other Within, is premature, but it is worth noting here that the Trickster would certainly never fail to take advantage of the opportunity presented in a case of mistaken identity; whether superior or inferior, the "mistake" would be exploited. The point is that we must *know* the imposition is mistaken, and only then *accept* the mythic correctness of the mistake.

There was a time when a huge, shapeless monster, Kammapa, spread terror everywhere. With a never-ending appetite for humans, he devoured every person living on earth save one, an old woman who had gone into hiding. She was the only person left on earth, and without the aid of a man, she gave birth to a child born wearing sacred amulets. The old woman knew this child was special, and she named him Lituolone, a name befitting a god. By the evening of his birth the child had already grown into a strong man who uttered words of great wisdom.

"Mother," said Lituolone, "is there no one else but you and I on the earth?"

"My child," replied the woman, trembling, "not long ago the valleys and mountains were covered with people, but the beast whose voice makes the rocks tremble has devoured them all."

Upon hearing this, Lituolone took up a knife and went in search of the monster, deaf to the entreaties of his mother. The two met in battle, but it was an uneven affair—Kammapa overwhelmed Lituolone, swallowing him whole. Still, even inside the great beast, Lituolone was not dead, and he struck out, tearing apart the monster's entrails and releasing himself and all the rest of humanity from the beast's belly.

Having freed himself and the others, Lituolone became the chief of the society.

THIS LITTLE STORY, from the African *Bastuo,* speaks to us of a different kind of confirmation—i.e., one that occurs, not inside community or within the bounds of structure, but prior to both—in liminality.

Here according to the ritual formula, "separation, liminality, aggregation," the story should end. Following his descent into the belly-of-the-beast Lituolone is reborn, whereupon his passage seems to be duly recognized and confirmed in society. If the story were typically European, at this point a wedding would take place, ritually recapitulating the *hieros gamos** —the sacred marriage that inaugurates the universe—and with creation thus renewed the tale of Lituolone would end—happily ever after:

> But people were not grateful to him, for they feared the power of one born only of a woman, one who had seen no childhood, one who had conquered the great formless monster Kammapa. So it was decided that Lituolone should be killed by being thrown into a deep pit. But Lituolone avoided it. Then his detractors built a great fire in the center of the village, intending to throw him in. But in the frenzy to capture Lituolone, another man was seized and thrown in the fire instead. Still Lituolone's pursuers would not relent; next they sought to push him over a high precipice. Once again Lituolone was spared when madness gripped his attackers and they pushed one of their own party over the cliff; this time Lituolone restored the poor man to life. So it was decided that a great hunt should be organized, which meant that the hunting party, with Lituolone as its chief, would be absent from the village for several days. One night, while the party prepared to sleep in a cave, Lituolone was persuaded to take a position farthest from the entrance. When the others thought the chief was asleep, they stole out and kindled a great fire at the cave's mouth. But when they looked around, they found Lituolone standing among them gazing at the blaze. Finally, Lituolone realized that nothing would ameliorate this deep hatred for him, and he grew weary of countering these attempts to do him harm. So he offered himself without resistance, allowing himself to be killed. It is said that when he died, his heart went out and escaped to become a bird.[13]

The second half of the story suggests the traditional sequence of the king's ritual descent into liminality, to prepare an incumbent king for investiture, or to revitalize the reigning king for another term. These rituals entail various privations, abuses, public humiliation, forced acts of criminality and taboo, the consumption of filth, and generally the total reduction of structural status. Recalling the previous discussion of liminality as related to the *descensus ad inferos,* the importance of such ritualization is clearly understood to rid the individual of any egocentric pretensions to structural superiority, and further to invoke an antistructural depth-perspective: the "crisis of humankindness" which is *communitas.* In terms of the present work the ritual degradation of the king is intended to isolate the implicate identity by temporarily destroying the imposed structural identity. In the story the ritual culminates in the king—who has now become a kind of Trickster—"allowing himself to be killed," thus breaking open his heart to release the invulnerable bird of the soul.

In its sequential order the story inverts the standard (Arnold van Gennep's) tripartite conception of the *rites of passage:** i.e., separation, liminality, re-aggregation; as Campbell states it: "The standard path of the mythological adventure of the hero is a magnification of the formula represented in the rites of passage: separation—initiation—return."[14] The story begins *and* ends outside social structure. For Lituolone, for The Fool of the tarot, for the Other Within, the sequence runs: liminality, aggregation, liminality.

When the strange child is born there is *no* social structure. He himself inculcates a new era and a new structure in which he, naturally, becomes the king. Yet his strangeness—his wyrdness—and his power preclude his ever becoming a "real member" of the flock. Hence, assuming the position of king—the very heart and icon of "order"— constitutes an *intolerable* contradiction of structural integrity. Prejudice and fear push him out, and yet in the end there is the hint of a wondrous transformation—in surrender to the dark Mystery of Death the heart-bird escapes—and one may well ask: to where does such a bird fly?

Anyone who has perused a handful of the world's creation myths could know that the "constant," the primordial condition, is *not* structure; it is, rather, undifferentiated chaos, darkness, the abysmal waters. Creation, life, consciousness, intelligence, all begin in liminality. Thus the uncompromising *faith* in structure—as fundamental and primary to life—is revised; a revision that constitutes a radical shift from the civilized perspective. Here "structure" and the "aggregate phase" comprise the illusory and transitory states; liminality is the primary ground of creation.

Descent into liminality is the beginning *and* the end, the enduring touchstone of identity and being. "The descent into hell is actually the ascent of soul"—when the heart-bird escapes—we return to our source, the original darkness—we go home.

The Bird with One Leg

HAVING PASSED THE DARK NIGHT, the initiand has now arrived by way of the shape-shifter: deer, dog, wolf, rat—each shape adding another facet to the mythopoeic consciousness. There awaits but one transformation to complete this initial cycle: that of "the one-legged bird." In the following passage from his elegantly particular and attentive prose poem "A Godwit," Robert Bly captures a deep feeling for the strange life of this avian outsider:

> One godwit, not as plump as the others, stands balanced on one leg, the other drawn up. My breath pauses as I notice that the foot is missing, and in fact the whole leg below the knee is gone. When he hops, his isolated knee bends like the other one; his single foot kicks a little sand away with each step. Feeding and hopping, he comes up near one of the plump ones, and with a swift motion, perfectly in rhythm, bites him in the ass. He then hops out of the flock and feeds alone.[1]

On Alexander's side of the Iron Gate the survivor knows when to employ the self-assertive cunning to "bite the ass" and when to employ the forbearing grace to "hop" quickly "out of the flock."

The poet's "breath pauses" at the moment of recognition—ten thousand years of exile are caught in that suspended breath:

It took me so long to notice that one bird was not a real member of the flock; the flock moves continually, striding or flying. Sometimes the flock strides away and leaves him; at other times feeds around him.

The flock, moving around the one-legged bird, instills the strange dyslexic sensation of one's outer and inner realities in complete antipathy. This scene depicts, with excruciating accuracy, the affective experience of the Other Within: the crowd envelops you, you appear to be one of them, maybe even let yourself pretend for a moment that you *are*—then the bell rings, or the light changes, they move off, and you are left alone and unchanged. Like a statue in a park; life moves around you. This is not sad; it is a matter of *knowing* one's ontic* reality—and how ridiculous it would be for the statue to abdicate its own "being" in favor of a longing to join the picnic or fly with the pigeons.

Lituolone might have done better in society had he taken the position of "counselor" to the king. The great wizard Merlin, as advisor to King Arthur, was an integral part of the structure, yet remained a mistrusted and shadowy outsider, a liminal figure who arrived and departed unpredictably and at will. The counselor, like the jester/fool, assumes a subordinate position to the king and yet who can say where the greater power lies? Something here is being hinted at regarding the old and quite offensive idea of knowing and keeping one's place. And yet, it is only when that "place" of structural status is accepted as one's ontic reality, value, and identity that one becomes trapped into proving self-worth in "the mirror of malicious eyes." If however one is *in-formed* by an identity and reality with a source and basis outside and independent of structure, then "keeping place" means that the sociostructural locus and the cosmo-liminal locus* overlap and permeate each other. In "the seat of the soul," at the crossroads of identity, the *coincidentia oppositorum,* the mandorla makes a mystic/revolutionary refuge/theater for the *in-formance* and *per-formance* of exactly who and what we are.

Sometimes a person cannot change the circumstances of structural inferiority; accepting this does not make it right, or fair, or just—but one must remember that righteousness, fairness, and even justice are conceptions of "structure." Outside, beyond, underneath, and above the structure-bound there is an-Other place; a hidden place which the eyes and minds of the massman cannot dismiss or even comprehend. In the *I Ching* it is written:

> In some situations indeed a man must hide his light, in order to make his will prevail in spite of difficulties in his immediate environment. Perseverance must dwell in inmost consciousness and should not be discernible from without. Only thus is a man able to maintain his will in the face of difficulties.

> *THE IMAGE*
> *The light has sunk into the earth:*
> *The image of DARKENING OF THE LIGHT.*
> *Thus does the superior man live with the great mass:*
> *He veils his light, yet still shines.*[2]

Sinking into the earth; *katabasis; descensus ad inferos;* liminality; the Rat's Way; *la chappe d'Hellequin*—facing Death, returning down to the "original darkness" from which all things are sprung. If the situation seems hopeless, then, the work is going well; for the Trickster performs heroics by mistake—the task *is* to make the right ones; this is clearly impossible and yet the task, with its generative misfortunes, remains. The wisdom—doomed vision—of the Trickster does not offer "hope": i.e., faith that one will "progress" to a better place. Instead, it offers nourishment and strength to sustain us, with courage and humor, just exactly *as* and *where* we are.

It is the fervent intent of this work to prise open the impossibilities of confirmation outside the capricious and arbitrary castigations of structure; to circumvent the annihilation of the overwhelmed and fallen soul. Lituolone finally resigned himself to the fact that there is no fixed place for this power in the center of the social order. Here is the Mythic Reality: the hierophany of betrayal breaks the heart open, to disclose a deeper invulnerable shape, not a structural, but a separate, kaleidoscopic, and primal shape, in which we find a place to stand strong—in the *poiesis* of the mandorla—*between man and what shines*. And all this, knowing at once that in our extremity we actualize the true human condition, the secret promise of life, this is our bond—the soul-perspective of *communitas*—our hidden and deep membership:

> The flock rises once more and flies toward the sea where the packed sand shines. The bird with one leg rises with them, but turns in the air, his long wings tipping among the winds, and lands at his old place to feed alone.

PART ONE

Trickster Wisdom

"O hag," said he, "great are the hardships I have encountered if you but knew; many a dreadful leap have I leaped from hill to hill, from fortress to fortress, from land to land, from valley to valley." "For God's sake," said the hag, "leap for us now one of the leaps you used to leap when you were mad." There upon he bounded over the bed-rail so that he reached the end of the bench. "My conscience!" said the hag, "I could leap that myself," and in the same manner she did so. He took another leap out through the skylight of the hostel. "I could leap that too," said the hag, and straightaway she leaped.

JOHN AND CAITLIN MATTHEWS,
"THE FRENZY OF SUIBHNE"[1]

IN THE ABOVE EPISODE "The Hag O' the Mill" provokes Suibhne [Sweeny] into the "leaping contest," and thereby leads him back into madness. The Hag is considered by both the Matthews as well as by Robert Graves to be a manifestation of the poet's muse or goddess. She appears to him after he has been captured by his "friends" and coerced into reentering society. Ostensibly the querulous Hag wishes to tempt him back to madness, but could it be that in truth she rescues *her* poet from the abdication of his soul's vocation?

"The Frenzy of Suibhne" is the Celtic tale of a seventh-century pagan king and poet who, as Graves has described, "quarrels with both the Church and the bards of the Academic Establishment, and is outlawed by them." Here, as usual, when the prevailing authority is seriously challenged, dire consequences result: stripped of standing—his title, holdings, and beloved wife irretrievably lost—Suibhne must forfeit all place and status in society. Having twice insulted St. Ronan, Suibhne's exile ensued after Ronan "vengefully threw in [Suibhne's] face a so called 'madman's wisp' (a magical handful of straw), which sent him fleeing crazily from the battlefield. . . . [This] flying madness is described as making his body so light that he could perch in the tops of trees, and leap desperate leaps of a hundred feet or more without injury. . . . Feathers then sprouted on Suibhne's body, and he lived like the wild things."[2]

If one considers that the "flying madness," which strips away life's domestic comforts, actually endows poetic-power—the ability to comprehend the secret speech of animals, and the capacity to shamanic-flight—it must be asked: is this condition a curse or a blessing?

Is it possible, where individual deviation is tolerated by society as foolishness, even madness, that the misfit may be freed from the constraints of societal expectation? And if "transgression"—blasphemy, profanity, wildness, lunacy, deformity—is dismissed and laughed-off as harmlessly eccentric, inscrutable, superstitious, whimsical . . . *the fool on the hill* may escape the scourge of a more serious inquiry. Perhaps then the camouflage of madness will prove to be innovation's best refuge against the harsher attentions of a puritanical, demythologizing, fundamentalist regime:

> Social power establishes its validity by means of a privileged language
> of reason and various structures of exclusion that support the crystal
> walls of reason's castle. These structures confine the unruly and
> silence the unreasonable, and become visible in the great institutions
> of confinement that were first established in the Age of Reason: the
> poorhouse, where an ethic of work makes poverty socially beneficial,

and the madhouse, where a metaphysics of reason strips certain men and women of humanity.[3]

Paul Youngquist has rightly understood Blake's myth-making to be a method of negotiating madness; but it is not a personal mental disorder that assails the great poet, rather it is his being at odds with a world gone mad; Blake, in his own words, is "mad as a refuge from unbelief."[4] Like Suibhne before him, William Blake, in defiance of a stifling doctrine, holds the cellar-door, just ajar, to the unreasonable depths, the wild and chaotic "divine night," and, thus, evades the straight-jacket and sterility of structural conformity. As in the words of another "mad" visionary—Hölderlin:

> Oh friend, we arrived too late. The divine energies
> Are still alive, but isolated above us, in the archetypal
>   world. . . .
>
> What is living now? Night dreams of them. But
>   craziness
> Helps, so does sleep. Grief and Night toughen us,
> Until people capable of sacrifice once more rock
> in the iron cradle, desire people, like the ancients. . . .
>
> . . . in the lean years who needs poets?
> But poets as you say are like the holy disciple of the
>   Wild One
> Who used to stroll over the fields through the whole
> divine night.[5]

What is living now? The following pages will consider the possible advantages afforded those individuals who are forced to inhabit societal margins—as well as any benefits they provide to the society which has excluded them. Moreover, we will seek to identify the cultural systems, mentalities, and perhaps instincts that lead societies to set up these exclusions. Finally, and most importantly, it is the purpose of this work to seek the individual consciousness and disposition that can flourish within such an ostensibly adverse circumstance, a consciousness identified herein unequivocally with the Mythic Trickster.

WILLIAM IRWIN THOMPSON has described a culturally beneficial "emergent mentality" which, whenever it occurs, is resisted and marginalized by the majority: "when an individual . . . parts company from the mentality of his companions, whether the companions are Catholics or Communists, this change is seen to be so profoundly threatening that the person is seen to have fallen from grace."[6] However, the work in hand will contend a reverse order of these events: showing that the isolation of being "fallen from grace" is conducive and perhaps essential to the genesis of that "emergent mentality"—a perspective affirmed by Jamake Highwater in his book *The Mythology of Transgression:*

> We live in a society in which science, religion, and government have consistently conspired to keep many exceptional people on the bench. Yet, for me being "left out" has always been a luxury, because it allowed me to evade the rules governing conformity. For me to be left out was to be forced into a personal quest I may not have dared if I had other less arduous options. For as long as I can recall, I have always seen my separateness as the basis of a cherished freedom from constraints, preconceptions, and social expectations. Not everyone is so fortunate. Many people internalize the mentality that disempowers them.[7]

Ironically, suffering fewer options to social inclusion may well free us from the narrow straits of normalcy. Ortega y Gasset has said: "socialization pulls man out of his life of solitude, which is his real authentic life."[8] Adding another reversal one might say "ostracism *pushes* us back *into* solitude, which is our real authentic life." Here, along with Suibhne, and unlike the case of the renunciant, solitude and authenticity are *forced* upon us as we are driven to interiority by the exclusions of social order.

Pushed out of the game and looking back in, we may *see* more clearly than those who remain inside. But to see clearly one must first withstand the temptation to the blind-rage of injustice or the bitterness of "sour-grapes." For even where the misfit is freed from traditional constraints and expectation, as Highwater observes, not *every* misfit recognizes or avails them-self of the potential opportunity. If one is overly attached to the personal insult—the injustice of the wrongs done to us—one will miss the opening to a deeper, more mature understanding; as in the words of Lao Tzu: "By bearing common defilements you become a sacrificer at the altar of earth. By bearing common evils you become a Lord of the world."[9]

CAUGHT BETWEEN THE EXTREMES of praise and pity, the lesson comes early on: seldom will anyone recognize *me*. As an infant polio took my body and sculpted it into a symbol, a gestic* hieroglyph which relentlessly super-imposed its message over mine. This interior/exterior disjunction is the consequence of the *imposed* shape—an external status assigned to a deformity, weakness, or poverty—experienced as a violation of the intra-personal *implicate* interior-shape. Split by the crisis of inner-knowing in collision with outer-experience, the fortunate soul rejects the veracity of both and seeks beyond them to a deeper personal/transpersonal life. Like the divinity *Kokopelli*—the Hunchbacked Flute-player—the gifts, dreams, seeds, songs, messages are stored and camouflaged within the deformity; thus, the mark of exclusion, the wound, becomes the fount of creative generosity, healing, and innovation. If we would gain authenticity and yet dispel the "mentality that disempowers" our task must be to bear the curse and discover within it that humble sanctuary which is our personal "refuge"; to discern the difficult blessing, as in Robinson Jeffers: "the destruction that brings an eagle from heaven is better than mercy."[10]

The Crucible
In the Iron Cradle

THE DESTRUCTION of the ordinary life, the divestment of status, privilege, and community, lays bare something indestructible, or invincible: the *Thunderbolt* at the core of the human being. This dissociation is the initiatory crisis which nominates the mystic, the shaman—a private and unreportable "breakthrough." Through this wound the individual may come to interpret the "ordinary" with an unprecedented and extraordinary nobility and wisdom; as Roethke posed, "What's madness but nobility of soul / at odds with circumstance?"[1] Creative behaviors and expressions may thus be said to "originate in [the] difficult confrontations between daily life and the unconscious"[2]; that is, the disequilibrium, the *asynchrony,* between conventional expectation (*circumstance*), and extraordinary experience (*nobility of soul*).

In his studies of creativity, Howard Gardner has identified certain contributing factors to the creative "breakthrough; of which two may be taken as fundamental to the emergent mentality which flourishes in adversity: (1) the "Faustian bargain" and (2) "fruitful asynchrony."* As Gardner describes it, "asynchrony" is experienced as dissonance between the nodes of the "triangle of creativity" (*the individual* creator, *the domain* of work, and *the field* of peers and critics). In negotiating this triangle these two factors enable and accelerate one another; for the greatest innovations made within "asynchrony"—the *difficult confrontations* of *being at odds,* dissonance—are the Faustian bargains," as Gardner says: "they resemble that kind of semimagical, semimystical arrangement that in the West we have come to associate with Dr. Faustus and Mephistopheles. Equally, they have a religious flavor, as if each creator had, so to speak, struck a deal with a personal god":

> What seems defining in the creative individual is the capacity to exploit, or profit from, an apparent *misfit* or *lack of smooth connections* within the triangle of creativity. . . . Individuals who avoid asynchrony . . . are unlikely to become creative people; those who experience asynchrony at all points may be overwhelmed.[3]

> The creators became embedded in some kind of bargain, deal or Faustian arrangement, executed as a means of ensuring the preservation of his or her unusual gifts. . . . What pervades these unusual arrangements is the conviction that unless the bargain has been compulsively adhered to, the talent may be compromised or even irretrievably lost.[4]

Fortunately in mass-civilization the operations of tolerated deviance often extend into a tacit, or sideways, approval; thus, passively promoting a psychosocial, and ritual function—i.e., the rupture of consciousness or creative breakthrough—smuggling in the unmentionable stuff of *cultural vitality*—as Thompson explains:

> Without noise and lunacy, culture would crystallize into a rigid theocracy. . . . The rigid hierarchy would attract its opposite in the form of external catastrophe, and the civilization would be overrun by primitives or sink beneath the Atlantean waves. So a healthier way to preserve the chaotic stability that does not call forth a complexity catastrophe* is to tolerate lunacy and noise within the noetic* system of the civilization as a whole. . . . One can learn as much from the mystics, crazies, and noisemakers, for they will be performing the new unconscious geometry that no one can yet see.[5]

In any system, intolerance of chaos will require increasingly rigid structures, safeguards, and measures against contamination, which will ultimately bring the system to a catastrophic level of complexity [complexity catastrophe]—chaotic stability, then, depends on "tolerated lunacy."

In this understanding it is submitted that the juggling Trickster exemplifies the flexible "unconscious geometry" as well as "the supreme capacity to survive, exploit, and profit from [any] *misfit or lack of smooth connections.*" In other words, the cultural significance of the trickster-mythos, its meaning and function, is to confirm and maintain the vital necessity of disorder, anomaly, deformity, deviance, error, accident, profanity, and transgression. Asynchrony, then, as shall be shown, will prove quite useful in the development and cultivation of Trickster Wisdom. For those asynchronous and negating messages: "you *can't* go in there, you *can't* do it, you'll *never* make it, you are *not* one of us," are taken by the Trickster as irresistible invitations to the contrary. It is further proposed that Trickster Wisdom's *chaotic stability* and radical *porosity** derives from the polyvalent and kaleidoscopic consciousness inherent in the *poiesis* of "Myth":

> Myth structures itself so as to preserve its own levels of knowledge, yet it is an epistemology* that is remarkably sensitive to patterns of change. The framing of types and qualities of knowledge means that nature is apprehended in her variety, in her distinctiveness, in her unpredictability, with energies crossing boundaries continually. Boundaries are permeable, and [the Trickster] Raven is always crossing them, causing exchanges, making things happen.[6]

MYTHOLOGICAL POROSITY or permeability of boundary begins where "the framing of types and qualities,"—i.e., the *patterning instinct*—expands the associative wholeness of consciousness and reality; an ontic and epistemic expansion of "oneness" into three elementary and bounded zones. Depending on what vantage one is looking from, these *three worlds* will be experienced as various triads: the "mystic-cosmic" Heaven, Earth, and Underworld; the "psychological" superconscious, conscious, unconscious; the "societal" elite, redeemed, and transgressor (or Noble, Freeman, and Thrall); the "temporal" past, present, and future; and finally the "somatic" inspiration, intellect, and instinct. Our first exemplar in accessing and traversing these simultaneous yet contradictory zones must be the *shaman*—here described by Mircea Eliade:

> The pre-eminently shamanic technique is the passage from one cosmic region to another—from earth to sky or from earth to the underworld. The shaman knows the mystery of the breakthrough in plane. This communication among the cosmic zones is made possible by the very structure of the universe. . . . [T]he universe is conceived as having three levels—sky, earth, underworld—connected by a central axis.[7]

Traversal of the various zones is accomplished at the point of connective flux and porosity, an axis or corridor. The power of the "axis" lies in its participation across all three zones.

Shamans throughout the world describe regions that are inaccessible and *incomprehensible* to ordinary consciousness. Exploration of why the "incomprehensible" is rejected and made anathema by the "rigid hierarchies" will continue; for now, however, suffice to say it is vital to our quest that a rapport with whatever excluded zones *be* re-established—the instincts, the past, the primitive, the unconscious, the underclass, and the underworld—"the divine energies have withdrawn," or been excluded, due to civilization's incessant need to eliminate competing worldviews, hence, these disallowed lunatic zones will inevitably be the sacred realm of origins and creativity:

> Among primitives, not only do rituals have their mythical model but any human act whatever acquires effectiveness to the extent to which it exactly *repeats* an act performed by a god, a hero, or an ancestor.[8]

All dances were originally sacred; in other words, they had an extra-human model (for every dance was created *in illo tempore,* in the mythical period, by an ancestor, a totemic animal, a god, or a hero) . . . a dance always imitates an archetypal gesture or commemorates a mythical moment.[9]

The ritual recapitulation of an "archetypal gesture" is the *renovatio:** renewal through the reiteration of a dance, a participation—across boundaries of space and of time—in and with a "first exemplary model." In this way the world (or worldview) is renovated, recreated, and made anew by virtue of an axial connection to its origin—the *renovatio* is both ontic and epistemic—it is a simultaneous de-struction and re-struction.

Given that the "archetypal gesture" presents an image, we can say the image is *archegestic:** "gestic," meaning to bear, to carry, combined with "arche," meaning original and primary. This archegestic renovation presents again the essential proposition of this book: that those who are identified with, or who inhabit, the aforementioned lunatic zones are *forced* into rapport with undifferentiated or "primary potential" through the liberating effects and alternate perspectives, the "other views" found in ostracism. For the outsider the normative categories become transparent; and outsiders may themselves become transparent, thus encountering a disjuncted experience of out-of-the-ordinary and unlimited possibilities, a condition which by its resemblance invokes the primordial condition of *participation mystique.** In this rapport, forced or not, the archegestic image reaches back to, and carries forward, an *archai:** the "optimum potential" of "primary process," leaping and connecting back and down into the body, the unconscious, the past—leaping across forbidden thresholds—the archegestic leap is an epistrophé*—*a point upon which one turns,* as James Hillman describes:

> Epistrophé, reversion, the recall of phenomena to their imaginal background. . . . Reversion through likeness, *resemblance* . . . "to lead something back to its origin and principle, to its archetype."[10]

By attempting the congruities between the imagination of the individual human soul with the imaginal patterns that myths call Gods, an archetypal therapy attempts . . . an *epistrophé* of the entire civilization to its root sources, its *archai.* This reversion begins where the Gods are fallen, where depth psychology has always worked with its eye attentive to the ugly.[11]

Now fallen, and with an "eye attentive to the ugly"—the taboo, profane, scatological, lewd, deformed—seeing all the world through the backward magic of the Trickster.

Epistrophé occurs through an image which carries and delivers to us an archegestic impulse. In other words, the image incites what could be called a *biomythic reflex,** a "release" in which the "archetypal gesture" is spontaneously and atavistically embodied, enacted, ritualized, and performed. The archegestic function of the central-axis can be more clearly understood in terms of Rupert Sheldrake's *morphic resonance:**

Morphic resonance occurs between . . . rhythmic structures of activity on the basis of similarity, and through this resonance past patterns of activity influence the fields of subsequent similar systems. The hypothesis assumes that this influence does not decline with distance in space or time . . . [it] postulates a two-way flow of influence: from fields to organisms and from organisms to fields.[12]

Unlike the rationally irrevocable events of historical, or linear time, here, as in the time of myth (and the time of song), the "two-way influence" of an event "does not decline with distance in space or time."

Any approach to center—which is in itself an archetypal gesture—incites the epistrophé, a return to undifferentiated flow. The "rhythmic structures of activity" in morphic resonance are the "archetypal gestures" of Eliade's cosmic dance. Again, contrary to the ordinary cause-and-effect progress of linearity, in which stimulus evokes response, epistrophé is "the mystery of the breakthrough in plane," the interpenetrating crossroads where response may invoke its stimulus. That is, the gesture or image, as enacted and performed, acts as a lightning-rod attractor to its associated *archai*. In this way the archegestic image creates the mandorla—a space, a vessel or container, a "crucible," the *coincidentia oppositorum*—the crossroads of identity, where one is imbued with a renewing and informing resonance, the simultaneous in-formance of per-formance. Proximity to and participation in this kind of axial corridor opens the kaleidoscopic field of origins and presents the *renovatio* of associative pathways.

The question now becomes, how does the alienation of exile to the lunatic margin constitute an approach to that connective axis—better known as center? This introduces what is perhaps the Trickster's preeminent feat: the conflation of the center with the edge or limen; in this conflation Trickster Wisdom is conservative *and* innovative at once. So it is not exactly right to say that trickster energy breaks down or overthrows conservatism—in fact, conservation is essential to Trickster's task: conserving ancient and discarded wisdoms by renewing root associations. Thus, the boundaries that Trickster attacks are those of a fixed and eviscerated ideal—the hollow structure of the empty granary. The transgressions of the Trickster deflate rigid idealism and allow an incursion of awe-inspiring chaos. The central-axis renews by its participation with its antithesis: the anti-structure of the "time of origins"—here, again following Eliade:

> Heroes share in an existential modality that is *sui generis** (superhuman, but not divine) and act in a primordial period. . . . Their activity takes place after the appearance of men but in a period of beginnings, when structures were not always fixed and norms not yet duly established. Their own mode of being is an expression of the incomplete and contradictory character of the time of origins.[13]

Being neither chaos nor yet cosmos the "incomplete and contradictory character" of the primordial period is understood as neither-this-nor-that—or, perhaps more horrifying (to the rational puritan), *both* this-*and*-that—the mongrel abomination of the miscreant dog-man.

When the archegestic image provokes the informance of primordial energy—a resonant flux of both chaos and cosmos—we experience a reinstatement of the initiatory liminal period. And the importance of this point cannot be overstated: the truly sacred center *is* liminal. In terms of society, the permeable function of myth is active only when the danger of the edge is in full rapport and exchange with the security and sanctity of the center: "Without a tension from without and an osmotic exchange across boundary lines, 'the center can not hold.' Its structures and institutions become ossified and incapable of withstanding inevitable change."[14] In this White confirms: the vitality provided by the center is dependent on an osmosis between the known and the *unknown*. Yet, if the functionality of the center is understood to be dependent on access to all three cosmic zones, why then, do we consistently find one or more zones ruled out? The rational mind rejects the asynchronous associations of the *axis mundi** reducing them to duality, and, ultimately, flattens that to a one-sided, one-way, one-god, one-world-view.

UNLIKE THE CONFORMITY of the civic or social center, the connective verticality* of the axis can be transformative only insofar as it is apprehended in a *personal sacred experience*—what the soul sees it is alone in seeing. We long for sacrality, however, it must be made duly and abundantly clear that when *hieros* (the sacred) shifts from hiero-*phan*y [*phany* = manifestation], to hier-*archy* [*archy* = governance] culture moves from hierophanic implication and participation to hierarchic imposition and control—thus, as Robert Bly says: "vertical longing has to do with *feeling*, and hierarchy with *power*."[15]

Kaleidoscope
The Ten Thousand Things

THE ATTEMPT TO MONOPOLIZE and regulate sacrality bars all subjective views; the imposed and authorized "reality" abides no competitor. "'Pure Reason' denies all possibilities that are outside itself."[1] Madness, heresy, and transgression have, in mass-civilization, become the underground lifeline to cultural vitality, as well as the mythopoet's only refuge from society's defensive horror of any undifferentiated or multivalent* experience—in Rothenberg's estimation:

> For 2,000 years at least (or, more accurately, 5,000) the impulse of "civilization" has been to supersede & annihilate its past . . . transforming that old savage/adam nature so as to get us full-clothed & scrubbed before return to paradise. Obviously they haven't utterly succeeded but been plagued by heresies & intellectual eccentrics— which failure acts finally to keep the options open . . . to stand with Blake's continuous desystematization, or Whitman's contradictions.[2]

In the civilizations of mass culture, the "options" to interior depth (authenticity) are kept open or porous, *within* the forms of "tolerated deviance," evading the straightjacket of conformity, ironically, by the very lack of personal options to social inclusion, and particularly by agency of that most unreasonable disposition which is Trickster Wisdom.

Civilization's imperative to elevate itself, "to supersede & annihilate its past," brings the total abrogation of epistrophé. Thus, the shamanic permeability of boundary is forsaken, and the Iron Gate, which guards the civil world from desecration, will ultimately stop the very sources— energies, in-formances, gnosis, or kinds of knowing—which we had once set out to sanctify. But why? What is the *need* in human nature to limit innovation and prefer blind conformity? What is the impulse which erects the structures of exclusion, the "crystal walls" of dogma and fundamentalism?

> Heaven and earth are in contact and combine their influences. . . . This stream of energy must be regulated by the ruler of men. It is done by a process of division. Thus men divide the uniform flow of time into the seasons . . . and mark off infinite space by the points of the compass. In this way nature in its overwhelming profusion of phenomena is bounded and controlled.[3]

Of course recognition of *pattern* is fundamental to intelligence—the succession of days, distribution of directions, constellations of the stars, migrations of animals, the alternations of life and death. This "process of division" is what Ernst Cassirer termed the "classifying instinct"; it is the ability to differentiate and designate patterns and variations and thus to *anticipate* outcomes.

In society the divisions of space and time are arranged into systems of shared meaning—the categories and conventions of "authorized" knowledge and consensus reality. Taken to extremes the nomenclatures of the "classifying instinct" limit not only our vision of reality but of our "selves"—as quantum physicist David Bohm remarks: "when this mode of thought is applied more broadly to man's notion of himself and the whole world in which he lives (i.e. to his self-world view), then man ceases to regard the resulting divisions as merely useful or convenient."[4] Such divisions and measures eventually became the imposed regulation of Law—in Bohm's words: "they appeared to be 'absolute truths about reality as it is', which men seemed always to have known . . . which it would be both dangerous and wicked to question."[5] Hence, all that falls outside this "divine order" will be excluded:

> Traditional cosmologies describe a centered universe in which the principle of order is ultimately paramount. Their social product is a cosmologically ordered form of civilization whose central symbol is the world-pole penetrating the earth. . . . As the locus of divine law, the cosmic pole is the most powerful symbol of authority and is regarded as the only legitimate source of human laws.[6]

The *axis mundi,* the world-connecting corridor—once the locus of shamanic departure—now toppled and eviscerated, becomes the symbol of imposed "authority," regulation, and Empire.

Thus come the Capital, the Seat-of-Power, the Throne and Scepter, the Lord of the Four Quarters. As the sages of the *I Ching* proclaim: the "overwhelming profusion of phenomena" is "regulated by the *ruler of men.* It is done by a process of division." John Michel's book (quoted above), seems hopeful of our return to such a divinely centered cosmology, he offers a conception of "authority above" the human world; but this worn-out top-down equation, of authority to celestiality, can be considered complete only if we entirely dismiss the underworld perspective of bottom-up authenticity—the sacred center, the "world-pole," needs "roots."

With this in mind the *descensus ad inferos* opens us to those outlawed and excluded perceptions which lie "below" the orderly, normative, daylight intelligence. Richard Schechner tells us that "the narrative-cognitive stimulus works from the cerebral cortex down while the movement-sonic stimulus works from the lower brain up. Performing a ritual, or ritualized theatre piece or exercise, is both narrative [cognitive] and affective."[7] It can be said, then, that the authority of codified consensus (reason) is top-down, while the authenticity of the embodied and enactive (imagination) is bottom-up. Authority is cognitive reason, authenticity is embodied expression; and what is called for here is both, *authentic* and *authoritative*. The narrative-cognitive leaps downward (epistrophé), the movement-sonic leaps upward (*renovatio*); what we need is to locate a connective axis that can conduct these extreme associations—what Bly has termed "*the leaping consciousness.*"

In the modern world, the vertical pole of the universe has been laid nearly flat to form a flawlessly level freeway, an endless on-ramp of concrete and information. No longer do we bow our heads in reverence, but, with chins held high, humanity marches forward, shoulder to equal shoulder, in an ever-rising progress to a lofty utopian future—such idealism rapidly turns to fundamentalism. In this is the mistake, or worse the intentional substitution of the "social" center replacing and displacing the "sacred" center. The delusion of this flat, spread-out, readily accessible center (something like a shopping center) is explicated in an image from the Grimms' story "Iron John": when the Wild Man is brought up from the depths, captured and placed in a cage which stands in a public courtyard of the castle. Here, the primal energy of the "nightworld" is locked up (packaged) and openly exhibited (put on display) in the "dayworld"; however, its deep vitality is no longer available, for it has been demythologized, commodified, and thus alienated from its ontic context; as James Hillman explains, the "energy" is alienated "based on the ontological disjunction between dayworld and nightworld. Drawn to extremes, each world tries to deny the other, and a diagnosis of madness or of evil is placed by each on the other."[8] In this way "the whole divine night," the mysteries of the forest, the madness of the underworld, of dream, of darkness, and the lunacy of the moon are vanquished or rendered impotent.

The human imperative to order, at its most inclusive, renders a fluid cosmology: as found in the shaman's threefold reality; a kaleidoscope of swirling, overlapping *mandalas,* images, and myths that reveal a continual creation and the inter-relatedness of each and every created thing. This deep inclusivity or underlying wholeness is described by Bohm as *Undivided Wholeness in Flowing Movement,* or, in a word, the "holomovement":*

The implicate order has its ground in the holomovement which is . . .
vast, rich, and in a state of unending flux of enfoldment and
unfoldment, with laws most of which are only vaguely known, and
which may even be ultimately unknowable in their totality. Thus
it cannot be grasped as something solid, tangible and stable to the
senses.[9]

The ever-enfolding-unfolding background is more enduring and permanently "real" than any of the transient laws, forms, or creatures
that emerge momentarily out of the flux—as Bohm says, the reality of
"*Undivided Wholeness in Flowing Movement* . . . is, in some sense, prior to
that of the 'things' that can be seen to form and dissolve in this flow."[10]

When the perceived pattern of cosmos is fixed and closed, the
purity of the "ideal" order is consequently vulnerable to degradation
and contamination; the reality/sanity model, established by the "ruler of
men," cannot admit the unaccounted-for, it must refuse the unnamed;
as Kenneth Patchen said: "the saner we are the more danger of madness
there is."[11]

In an utterly idealistic mythos the unaccounted for threatens
a corruption of the pattern: a rupture of the heart (*cor*), as found in
the bottom-up-wisdom of Blake's inversion: "The Elect shall meet
the Redeemed on Albions Rocks they shall meet Astonish'd at the
Transgressor, in him beholding the Savior."[12] Thus, "Astonish'd at
the Transgressor" Trickster Wisdom delivers to us the "primary-
process," the "optimum potential" of cultural vitality. Furthermore, the
monumental structure of civilized idealism if un-*cor*-rupted—un-moved
in the heart—must savagely and heartlessly impose itself, overwhelming
the contrary, indigenous, imaginative, and innovative.

Regarding order as imposition, Richard Leakey remarks: "Imposition
of order is a human obsession: it's a form of behavior that demands
a sophisticated spoken language for its fullest elaboration. Without
language, the arbitrariness of human-imposed order would be impossible."[13] What gets said obscures what actually gets done. The explicate

suppositions of lexic* designation efface the implicate informance of gestic and intrinsic discernment. Hence, when the "ruler of men," that tight-fisted emperor, decrees the one right order, there follows an enforced and unquestioning catechism of "belief learned by rote"—the nomenclature and "taxonomy" (arrangement of names)—the infinite classes and orders of the *ten thousand things:*

> *Heaven and earth*
> *Begin in the unnamed:*
> *name's the mother*
> *of the ten thousand things . . .*[14]

The ever-burgeoning kaleidoscope of the "unnamed" cannot be regulated, it cannot be limited to the ratio of human perception, nor can it be stopped. Though we *name* ten thousand or ten billion "things," the attempt to keep "nature in its overwhelming profusion of phenomena bounded and controlled" must fail:

> *To order, to govern*
> *is to begin naming;*
> *when names proliferate*
> *it's time to stop.*[15]

Knowing that all *things* "begin in the unnamed," a flexible or "open" society would avoid such a failure by maintaining reciprocity with the "holomovement"—the implicate, undifferentiated, and unnamable. Considering the departure from the imposed order, the rigidly explicate and "known," into the flux of cultural and epistemic "porosity" Schechner observes:

Certain systems are more porous in relation to the unconscious than other systems. But the ways in which this porosity is encouraged or repressed, guarded, regulated, and used, differ vastly not only from culture to culture but within every culture, and even within each individual. Children, crazies, and "technicians of the sacred" each encounter and filter differently what Anton Ehrenzweig . . . calls "primary process." Account after account tells the story: a future shaman is "called" but resists the call. But s/he cannot control the experience "coming" in the form of dreams, visions, uncontrollable impulses, and sickness. . . . In modern Western culture it might be said that the impulses from which art is made—the experiences of the artist (the shaman's "call," the artist's "raw material")—originate in difficult confrontations between daily life and the unconscious. . . . Ehrenzweig . . . says that "the truly unconscious and potentially disruptive quality of undifferentiation" threaten to introduce the catastrophic chaos which we are wont to associate with the "primary process."[16]

Where the undifferentiated *kaleidoscopic chaos* and the differentiated *taxonomic order* meet and overlap, in the mandorla, is precisely the "poetic" domain of the Trickster: mythic porosity depends on the unspeakably deep "dreams, visions, [and] uncontrollable impulses" which shatter the "absolute truths about reality"—as Anne Doueihi notes: "This deeper wisdom about the linguisticality of our constructed world and the illusoriness of that construction is where trickster stories open onto the sacred."[17]

In the *Book of Changes* one finds the more ancient and indigenous patterns of *Taoism,* overlaid and obscured with the controlled invasive rigor of *Confucianism.* David Gordon White compares "Taoists, for whom chaos was an optimum potential or force and a desideratum"* to "the Confucians, who were meddling busybodies . . . the Confucians, with their rites and etiquette, their mandarins and sage kings, were fuddy-duddies."[18] These two antithetic approaches to the patterning instinct constitute the imposed-hierarchical vs. the implicate-hierophanous—sacred order vs. sacred experience. The Confucian-insider seeks top-down "control," while the Taoist-outsider seeks bottom-up "accord." Imposed order employs a closed structure to deflect and subdue the forces which threaten its control; implicate order employs a kaleidoscopic openness to align *itself* to those very same forces. And it is with the loss of implicate order, with the top-down imposition of unauthentic-authority and bureaucratic constraint—fuddy-duddyism—that the necessity of "tolerated lunacy" is born.

JOSEPH CAMPBELL DEFINED four functions of myth: "mystic; cosmological; social-historical; and psychological." At this point, we are concerned primarily with the third, socio-historical, function—as Campbell explained it: "the shaping of the individual to the requirements of his geographically and historically conditioned social group."[19] Additionally he says, "In the context of a traditional mythology, the symbols are presented in socially maintained rites, through which the individual is required to experience, or will pretend to have experienced, certain insights, sentiments, and commitments."[20] Rendered thus the "socio-historic" function is *conservative;* providing a system of shared meaning—but this definition is incomplete, something is missing which can be called *the adoptive capacity* of myth*. And this is to be set alongside Campbell's definition which is here termed the *adaptive capacity*. These terms are given following their usage "in current OED lexicographical practice, [where] 'adopted' is used to refer to words [images, and individuals] that have entered the language [consciousness] without change, while words [images, and individuals] which are altered in some way are considered to be adapted."[21]

One "adapts" oneself to the group when the need to be accepted (*as is*) is overwhelmed by the imperative to simply *be* accepted on any terms. The universal desire to gain membership in the social group can be traced to the essential human need for *confirmation*. In its elementary form, confirmation comes in that moment when we ask our companions, "did you see that?" and they reply, "yes, we saw that too," implying "your vision is accurate, you are like us, you are not insane." The counterpart to this conservative confirmation is the confirmatory adoption of intrusive or radical change: where the individual confronts the group with an ideological break-through, and opens collective consciousness to metaphor, innovation, and a revelation which cannot be denied and therefore is "adopted" as is.

The adoption is not enforced, it is insinuated; it works in reverse, from the bottom up, shaping the social group to the anomalous, thus permitting the collective adoption of the exceptional, deviant, and unforeseen particular. Such openness requires a structural and categorical permeability (or play) that is not accounted for in Campbell's four functions of myth. Yet he did envision the necessary reversal of social imposition, in what he referred to as "the other function . . . of 'the Mythology of the forest, the Quest, the Individual': the SILENCE."[22]

We could say that the village mythos has to do with the cosmic and social-historic functions of myth, whereas the forest mythos has to do with the mystic and the psyche. The adoptive capacity allows the forest experience back into the village; in Campbell's words: "the individual has had an experience of his own—of order, horror, beauty, or even mere exhilaration—which he seeks to communicate through signs; and if his realization has been of a certain depth and import, his communication will have the value and force of living myth."[23]

If the shamanic breakthrough, the expansive permeability of boundary, is to be reclaimed, the task here must be to enlarge the "social-historic function of myth," beyond the merely "adaptive" to include the "adoptive capacity." Moreover, this effort is predicated on the conviction that "myth" (if considered whole) is always and has always been *both* adaptive *and* adoptive. Clearly, Campbell understood the dangers in a lack of adoptive porosity, a danger which he termed "exploitative myth," to wit: "in some traditions—the biblical, Judeo-Christian-Muslim, for example—the exploitative, racial or institutional, as well as masculine-sexual accent, has been to such a degree dominant that everything else has been structured to support it."[24] Can such narrowly structured traditions, calculated to exploit, manipulate, and coerce, be accurately labeled myth?

Where this so-called "myth" commands unquestioning conformity and assimilation it must be disqualified as pseudo-myth, half-myth, one-sided-myth, etc.; this premise is explored insightfully in the work of Adolf Guggenbühl-Craig:

> I believe the mythologies of chauvinism and racism lack something: they are one-sided myths. In human relationships there is always a longing for the foreign, an admiration of the exotic: "the mysterious stranger," for example. For a mythology of group affiliation to be complete, it must include superiority *and* inferiority. . . . It is the one-sidedness of a mythology that poses a danger. To put it more precisely: any single myth is one-sided. It is the obligation of the person influenced by it to complement it with its polar opposite. . . . A myth of the evil male, for example, needs its counter-myth, in which women express their admiration for men.[25]

> Every human being interested in his well-being and his salvation is entitled to foster myths which seem to contradict one another. In fact, a person without contradictory myths cannot be trusted . . . the ego always experiences its own soul in contradictions: alternately as pleasant and unpleasant, as enjoyable and frightening, as constructive and destructive. This contrasting quality of psychic experience must be expressed in symbolism if it is to be really complete and not one-sided.[26]

In the mythopoeic state of mind there is an inherent openness, inclusivity, adoptivity, incorporating the Other without significant modification, and allowing the "difference" to exert its influence on the whole. In contrast, where the blind repetition and rigorous duplication of dogmatic-order is taken as the key to solidarity and sanity, such associative openness is discarded. Moreover, dogma—myth without *poiesis*—brings about myth by rote, imposing a one-sided ideal that is oppressive, abusive, and exploitative. As Blake realized: "I must Create a System, or be enslav'd by another Man's."[27]

Surrender of the imagination to the fixed (explicate) "ideal" is the move to one-sidedness, the move from implicate experience ("what the soul really sees") to imposed belief. The imperative to enforce cosmic-order requires that all exceptional and extra-ordinary elements be either neutralized, indoctrinated, or exiled, as in Plato's famous exclusion of the poet: where poetry, identified as a contaminant, is swept out of the house with the rest of the "dirt":

> In the *Republic* itself Plato could not forbear professing his love
> and deep admiration for the Homeric poems. But here he was no
> longer speaking as an individual, and he does not allow himself to
> be influenced by personal inclinations. He speaks and thinks as a
> lawgiver, who estimates and judges the social and educational values
> of art. "You and I," says Socrates addressing Adeimantus, "are not,
> for the moment, poets, but founders of a commonwealth. As such,
> it is not our business to invent stories ourselves, but only to be clear
> as to the main outlines to be followed by the poets in making their
> stories, and the limits beyond which they must not be allowed to go."
> What are these limits that no poet, neither the epic nor the lyric and
> tragic poet, is allowed to transgress? What is combated and rejected
> by Plato is not poetry in itself, but the myth-making function.[28]

Henceforward in Western civilization, as Cassirer here recognizes, the multivalent myth-making function of the unprecedented extraordinary individual is "combated and rejected," and the triality of the vertical dimension is cut-down and laid flat.

Where the ever-shifting nature of kaleidoscopic consciousness is shut-down or cut-off, there the one-sided and exploitative pseudo-myth becomes expert in the rigorous detection and expulsion of filth—as White says: "It is this sort of reduction that makes the forces of chaos, impurity, marginality, criminality, and foreignness all synonymous. . . .[29] The ideological domestication of chaos may be cast in terms of how a society deals with its dirt."[30]

Betwixt two great mountains, at the edge of the civilized world, looms the Great Wall; built by the civilizing law-giving hero to prevent the corrupting dirt and chaotic hordes of dog-men from swarming through the "sole gap" (soul gap?). "What is combated and rejected . . . is not poetry in itself, but the myth-making function." For the Other Within the liminal revelations of a *lived poiesis* have always been the transgressive works of deviance, resistance, and exception to the over-waxing and hollow authority of those who "no longer speak as individuals" who "speak and think as lawgivers." The myth-making function is the heart of Trickster Wisdom. The mythopoeic imagination demands a radical associativity, demands access, whether forbidden or not, to the *Other*-side of one-sidedness—to explore, in Lawrence's words: "the other universe of the heart of man, that we know nothing of, that we dare not explore."[31]

How to begin then, and take the first step to integrate the dark wilderness, the Other-side of the one-sided wall? Although Campbell did not centrally define an adoptive function of myth, he did write extensively on the individual-heroic departure from societal norms, a move which for him was the artist-hero's answer to the singular call of the *wyrd*. This valiant departure he characterized as "the mythology of the forest," in contrast to "the mythology of the village"[32]; a marriage of images that sheds a certain uncanny light on "The Frenzy of Suibhne," as well as his poetic heir, William Blake, as Bly says, "Blake took the first step: he abducted the thought of poetry and took it off to some obscure psychic woods. Those woods were real woods, occult ceremonies took place in them, as they had in ancient woods."[33]

The *village* is conservative and the ancient *forest* provides its counter-myth: the extraordinary individual in the wilderness, traveling through the dark, and always down, in a *descensus ad inferos* into the underworld, the unconscious, the lower classes, and further down into the chaos of the body and beyond.

If we want the Other-side, the implicate, mysterious, kaleidoscopic, then pseudo-myth, half-myth, one-sided myth will not deliver. Hence the division of mythology into "myth" (above) and "counter-myth" (below) is really a dismembering, a mutilation of the originary body of myth; as Wendy Doniger explains, "myth" always encompasses its own contradictions:

> A myth is a much-retold narrative that is transparent to a variety of constructions of meaning, a neutral structure that allows paradoxical meanings to be held in a charged tension. This transparency—the quality of a lens—allows a myth, more than other forms of narrative, to be shared by a group (who, as individuals, have various points of view) and to survive through time (through different generations with different points of view).[34]

Myth, in its essence, is adoptive. Clearly the capacity to hold this "charged tension," to form wider and wilder associative leaps, will be fundamental to any socio-adoptive function of myth; the farther we move into one-sidedness the farther away we are from the "paradoxical meanings" of myth and poiesis.

The ability to hold the paradox of the myth/counter-myth polarity is key to the mythopoesis of Trickster Wisdom and to the ability to *think* mythologically at all. One can deduce, then, that any facility to mythopoeic intelligence will evince such resonant tensions. Here we confront the notion of liminality as a personally sacred condition; where one's deeply personal and singular difficulties—asynchronies— drive consciousness away from local conventions to the multivalent crossroads of identity—as in Eliade:

> Only later did I understand that part of my destiny demanded that I live "paradoxically," in contradiction with myself and my era; which compelled me to exist concurrently in "History" and beyond it; to be alive, involved in current events, and at the same time with-drawn, occupying myself with apparently antiquated, extra-historic

problems and subjects; to assume the Romanian mode of being in the world and at the same time to live in foreign, far-off, exotic universes; to be simultaneously an "authentic Bucharestian" and a "universal man." Not *les extremes me touchent**—but *coincidentia oppositorum*. It was not, I think, an inclination toward extravagance and paradox. It was rather—camouflaged in biographical incidents and creations of a cultural order—my religious mode of being in the world. *Coincidentia oppositorum* is just as integral to folk religiosity in Eastern Europe as to the religious experience of an Oriental or archaic type. I should go even further and say that the paradox of the coincidence of opposites is found at the base of every religious experience. Indeed, any hierophany, any manifestation of the sacred in the world illustrates a *coincidentia oppositorum:* an object, a creature, a gesture becomes sacred—that is, transcends *this* world—yet continues to remain what it was before: an object, a creature, a gesture; it participates in the world and at the same time transcends it.[35]

The contradictory claims of *forest* and *village* struggle for dominion of the heart; the capacity to endure this kind of existential ambivalence—to live on both sides of the wall; to contain inner-knowing along with outer-experience and not defer to either claim—is key to the leaping imagination of Trickster Wisdom; it is the capacity to survive the asynchrony between the village's demanded conformity, and the dark forest's unprecedented innovations of self and soul.

Here is a "consciousness" leaping between the "unspeakable visions of the individual" and "the reconstructed tale of the tribe."[36] In this *coincidentia oppositorum* is one more, perhaps the ultimate, biomythic triad: the universal, the local, and the personal. It is only through the multivalent and abundantly fruitful asynchronies of this triangle—the hierophanic and implicate in exchange with the conventional local/imposed—that archetypes, symbols, and images emerge as transcendently "universal." In this, the individual speaks *not* as Plato's universalizing "lawgiver," but in the most deeply personal voice of poiesis—where the utterly individual *and* the utterly universal embrace in the *plurality* of the mythopoeic consciousness.

Without the inclusive and dynamic ambivalence generated in this trialogue—local, personal, universal—the imagination collapses into dualistic fundamentalism; myth is eviscerated, and there can be no adoptivity. The insider looks into the mirror and sees only the projected consensus ideal, the monovalent identity of conformity. If one reflects nothing "personal" in return, then nothing of authentic or original depth is offered back to community or cosmos. But if, by some chance, that contemporary-local mirror can be shattered, through that epistemic and ontic catastrophe—the hierophany of betrayal—some strange and ancient image steps forward, from the Other-side, appearing through the breach:

> There I stooped to drink at a pool, and I saw myself in the chill water. I saw that I was hairy and tufty and bristled as a savage boar; that I was lean as a stripped bush; that I was greyer than a badger; withered and wrinkled like an empty sack; naked as a fish; wretched as a starving crow in winter; and on my fingers and toes there were great curving claws, so that I looked like nothing that was known, like nothing that was animal or divine.[37]

Chymera
Mirror of the Beast

The evisceration of tradition takes place when the heart loses its relation with organic nature, its empathy with all things, when the core of our breast moves from an animal to a mechanical imagination.

JAMES HILLMAN, *THE THOUGHT OF THE HEART AND THE SOUL OF THE WORLD*[1]

WHEN "ORGANIC NATURE" and "animal imagination" are excluded from the heart, tradition is eviscerated: hollowed-out, superficial. An eviscerated culture is heartless: "the center will not hold" and the "dark beast slouching toward Bethlehem" may be our only salvation.

In one version of a cherished tale, when the Beast gives the mirror to Beauty, there is an inscription: *reflect for me, and I will reflect for you*; this is *her* task, the ultimate *narcissine task** of the soul to see through the self, deeper than appearance—not merely to observe, but to penetrate and participate, across boundaries, in rapport with the Other-half, the excommunicated half of being. In this way the "ideal" can be penetrated and broken-down, and a deeper undomesticated image, a wild visceral-image takes shape and enters the scene: "In the epic of Gilgamesh, which takes place in a settled society, psychic forces suddenly create Enkidu, 'the hairy man', as a companion for Gilgamesh, who is becoming too successful. The reader has to leap back and forth between the white man, 'Gilgamesh', and the 'hairy man.'"[2]

They say that Gilgamesh, *the ruler of men,* two-thirds-god, "Lord of Four Quarters," enjoying his divine privilege and royal status as the center and supreme embodiment of "Law," had become abusive of the common people and yet Gilgamesh was not so far elevated that he could not stoop to recognize his counterpart and embrace the wild Enkidu as his "friend." Most kings and petty tyrants, however, will refuse to be so humbled; they cannot resolve to trust their lowly twin for fear of losing control:

> The Emperor—the mythic insider—believes that facts inform us. Unlike the dauntless, medieval outsider on his fabled quest, who lets the reins lie slack on the horse's neck as he ventures into the very darkest part of the forest, the Emperor anxiously tugs at the reins, fearful of being carried away. The insider in us dreads the impetuousness of the horse, for the mythic horse represents the boundless possibilities of nature. And so the fainthearted Emperor insists on retaining control of the beast.[3]

Images of "slack reins" recall the exile of the Celtic hero, Con-Eda, who, in order to accomplish his quest and inherit the throne, must not only submit to the indignity of riding a shaggy little pony, but, significantly, must drop the reins and let the ignominious animal lead the way—submitting to the inferior, as Michael Meade elaborates: "Little horses like this often inhabit fairy stories. They are lame or hobbled, they don't go full speed, or they go the wrong way. They are the only horse left in the stable after all the warriors have mounted up and ridden away. They're the overlooked, left-behind, unwanted horses that wait until we're ready to drop down to them, then they carry us to the trials of fire and water that await us."[4]

There will be more to say on the wisdom of submitting to the horse later on, for now suffice to say that in each of us, as in the world, the controlling forces represented by Gilgamesh (the god-man) call for the balance of the counter-myth in the form of an unbridled animal-man—Enkidu the Wild One. In this mythic polarity there is an interesting correspondence with a particular story of Coyote and Bear:

> Coyote heard someone halloo. Then he saw Eagle a long way off. Eagle said that far off there was a country where there were buffalo all the time. Eagle said, "I am going there, but you cannot. You are too poor." Then Coyote was angry. In fifteen days he reached the place. It was near Great Falls. There was a big camp there and the chief's name was Bear. The people did not like Bear. When buffalo were killed, Bear would take the best pieces for himself—all the good meat and the chunks of fat.
>
> Coyote killed a big buffalo and stripped off all the fat. Bear heard that Coyote had killed a buffalo, so he came to look at the meat. Bear said, "This is nice meat. I will take it." Then Coyote took a red hot stone, wrapped it in fat, and put it in Bear's mouth. Thus Coyote killed Bear. Then the people made Coyote chief. Now Bear was a great medicine man. Whatever he wished came true. After Coyote became chief all the buffalo went away. Then the people said "Coyote is a bad chief."[5]

Eagle is the messenger of Great Spirit; and surely Eagle knows his saying "you *can't* go to the land of buffalo" will compel Coyote to go straight there. So just as the Great Mother sends Enkidu to challenge the oppressive Gilgamesh, Great Spirit sends Coyote to challenge the oppressive Bear. Here, however, the Empire of Bear is overwhelmed by the wildness of Coyote, revealing the consequence of a complete reversal: *no more buffalo*—i.e., scarcity, famine, ignorance.

The crucial point to be taken from this result is that when the creative abundance of the wild, unbridled, instinctual, and forgotten is accepted and integrated one will perforce relinquish a full portion of political, domestic, and civilized comfort, approval, safety, and wealth.

In the "Faustian bargain" we recognize the loss of this particular kind of "buffalo" as the requisite payment for a rare and generative freedom from the superficial life of conformity, denial, and one-sidedness.

> In ancient times, in the "time of inspiration", the poet flew from one world to another, "riding on dragons", as the Chinese said. Isaiah rode on those dragons, so did Li Po and Pindar. They dragged behind them long tails of dragon smoke. Some of that dragon smoke still boils out of Beowulf. . . . This dragon smoke means that a leap has taken place.[6]

THE ABOVE AND THE BELOW are met and mingled in this archegestic leap—displayed in the subterranean dragon's sulphurous spume trailing high across the sky. Of course "good citizens" don't want to see the offensive blemish of monster fumes marring their cheerful blue skies, and they certainly don't want to know what the dragon knows.

Riding the dragon we descend from the mammalian world, deeper down, to the reptilian: "the dragon is the paradigmatic figure of the marine monster, of the primordial snake, symbol of the cosmic waters, of darkness, night, and death—in short, of the amorphous and virtual, of everything that has not yet acquired a form."[7] The dragon is, in short, pure anti-structure. And the creative-soul in-touch with such hierophanous chaos, yet confronted with a terrified society's denial and proscription, is the definitive "soul at odds with circumstance." So if the dragon-rider is to dwell in the light-world, resist assimilation, and maintain a living connection to the abominable Beast of the Abyss, a "trick" or two will be needed. In this transgressive effort one must cultivate a great deal of *cunning*:

> The first experience . . . is interior. When the poet realizes for the first time . . . when he touches for the first time, something far inside him. It's connected with what the ancients called The Mysteries, and it's wrong to talk of it very much. . . . Then there's the second

necessary stage . . . which I would call something like cunning. And cunning involves the person rearranging his life in such a way that he can feel the first experience again.[8]

In this, Bly has given a cogent instance of trickster-energy abetting the individual departure to the creative life; "rearranging one's life" so as to feed the soul, to see what the soul really sees, to foster a personal living connection to *Mystery*.

Cunning is required to develop a mature connection with all those regions, ideas, and energies which have been disallowed: the "Trickster offers astonishing advice to adults . . . to survive in maturity, we must give up the role of the idealistic, innocent, virtuous hero, so prominent in children's tales, in favor of the cunning, aggressive, practical Trickster."[9] While it may seem true that the "virtuous hero" appears more often and so displaces the trickster figure, we should consider the preponderance in myth and fairy-stories of the "trickster-situation"; when characters are forbidden to enter a certain room, open a certain box, eat a certain fruit, they are being initiated into trickster-energy—for, as we know, to the Trickster a taboo is a summons.

In order to more fully grasp the initiatory potential of this dilemma, and the cunning it demands, consider the following story, "The Lind Würm," where we find a King and Queen presiding over a happy and abundant kingdom:

When the Queen is in labor with her first child she is attended by a Midwife, who seeing that the first-born is a small snake, discretely removes it from the birth bed and tosses it out the window. After which the Queen gives birth to a perfect baby boy; and the snake is never mentioned. Years later on his way to meet his bride the young prince comes to a crossroads where he is accosted by a huge dragon [würm] who bellows: "A bride for the elder brother first! No bride for the younger till the elder has his marriage!"

When the boy returns home and asks his parents about an older brother they truthfully reply that they "know nothing." The Midwife, however, is still alive and she recalls something about an embarrassing little snake she thought best thrown out the window. Once the truth is known all concerned agree that the dragon should be brought to the castle and a bride should be found. This proves problematic, however, when they discover that the groom devours his bride the moment he is alone with her. Soon there are no more princesses available.

Now a young woman living with her father in the forest, hearing of this situation decides to try her luck with the monstrous groom. She visits a wise woman, obtains her advice, and then heads for the castle. When she arrives and tells them what she wants they are delighted, and soon enough the betrothal is performed and she finds herself alone in the wedding chamber with the huge monster. He asks her to remove her skirt, and she replies that he must first remove his skin. The dragon complies only to reveal another, perhaps somewhat softer skin. In her turn the girl removes her skirt revealing of course another in its place. This exchange goes back and forth until the dragon is reduced to a quivering amorphous lump. Where upon the girl, having been instructed by the wise woman, fetches buckets of lye and steel brushes, and begins the arduous task of scrubbing; ultimately revealing the true and noble countenance of the elder undomesticated brother. After which, of course, a fabulous double wedding is celebrated.[10]

Again Gilgamesh meets Enkidu. In this case, however, the wild half gets *thrown out the window*—all the way down to the reptilian abyss—and our parents can tell us nothing about it. This calculated ignorance frees parents from any feeling of responsibility for the betrayal of their children; "it is not our fault, things aren't up to us, it's the government and the corporations (The International Guild of Midwifery), we cannot help." The only way out is to make the leap from the life of courtesy to the life of the forest and so to take-up the obscure cunning of the Wild One, the wise trickster-woman wearing seven skirts.

Cunning is foremost a wild intelligence. The Mythic Trickster is most often portrayed as a clever and wily animal and, more often than not, that animal is a scavenger: the filthy eater of carrion, the most cunning sneak-thief of all. Thus, Trickster tales bring the idea of food and nourishment together with the smell of death and decay, confronting life in the world "as it is" through the pores and membranes of our own flesh and blood, through the senses, which Blake called "The chief inlets of soul":

> The lining surrounds the cell; bark surrounds the tree; skin surrounds the animal. These membranes act in a selectively permeable way, allowing nourishment in, keeping poisons out, expelling wastes or, in the case of the nursing mother, expressing food. . . . Boundaries are the magic points where worlds impinge. . . . If one thinks of the human body as a bounded entity, one has an idea of what boundary permits and does not permit. Exchange with the world is made at the mouth, nose, ears, eyes, anus, sexual organs, and the skin itself.[11]

In this "porosity" the vital connection to the wild animal-Other is achieved through the visceral sensuality of our own bodies—as Sean Kane says, at "the magic points where worlds impinge."

MANY MYTHOLOGIES have so valorized the powers of the body as to interpret the entire creation in terms of human physiognomy. In the case of the *Ndembu* "mystery of three rivers": "Three trenches are dug in a consecrated site and filled respectively with white, red, and black water. These 'rivers' are said to 'flow from Nzambi,' the High God. . . . Each 'river' is a multivocal symbol with a fan of referents ranging from life values, ethical ideas, and social norms, to grossly physiological processes and phenomena."[12]

Victor Turner's long study of the *Ndembu* reveals their central ritual—*The Mystery of Three Rivers*—to be a vast and cosmic augmentation of basic body functions. In its most rudimentary associations the

Black River is *feces,* the Red River is *blood,* and the White River is *milk/semen.* All created things are then derived from, or associated to, these three ambivalent—sacred/dangerous—yet nutritive and life-actuating substances.

For the tribal consciousness the visceral experiences of the body are beyond category, life affirming, quintessentially sacred, and powerfully informative. For us, however, as Morris Berman explains it:

> Substances such as blood, semen, saliva, a whole variety of foods, and even "dirt" . . . symbolically [stand] for disorder. And to be disordered, from the Neolithic revolution onward, has been to fall outside the categories of Self and Other. . . . Fluids that come out of the human body, such as blood and semen, are taboo because they echo the fundamental problem of the infant: where does me end and not-me begin? Intermediate substances leave the boundaries of the body unclear, and this can evoke a primal fear.[13]

Here is the massman's terror of the "crossroads," the primal fear of the neither-*me*-nor-*not-me.* One clear task of Trickster Wisdom is to allay those fears, however humorously or unpleasantly, to reacquaint civilized society with the "intermediate" powers of our own bodies—again citing Berman:

> For many centuries now, and I suspect many millennia, "we" (i.e., our minds) have regarded our bodies as somehow untame, unruly—animalistic. They give birth, they die, they generate stomach aches or menstrual cramps, they contract diseases, they tingle with excitement, they get fired, and all without "our" voluntary control. Like animals, they don't "listen to reason." And so in animal species we see reflections of our own physicality.[14]

Hence, before moving on through the mirror of the Beast, the West's long-standing hatred of the body must be dealt with. It may sound absurd to speak of a "body-hatred" in a culture that is obsessed with body-image; however, the object of that obsession is an "ideal" of appearance, health, and youthfulness, which has nothing to do with experiencing the actual living body.

In what William G. Doty accurately calls the "tyranny of the svelte young body"[15] we are presented with an ideal or "virtual" body which can be sustained only by a prodigious denial (i.e., the exclusion of the "actual" body's demands and processes). This idealized-body cannot *admit* the inevitable betrayals of life: the urinating, defecating, incontinent, hungry, lust-driven, decrepit, childish, dirty, weak, smelly, uncoordinated, pre-ejaculating, frigid, flatulent, diseased, wounded, sweating, unresponsive, and capricious flesh. We have lost our reverence for the true human body; and the cruel demands of this artificial and idyllic "substitute-reality" have robbed us numb and blind—we cannot take the body seriously as the ancient Trickster Wisdom of Lao Tzu advises: "To take the body seriously is to admit one can suffer."[16]

Indeed, the body's suffering can be astonishingly cruel; but is not the denial of suffering yet more cruel?—as Stafford wrote: "I call it cruel and maybe the root of all cruelty / to know what occurs but not recognize the fact."[17] To "know" of suffering and yet refuse to "recognize" its occurrence is the essence of oppression.

The extensive damage done by such arrogance is epitomized in Trickster's adamant contention, "I will *not* defecate." Refusing to "recognize the fact," and so eating the laxative-plant, Trickster tries to escape his disobedient bowels by *ascending* a tree. No amount of elevationism, however, can out-pace the rising pile of natural consequence; ultimately, from the highest branches, he falls and is buried in a mountain of his own excrement. Thus demonstrating clearly how the effort of denial is exacerbated: one must dig their way out, groping helplessly, covered with, and blinded by, the substance of their own exclusions. As Paul Radin comments: "Broadly speaking, a Winnebago would say this is an illustration of what happens when one defies nature even in a minor fashion."[18]

Once the constraints of order have been established it is only Trickster who can continue to handle, with impunity, this anti-structural intermediate-material—the taboo and chaotic. Trickster's incessant handling of the anatomical, scatological, bestial, obscene, and blasphemous calls us back to certain realities and common sense. As James Taggart has shown "blasphemous and scatological speech also represents a stance towards authority, particularly religious authority."[19] That is to say, one may display a palpable autonomy, ferocity, and independence—i.e., self-assertive resistance to assimilation in the village—through transgressive expression. Today the Trickster speaks to us, from T-shirts and bumper stickers, in the flippant, yet impotent reminder, "shit happens"; few take this saying seriously, for that would be to admit too much: *to admit one can suffer.*

> The view of nature which has predominated in the West down to the eve of the Scientific Revolution was that of an enchanted world. Rocks, trees, rivers, and clouds were all seen as wondrous, alive, and human beings felt at home in that environment. The cosmos, in short, was a place of belonging. A member of this cosmos was not an alienated observer of it but a direct participant in its drama. His personal destiny was bound up with its destiny, and this relationship gave meaning to his life. This type of consciousness—what I shall refer to as . . . "participating consciousness"—involves merger, or identification, with one's surroundings, and bespeaks a psychic wholeness that has long since passed from the scene.[20]

How are we to embody this profound kind of *belonging*—relatedness, associativity, and participation—in a world which demands the alienation of animal-intelligence, instinct, and the dissociation of one's very body, in favor of a tyrannous ideal which assails us on every side a thousand times a day? Certainly not without cunning, not without the full realization that my body, with all its frailties of flesh and blood, is an integral source of earthly wisdom and authenticity, of connectedness to the rest of life, and *biophilia**[21]—the "innately emotional affiliation" to all living things.

If E. O. Wilson is correct that this instinctive "feeling" of connectedness to all life is biologically prepared, then—if biophilia is to be more than just a concept—we will have to drop down below the "linguistically constructed world" to actually experience those primal intelligences which have been *thrown out the window*—submit to the heading of the shameful little horse, embrace the fearsome reptilian brother, and take to heart the visceral intermediations and gnostic whisperings of flesh, bone, and blood. Let us recall the wise words of James Hillman that began our contemplation of the Beast: "the evisceration of tradition takes place when the heart loses its relation with organic nature, its empathy with all things, when the core of our breast moves from an animal to a mechanical imagination."[22]

In his book *The Gift,* Lewis Hyde makes the very important point that in a "gift economy" the boundary which defines the "insider" is the perimeter of the group, while in a market, or commodity economy, that same boundary shrinks to the immediate skin of the individual person. No one is exempt from exploitation.[23] With this in mind one may begin to appreciate the ubiquity of the alienation and isolation—the *not*-belonging and *non*-participation—experienced as dis-confirmation in mass-society. Victor Turner said that ritual transformation is "individual" while ceremonial confirmation is "communal"; that is, ritual is a *forest* experience, while the counter-part, which happens in the *village,* is ceremonial confirmation. Hence, in the commodity economy of mass-civilization no one can confirm another's transformations because the individual is not "a real member" of any exterior community, and there is no village to which any individual truly "belongs." There can be no sanctioned "crisis of humankindness," no *descensus ad inferos,* to transform secular outsiderhood into the efficacious "condition of *sacred* outsiderhood."

In ritual, the separation from community has the initiatory meaning and function of "liminality" and "descent"—where the separateness is valorized by all as a sacred and efficacious (albeit dangerous) condition. In the modern world, due to the complete absence of any confirmatory community, the traumatic and isolating passages of life become meaningless; far from entailing sacrality and efficacity, now the creative potential of liminality is belittled, skipped-over, and denied. If the village cannot confirm ritual-transformation then it must do without the creative vitality of the forest:

> Liminality is the domain of the *interesting,* or of *uncommon sense* . . . it represents a limitless freedom, a symbolic freedom, of action which is denied to the norm-bound incumbent of a status in a social structure. . . . Liminality is pure potency, where anything can happen . . . where the elements of culture and society are released from their customary configurations and recombined in bizarre and terrifying images.[24]

Clearly Turner saw the necessity of this creative source, as Schechner notes: "Turner searched for ritual's creative powers. . . . He wanted to show how ritual was not just a conservator of evolutionary and cultural behavior, but a generator of new images, new ideas, and new practices."[25] When there is no authorized "sacred context" our secular isolations and secret sufferings may resemble, but are not truly "liminal"—they are "liminoid."*

Here, Turner's word, "liminoid," is taken and turned to a slightly different meaning: it is not the modern or secular equivalent of the liminal, but a degraded, demythologized, depotentiated, and eviscerated remnant or vestige. The liminoid is *seemingly* an insider, a real member, while secretly faking it, "passing" as a good and valid citizen, hiding their wyrdness—even from themselves—at all costs, living in fear of discovery, and with a repressed disappointment (sometimes outrage) at never finding the healing and forgiveness of "confirmation" in the village.

Everyone in mass-culture will, to some degree, experience this disquieting sense of alienation and unworthiness. Yet this isolation is really superficial, an imposed epistemic construction; across the board, in the science, religion, and politics of mass-civilization, only the subversive wisdom of the heretic, or madman, may reintroduce the implicate flow of undifferentiated chaos. And yet as Hyde tells us: "most of [these] modern thieves and wanderers lack an important element of trickster's world, his sacred context. If the ritual setting is missing, trickster is missing."[26] It must be established, therefore, beyond all doubt, that deviance, cunning, trickery, in and of itself, is not enough; for the real fruits and blessings of our cursed asynchrony are the undifferentiated, unprecedented, and hierophanous generations of liminality.

In Colin Turnbull's view "as long as we insist on taking liminality to imply a transitory in-between state of being, we are far from the truth . . . it would be better seen as a timeless state of being, of 'holiness,' that lies parallel to our 'normal' state of being."[27] Yes! and what is more, this liminality is the constant, underlying, fundamental, and primary reality—as Bohm tells us: "every immediately perceptible aspect of the world is to be regarded as coming out of a more comprehensive implicate order, in which all aspects ultimately merge in the undefinable and immeasurable holomovement."[28] Thus, the liminoid constraint to imagine structure as fundamental and secure is mistaken: the forms and figures of "structure" and the "aggregate phase" are in-between, illusory, abstract, and transitory.

The counter-move, then, to liminoid one-sidedness, is extension into "depth," into the soulful perspective of the *descensus ad inferos.* This is not simply the withdrawal to the interior of one's private little inner-world, but a painful descent, deep down, into a holiness (Bohm's "undivided wholeness") that opens out behind, beneath, and within each of the ten thousand things, all creatures and peoples, invisibly connected in the depths—not the interior of the world, but the "world interiority"—the *Mundus Inferorum.**

The choice is a simple one; it is the choice offered to Beauty and her sisters: What do you want? What is your desire? Will you choose the bright bows, buttons, and fine silks of the persona's bright society? Or the soul's desire, from which all troubles and sufferings flow—a single rose; but not just any common rose, it is the blossom plucked, on pain of death, from the deep forest garden of the Beast.

THE DIMENSION OF authenticity is "depth": looking through the mirror to interiority, ancestry, primality. To survive civilization's barren plateau one must descend to the "roots": the cunning, instinct, and initiatory wisdom preserved in the mythos of the Trickster.

In the Celtic myth "The Transformation of Gwion Bach," the whole initiatory process revolves around the triple ritual/alchemical vessel—cauldron, womb, and coracle.* First, is the "cauldron" of the Hag Cerridwen (The Hag O' the Mill) which endows the gift of poetic wisdom—the knowledge of past, present, and future; fleeing the scene Gwion transforms into a grain of wheat; and pursuing, in the shape of a hen, Cerridwen swallows the grain and becomes pregnant. Secondly, then, the "womb" of the Hag incubates the initiand who is reborn purified and transformed; Gwion, now Taliesin, has become, in essence, the "son" of the goddess/muse. Thirdly, Cerridwen casts the babe away, alone in the "coracle," drifting to his doom on the cold Northern sea. Cauldron, womb, and coracle are one, as the initiand floats, in uterine darkness, for three days, or nine months, or forty years, traversing the primordial waters of life and death: "I was born during the night sea-journey. . . . I am all alone; floating in the cooking pot / on the sea, through the night I am alone."[29] Alone and anonymous, on such a limitless and bottomless sea, one must follow Machado:

> *Mankind owns four things*
> *That are no good at sea;*
> *Rudder, anchor, oars,*
> *And the fear of going down.*[30]

To be initiated by life's inevitable betrayals one must drop all such well-known conventional and trusted "controls," entering into collaboration with a deeper kind of knowing. Of course, one may face descent to these abysmal waters with some trepidation, that is only to be expected, but surely not with the Emperor's tight fisted refusal; for is it not the norm-bound "fear of going down," the terror of being out-of-control and dragged under, which promulgates the inflated rigor of fundamentalist inhibition?

Setting fear aside, putting to sea, and "going down," riding Con-Eda's little horse to a submarine world, the diluvian underworld where the Wild Man awaits in the hidden forest pond. This chaotic wisdom provokes us to great risks, incongruous and deformative associations, summoning the Thunderbolt of heaven down into the slums, the forests, the flesh; unhinging the mind, bequeathing madness as a refuge from the stiff formalities and pretentious rigors of false pride, as in the raving voice of Yeats's mad and broken-down old hag *Crazy Jane*:

> *A woman can be proud and stiff*
> *When on love intent;*
> *But Love has pitched his mansion in*
> *The place of excrement;*
> *For nothing can be sole or whole*
> *That has not first been rent!*[31]

Neither sole nor whole—till ruptured in the heart—broken-open to the depths, fallen to *the no-place of excrement*, where "shit" unquestionably "happens." Like the Hag O' the Mill, or The Lord of the Beasts, Crazy Jane summons us down and away from seduction and abdication to the wilds and a long forgotten authenticity. Only by epistrophé to this fertile darkness, only by admission of, and surrender to, the deformities and defects of self and soul, can we experience any portion of "wholeness." This is the task, the mad task, of the Other Within. In summary of this all embracing and vital depth, Robert Duncan cannot be quoted too often:

> All the old excluded orders must be included. The female, the proletariat, the foreign; the animal and vegetative; the unconscious and the unknown; the criminal and failure—all that has been outcast and vagabond must return to be admitted in the creation of what we consider we are.[32]

PART TWO

The Leaping Consciousness

IF WE ARE WISE, we are inclusive. Wisdom takes advantage of multiple perspectives and intelligences. Wisdom is never one-sided. Howard Gardner says: "Wisdom or synthesis offers by its very nature the widest view . . . considerable common sense and originality . . . coupled with a seasoned metaphorizing or analogizing capacity."[1] The mythos of pre-civilized native-wisdom is alive with an inclusive *poiesis,* allowing, even seeking, the kaleidoscopic unfoldment of ever-shifting cosmic and cultural patterns.

Many have described "tolerated lunacy" as a Saturnalian* outlet, a kind of pressure valve to drain off the excessive build-up of violent tensions, an hierarchic control process or "governor" for the elimination of accumulated cultural waste. The view taken herein is precisely the opposite: Trickster Wisdom creates play within a "system"—a social and/or psychic structure—it functions as an alimentary organ for the ingestion of undifferentiated chaos, the *prima materia,** the food of cultural and soulful vitality:

> The catastrophe of the previously unforeseen is what breaks the world progression forward, and the moment the catastrophe has come to pass it appears to be what was intended all the while. For it is creative in a deeper way than the planning creative spirit supposes. It transforms the situation, forces an alteration on the creative spirit, and throws it into a play that carries it beyond itself, carries

it, that is to say, really and properly into play, and into a play that entrains the entirety of creation. The planner, the watcher, is compelled to become the endurer, the sufferer. Such a metamorphosis into the opposite, into the absolutely alien, is what throws the knots that reticulate the net of the living whole and mesh the individual alive, into the fabric.[2]

The brooding effort of the beginning, the surprise that abruptly cuts across it, the meaning-bestowing understanding that links the unintended back into the plot by assigning it its proper place, are elements playing into the style of the whole continuity of the cosmic course, the cosmic "permanence," which is "continuous creation." . . . Everything has been down there all the time; things only come to view, assume, and shift their forms. What had reposed within the God like a dream, self-enclosed, and all-comprised, arises, steps into shapes, and variously confronts itself, to work effects upon itself. That is the continuous creation, that is the play of the world.[3]

Everything has been *down there* all the time! Here, at last, in Zimmer's elegant prose, is the sought-for model: the socio-adoptive function of myth—where the implicate or "emergent" is immediately welcomed, valorized, and adopted as original. Out of this "cosmic permanence," the mind of Brahma—the most ancient and originary—"things only come to view, assume, and shift their forms," in the ever-enfolding-unfolding holomovement, the *creatio continua** of kaleidoscopic consciousness.

The creative catastrophe is initiatory: as in the shaman's death, the "breakthrough in plane," the creative breakthrough is the rupture/betrayal of traditional, ordinary, structure-bound life, an opening which inaugurates a new unprecedented consciousness. The "meaning-bestowing understanding" then weaves the emergent or unforeseen, "back into the plot," back into the pattern as if it "was intended all the while." This is the *creatio continua,* the adoptive mytho-poiesis (myth-making) of Trickster Wisdom, the vast associative range of the leaping consciousness. As Gardner says, the creative breakthrough "involves a strange amalgam of the most elemental impulses with the most sophisticated understandings."[4] The distance conjoined between the old and the new, the primal and the rational, the above and below, is the proportion of creativity as inherent in "the leap."

Various cultures have fostered, to some extent, the widened adoptivity of this continual mythopoesis. It is of pointed interest to note that in many cases where this adoptive readiness to valorize the unprecedented is observed through the constrained acuity of experts and scholars, such adoptivity is reported as cultural weakness, inferiority, and shallowness of moral conviction and intelligence; this Western bias in favor of eternal, unchanging, monovalent, God-given social norms, is rampant—there are, however, helpful exceptions:

> I had been led to believe in the spring that the Coronation Gulf people never had had any knowledge of the killing of bowhead whales . . . [nor] ever seen a live one . . . after vain inquiries all summer, we heard various stories of whale killings, most of them centering about a single man who they called Kaplavinna. They told how this person had a very large boat. This again was new . . . up to that time we had heard nothing about anything but kayaks. . . . It turned out on investigation that my own man, Natkusiak, was the fountainhead of all these stories. . . . Kaplavinna was none other than Natkusiak's former employer, Captain Levitt of the steamer whaler *Narwhal*. These were the local versions . . . translated into terms comprehensible to the Coppermine Eskimo. Another story which we picked up at this time was that of . . . vague and strange animals living in an unknown land to the west. . . . These people were . . . unfamiliar with the dangers involved in the possible snow-slides and other peculiar conditions of mountain hunting. They had received from Natkusiak the general idea that mountain sheep hunting was dangerous . . . the dangerousness of . . . hairbreadth escapes from snow-slides . . . became in their versions hairbreadth

escapes from the teeth and claws of ferocious mountain sheep. . . . The Kiligavait, which they had associated with the mountain sheep in these narratives, were nothing but the mammoth, known to all branches of the Eskimo race. . . . Thus we had a side-light, not only on the origin of myths among primitive people, but also upon the startling rapidity with which they grow and change their form.[5]

As ludicrous as the image of bloodthirsty sheep may be, the mythopoeic imagination is here revealed to function as the mind of Brahma described by Zimmer as *the continuous creation, that is the play of the world.*

Surprised and delighted by the unforeseen and, at the same time, affirming it as issuing from the seat of origins, where the dangers of hunting sheep may be associated to the deep memory of hunting *Kiligavait,* the great mammoth. The adoptive mentality works in "the meaning-bestowing understanding" as Eliade affirms: "The historical event in itself, however important, does not remain in the popular memory, nor does its recollection kindle the poetic imagination save insofar as the particular historical event closely approaches a mythical model."[6] Mere facts and details are insufficient to convey the deeper meaning—as Eliade goes on: "We might say that popular memory restores to the historical personage [or thing] of modern times its meaning as imitator of the archetype and reproducer of archetypal gestures—a meaning of which the members of archaic societies have always been, and continue to be, conscious."[7]

Insofar as meaning is lacking or depleted, ossified, or flattened, its vitality may be restored and renovated by an association, through the archetypal gesture, to the energies of those deep images that linger in historical obscurity, lurking behind the rational facts. The *renovatio* occurs through "the meaning-bestowing understanding that links the unintended back into the plot by assigning it its proper place . . . playing into the style of the whole . . . which is continuous creation" (i.e., the ever-enfolding-unfolding holomovement of the implicate order). Ignorant of this deeper movement, the cut-and-dried explanations offered for our lot in life are maddeningly deficient, flat, and oppressive:

> The Romanian folklorist Constantin Brailoiu had occasion to record an admirable ballad in a village in the Maramures [northwest Romania, a geographically isolated region]. Its subject was a tragedy of love . . . he was told that it was a very old story, which happened "long ago." Pursuing his inquiries, however, he learned that the event had taken place not quite forty years earlier. . . . Almost all the people of the village had been contemporaries of the authentic historical fact; but this fact, as such, could not satisfy them: the tragic death of a young man on the eve of his marriage was something different from a simple death by accident; it had an occult meaning that could only be revealed by its identification with the category of myth. . . . It was the myth that told the truth: the real story was already only a falsification. Besides, was not the myth truer by the fact that it made the real story yield a deeper and richer meaning, revealing a tragic destiny?[8]

History wants to know "what really happened?" And the mythopoeic intelligence when presented with the proven historical version will return the very same question: "Yes, of course, but what *really* happened? What is the *truer* truth?" If the Mythic Reality is excluded, the "real" is limited to one ontological zone; consensual sanity/reality becomes one-sided, and one-sidedness will never answer the need of the heart.

The mythic imagination seeks to illuminate the hidden forces at work—or at play—behind the superficial scenes and day-lit details of a factual report. For the soul a literal repetition of facts alone is blatantly half-hearted. In myth, as in all orality, there can be no "one" original, fixed, or final version; every style, every personal rendition contributes to the whole. Every version is the true version, so long as the "teller" remains true, and the possible meanings remain multivalent and unlimited. The connective threads of many meanings, versions, and stories may widen one's heart enough to recognize and engage the extraordinary:

> Today I went into the hills. The sun was shining, I sat down beside a stream and a cow approached to drink. She had a good look in her eyes and I felt lonely.
>
> "What is it like to be a cow?" I asked.
>
> "Why should I tell you?" she answered politely, dripping water from her spongy lips.
>
> "I'm writing a book and I'd like to record your point of view."
>
> "In that case," she said, "I'll tell you. Do you know the story of the wren and the mole?"
>
> I was compelled to admit that I did not.
>
> "Then the story of the grasshopper who fell in love with a water-lily—surely you know that?"
>
> Again, no.
>
> "Do you know why the little men in the grass are unable to eat barley?"
>
> I shook my head.
>
> "I can't explain anything to you."[9]

In this scene from Kenneth Patchen's novel, *The Journal of Albion Moonlight,* we find the animal imagination conversing with the rational mind. The implication is that the cognitive-linguistic and the movement-sonic are able to converse via "Image." We must hold many stories, store up images, many truths, in the granary of the heart (what Bly has called "The granary of images"[10]), for the heart is the axial locus of participation in the above *and* the below, intellect *and* instinct. Only when prepared in this way can we readily greet the unforeseen. If the many-storied imagination is denied and impoverished, if we cannot imagine the wren and the mole, the grasshopper and water lily, the little men in the grass, then, when the unforeseen presents itself, when the paraclete arrives, we too will understand nothing.

RICHARD SCHECHNER OFFERS us yet another view into a people's adoptive capacity: the imagination of the Yaqui Indians who have weathered the tides of both Spanish and Anglo conquest. The Yaqui's cultural strength seems in part derived from a remarkable flexibility of incorporating indigenous with exotic/invasive symbols:

> In their own view, the Yaquis have never been conquered. Even after the terrible genocidal diaspora of the nineteenth century. . . . [T]he Yaqui struggle to remain Yaqui expresses itself most clearly in their need to perform Waehma. . . . [In this] The Yaquis are masters at appropriating what has been imposed: Catholicism, Spanish and English Languages, towns organized around a church and its plaza . . . the Yaquis have prevailed over diaspora by *performing their identity* as Yaquis.[11]

To remain unconquered, in this sense, is to prevent one's identity, meaning, and purpose from being displaced and disempowered. Certain performances—rituals and ceremonies—help define and protect identity. Speaking of such "definitional ceremonies" Turner says they are "a kind of collective 'autobiography,' a means by which a group creates its identity by telling itself a story about itself, in the course of which it brings to life 'its Definite and Determinate Identity' (to cite William Blake)."[12]

To cultivate and maintain the inter-personal—societal or tribal—identity is key to remaining "unconquered," but perhaps even more crucial is the "performance of identity" in the intra-personal sphere.

In this regard Blake can again be appropriately cited: "To be in a Passion you Good may Do / But no Good if a Passion is in you."[13] In other words, "when *in* a passion" I still know who I am, my identity and meaning are maintained, but when the passion (or the imposition) fills me up, I am possessed, my sense of identity is displaced and obliterated. Instead of "appropriating what has been imposed" and retaining an accurate sense of identity the individual is inundated with: "That defiling and disfigured shape / The mirror of malicious eyes / Casts upon his eye until at last / He thinks that shape must be his shape."[14]

In the face of such invasive, overwhelming, oppression and disconfirmation the consciousness of ritual display is the stronghold of resistance. In the struggle to remain "who and what we are"—for us, just as for the Yaqui—the mythopoeic "performance of identity" establishes a container, a sacred precinct: the "refuge from unbelief." Hence, the in-formance of per-formance, the imaginal exchange across reality boundaries via expressive display, is key to finding the blessing in the curse, and dispelling "the mentality that disempowers."

In modern society such a move entails a breakthrough to the contents of depth, "the place of excrement," the Mythic Reality, a radical move toward all that has been exiled from the explicate domain of the reality/sanity structure. Whether for a people or an individual, a refuge for ever unfolding soul is constellated by associative valor—the poetic synthesis of incompatibles—in the archegestic resonance, the *coincidentia oppositorum,* of the "deep image." Representing all that has been outcast—death, the ghettos, the Beast, the body, the unconscious, the abyss—the leaping Trickster is the liminal ambassador of the axial corridor, the one who is conversant at once with above-*and*-below, center-*and*-edge, spirit-*and*-flesh:

Depth is the measure of vision. If one sees deeply enough, one lets in the light. The poet is a seer or better, a shaman, defined by the Copper Eskimo as "the one who has eyes." So "Deep image (if it was more than a gimmick) carried the hope, like poetry in general, of 'finding the center,' which is an activity the ancestors in the old myths of founding engaged in at the start and that we have to learn to do again."[15]

Dragon Smoke
The Marriage of Heaven and Hell

*In many ancient works of art we notice a long floating leap
at the center of the work. That leap can be described as a
leap from the conscious to the unconscious and back again,
a leap from the known part of the mind to the unknown
part and back to the known. . . . Powerful feeling makes
the mind associate faster, and evidently the presence of
swift association makes the emotions still more alive.*

ROBERT BLY, *LEAPING POETRY:*
AN IDEA WITH POEMS AND TRANSLATIONS[1]

CONNECTING SELF TO OTHERNESS, the leaping consciousness is
the antithesis of one-sidedness. The wisdom of whole-heartedness,
Trickster Wisdom, and the mythopoeic imagination are dependent
on this associative alacrity.* The hierophanic provocation of the
archegestic image is not merely to form an association, but to breach—
to de-form—a previously established border of consciousness, and thus,
to widen the heart. The normative consciousness-boundary represents
the spatiotemporal*-psychosomatic compass of consensus reality; the
broach of which limit presents the dissolution of structure, the crisis of
shamanic-death, the rupture of the heart—*cor-ruption*—widening and
allowing all that has been excluded to return:

Bly's most explicit statement on the image is in his essay, "Recognizing the Image as a Form of Intelligence," in which he says, "The image joins the light and dark worlds . . . when a poet creates a true image, he is gaining knowledge, he is bringing up into consciousness a connection that has been forgotten." Further, images "present intellectual evidence against . . . the notion that human reason is alone in its intelligence, isolated, and unchangeably remote from the natural world."[2]

The "deep image," the archetypal gesture, the biomythic reflex, the epi-strophé and *renovatio,* the *arche / gestic* in-formance of performance— re-membering "a connection that has been forgotten," connecting to the outlawed, suppressed, and excluded, simultaneously and indivisibly in myth, psyche, and culture.

In Sean Kane's mytho-ecological view this "forgotten connection" may be found in reaching, beyond the more recent agricultural bias, back to the paleolithic hunters and down to our shamanic roots: "it is practically impossible for us to feel our way to the spirituality of human beings who lived without agriculture. These were people who greeted all forms of life as intelligent kin."[3] This "biophilia" changed dramatically with the advent of agriculture, as Kane explains, "with the crossing into the Neolithic . . . the barriers go up between human effort and providen-tial nature." The history of the "human effort" to barricade "the sole gap between the civilized and savage races and worlds," to divide and regu-late "providential nature," reaches its apex in the ideology of Alexander's Iron Gate.[4] The sedentary and settled world-view of property-rights, with fenced-in and controlled resources, represents a monumental shift in consciousness, as Morris Berman corroborates: "domestication was a profound redirection of human reason, from the subtle to the coarse, i.e., from polymorphous and kaleidoscopic thinking to that which is binary, mechanical, ideological."[5] The leaping consciousness, then, is probably as close as any post-agrarian can get to what Berman calls *participating con-sciousness.* In the associative leap we have what Kane calls "the music of pattern . . . a polyphony, with each voice, each being, singing its own song or story."[6] Conjoining the modern-human-village and the archaic-bestial-forest, the leaping consciousness attempts an archegestic epistrophé from the solar thunderbird to the lunar serpent:

> *No instruction is certain, no knowledge complete.*
> *If I speak for the serpent, the serpent*
> *may speak for the bird. My position*
> *is that I have no position.*[7]

Leaping ten thousand years and more Robert Bringhurst opens the axial corridor between the celestial bird of cosmos and the underworld serpent of chaos. One can agree when he adds, "all positions are prisons and no truth is true," because the trap of the fenced-in and fixed position has been laid bare.

The leaping consciousness is not satisfied to make a single heroic dive to the *archai* of the underworld, then return up to this world, and call the job done. Its achievement is more cyclical and oscillatory, like Persephone's seasonal rhythms—back and forth between the worlds repeatedly. Or better, like swift Hermes, leaping between the extremes of Olympus and Hades and through the ordinary world of middle-earth at will. This kind of multidimensionality demands the "no position" of the leap. The rational mind cannot come to rest upon a clear concept here; the image stays in motion, it dances—and as Marion Woodman has said: "What does not move dies."[8]

While this leaping wit is mercurial, it should not be confused with duplicitous deceit, or indecisive weakness. The insider's inability to endure the crisis of extremes is best characterized as "shiftless": immovable, uninspired, obtuse, and trivial; while the polyvalent Trickster, by subtle contrast, is "shifty": multifaceted, unpredictable, irrepressible. Like the ever-changing surface of water Trickster Wisdom is deceptively deep. This "multivalence" (evaluative plurality) is essential to depth—in Turner's view:

I discovered that what I called dominant or pivotal symbols . . . were not only possessors of multiple meanings but also had the property of polarization. [On one hand there is] the physiological or orectic* pole of . . . meaning. "Orectic" is a term . . . meaning "of or characterized by appetite or desire." [On the other hand there is] the normative or ideological pole, since it refers to principles of social organization, social categories, and values . . . the orectic pole . . . surely has something to do with the functions of the limbic system, the old mammalian brain. . . . It is interesting to me that a dominant [multivalent] symbol—every ritual system has several of them—should replicate in its structural and semantic make-up what are coming to be seen as key neurological features of the brain and central nervous system.[9]

Ergo Jung's emphasis, as well as Eliade's and Campbell's, on the *coincidentia oppositorum,* the neither-this-nor-that of liminality, the crossroads, the mandorla, the *no position* of the creative breakthrough, where the contradictions of the "orectic" forest and the "normative" village are not resolved but bound together—married in a dance.

With reference to the "central nervous system" Turner opens the way to speculations on brain and neural function, which he relates to "play," and which Bly relates to the workings of the leaping consciousness—a consciousness essential to the generations of Trickster Wisdom. Therefore the descent now proceeds in a brief look at "the 'triune brain' . . . three brains in one . . . each [with] its own special intelligence, its own sense of time and space."[10]

ANATOMICALLY IT IS a fact that these three distinct parts of the human brain—arche-cortex, meso-cortex, and neo-cortex—are stratified somewhat like an archaeological site: the deeper you dig the older the information. Right away one should notice a reoccurrence of *triality,* rendering one more microcosm to be trisected by some transcortical axis. If we prefer the new and the higher we will naturally exalt the neo-cortex; some go so far as to name the frontal lobes (a division of the neo-cortex) the "angel brain." One should, however, if spending any time at all in this matter, be primarily seeking the connective axis. Hence, continuing the emphasis on descent to the *archai,* rather than vilify the elder and lower "animal" cortices, the quest, herein, should aim to valorize their vital contribution—as Anthony Stevens suggests: "it seems probable that Jung was right when he guessed that the archetypal systems, if they could be given a local habitation and a name, must have their neuronal substrate located in the phylogenetically much older parts of the brain."[11] It will not suffice to describe "animality" as inevitably leading to a *Lord of the Flies* catastrophe; and it should not be too difficult to connect the malevolent contributions of the "new brain" to the ceaseless torrent of human atrocity. If the neo-cortex is the angel brain then it is also the devil brain: the infernal side of humankind must be understood to exceed and eclipse mere animal brutality.

In this context revisiting Schechner is pertinent: "the narrative-cognitive stimulus works from the cerebral cortex down while the movement-sonic stimulus works from the lower brain up. Performing a ritual . . . is both narrative (cognitive) and affective"—top-down control *and* bottom-up abandon. Let it be said, then, that top-down control is angelic *and* demonic, and that bottom-up abandon is equally innocent *and* savage. Furthermore, as it is with *yin* and *yang,* opposites associate and *reverse* at their points of excess, at the point of conflict, "where disparate reality spheres hinge," as in Blake: "Excess of sorrow laughs. Excess of joy weeps."[12]

If on one hand the village-normative is likened to the narrative-cognitive, and on the other hand the forest-orectic to the movement-sonic, it becomes clear that the embodied, performative arts—song, dance, oratory, ritual—are forest-orectic, movement-sonic, bottom-up in character. Although the present work mainly strives to revalorize the exiled depths, it should be pointed out that whether one pursues the mental meditative-contemplative or the somatic ritual-enactive pathways, ultimately neither will succeed unless there occurs a coincidence, a breakthrough from one side (hemisphere) to the other, arcing through the intervallic* void of the *coincidentia oppositorum:*

> The associative paths . . . allow us to leap from one part of the brain to another and lay out their contraries. Moreover it's possible that what we call "mythology" deals precisely with these abrupt juxtapositions . . . using what Joseph Campbell called "mythological thinking," it moves the energy along a spectrum—either up or down. [It] can awaken the "lost music," walk on the sea, cross the river from instinct to spirit.[13]

The mythical and logical bases and processes of the leaping consciousness, of Trickster Wisdom, and of mythopoesis itself, take place in a holographic *trialogue* associating across the nexus of "abrupt juxtapositions" between every macro-, meso-, and micro-cosmic zone of one's biological, psychological, and sociological being:

> It's clear that Lorca is often leaping from one brain to another. . . . Lorca pulls an image out of the memory bank of the mammal brain: "The creatures of the moon sniff and prowl about their cabins," and then immediately follows with an image from the memory bank of the reptile brain, "The living iguanas will come to bite the men who do not dream," and then an image from the memory bank of the new brain comes in: "The man who rushes out with his spirit broken . . ." He doesn't do it deliberately—that's simply how the brain works when it is confident and excited.[14]

It is preferable, in the present context, to say "that is how the *imagination* works," so to avoid the whole debate over localized brain function (the question of which is, here, actually somewhat irrelevant). Bly's description of "leaping from one brain to another" is quite befitting in light of the shamanic axis, in that it shows how the participation of all three ontic streams—heaven, earth, and underworld—contribute to a feeling of centeredness and depth and, therefore, of authenticity, participation, and *confidence*. The confidence that Bly mentions is essential to the Other Within's long-sought capacity to perform identity and exploit asynchrony. It confirms us in a confidential rapport *between* the "three brains," in which each is the other's *confidant*. The deep confidence of this interior and confirmatory trialogue is a wellspring of resistance to assimilation.

In traditional society the transformative departure from the normative ordinary life into a liminal condition is supported and facilitated by the village culture—the initiand is conducted from a zone of structure into liminal isolation and there allowed, or guided, to *change*— within certain limits and safeguards. However, as we have seen: when culture expands to Empire so, in turn, expands its top-down imperative to control consciousness and stamp out all deviation: "Does socio-culturally transmitted information take over control in humankind and, if so, what are the limits, if any, to its control? Does the genotype take a permanent back seat, and is social conditioning now all in all?"[15] In other words, Turner is asking: when, if ever, do we set aside oar, rudder, anchor, and the fear of going down? When do we drop the reins and let the "horse"—the "phylogenetically older parts of the brain," the genotype, the forest-orectic, movement-sonic—lead the way? When do we allow ourselves to enter into an exchange with the exiled portion of self and soul? And this question pulls us back into that ancient tension held betwixt the Emperor and Con-Eda—rivals who stand here as the symbolic poles of a single rider:

> By the rider we understand that changeable part born to specific parents, flexible even whimsical, capable of altering course quickly: the reader of books, the self-transformer, owner of rapidly changing opinions, embedded in family life. . . .
>
> By the term "horse," we understand the more instinctual part, more willful than the rider or less obedient to the rider's will, associated more with the physical, instinctual, muscular, hormonal body

than with its alert and inventive rider. The "horse" is less open to change; the horse retains patterns known for thousands perhaps millions of years. We could say that the "horse" is utterly absorbed by the ancestors, hardly aware of any inventions since the flint arrowhead; the horse is slow, conservative, powerful, unheeding, many times stronger than the rider. . . .

To take one more step we might imagine a hawk or falcon perched on the rider's shoulder. This predatory bird stands for the part of us which frees itself from both the rider and horse, flies high into the clouds, sees the countryside from afar, lives in air. . . .

We notice the men and women who study initiation in our culture usually choose one of the three roads I've mentioned, and ignore the other two.[16]

Although he does not mention it specifically, we can deduce that Bly is thinking of the incompatible imperatives of what can be recognized as "the three brains," which have been linked here to the trialities of Hell, Earth, and Heaven; the Black, Red, and White rivers; past, present, and future; instinct, intellect, and inspiration; thrall, freeman, and noble— *ad infinitum.*

The Emperor's way is the village mythos (the *normative* pole), which is concerned with adapting the rider to its control—the domination and harnessing of "horse-power"—so as to subordinate individuals and regulate social bonding; while Con-Eda's way is the forest mythos (the *orectic* pole) which calls both the horse and the hawk away from the agrarian-village domestic life to the soul's heights and depths, the peaks and valleys, of personal hierophanic experience beyond the borders of what is fixed and settled. The trialogue of *confidants* cannot be achieved without the mature axial involvement of all three ontological zones. Just as scholars tend to choose only *one* of the roads Bly lays out, it is clear that people prefer to valorize a single cosmic zone—a shiftless one-sidedness which precludes all leaping. The horse, then, represents the archaic energy of the genotype that is most often subverted, denied, and turned against us; therefore, in order to include it, we must proceed to explore its associations, beyond Single-vision, as a *dominant,* or multivalent symbol:

> In the noonday sun, the horse gallops blindly on, while the horseman, clear-sighted, anticipates its fears and guides it towards its predetermined goal. At night, however, when the horseman himself becomes blind, it is the horse which sees and guides, and it is the horse which takes control, since it alone can with impunity pass through the gates of mystery beyond the reach of reason.
>
> The horse . . . reaches the acme of its positive valence when both the upper and lower planes are made manifest without distinction through its mediation, that is to say when its significance becomes cosmic.[17]

With the above and below manifest, the horse is revealed to be an axial image fully capable of participation in the trialogue of a wholehearted creativity:

> [In the Kirghiz epic poem, *Er-Töshtük,* the hero must] abdicate his own individuality and trust the paranormal powers of his magic horse, Chal-Kuiruk, which enables him to reach the Underworld and escape all its traps. . . . At the outset of this fantastic ride, it warns its master. . . .
>
> "Your chest is broad, but your spirit is narrow. You are heedless. You do not see what I see, you do not know what I know. . . . You are brave but stupid." . . . Lastly, to add the finishing touch to its powers, it says: "I can walk through the depths of the seas."[18]

Walking, without *anchor, rudder, oar,* "through the depths of the seas," the tricksterish voice of *Chal-Kuiruk* is the playful voice of liminality itself—speaking to loosen the control narrowed spirit of the liminoid massman.

When the horse addresses the rider we have something quite different from the situation where animality simply takes control, inhibiting the consciousness of the rider. In this exchange, there is interaction and interplay, the reverse of the tight-fisted, control-narrowed spirit. In this way, as Zimmer said, allowing ourselves to be carried away "transforms the situation, forces an alteration on the creative spirit, and throws it into a play that carries it beyond itself, carries it, that is to say, really and properly into play, and into a play that entrains the entirety of creation"—as Turner explains:

> Play can be everywhere and nowhere, imitate anything, yet be identified with nothing. Play is "transcendent" . . . though only just so, brushing the surfaces of more specialized neural organizations rather than existing apart from them or looking down from a godlike height on them. Play is the supreme *bricoleur** of frail transient constructions, like a caddis worm's case or a magpie's nest in nature. Its metamessages are composed of a potpourri of apparently incongruous elements: products of both hemispheres are juxtaposed and intermingled. . . . You may have guessed that play is, for me, a liminal . . . mode, essentially interstitial, betwixt-and-between all standard taxonomic nodes, essentially "elusive"—a term derived from the Latin *ex* for "away" plus *ludere,* "to play"; hence the Latin verb *eludere* acquired the sense of "to take away from someone at play," thus "to cheat" or "to deceive." As such play cannot be pinned down. . . . Like many Trickster figures in myths (or should these be "antimyths" . . .) play can deceive, betray, beguile, delude (another derivation of *ludere* "to play"), dupe, hoodwink, bamboozle, and gull.[19]

"Play," in terms of the work in hand, is the life-and-death matter of myth, ritual, and art. Trickster Wisdom is serious play, sacred play; it is not transgression for transgression's sake, nor is it simply a preference for flamboyance or rebelliousness. Trickster plays to break out of the *rigor mortis* of thoughtless imitation into the Life and Death dance of the deep imagination.

And with imagination comes the loosening of controls and constraints which leaves a little "play" in the works, an unbridled associative range, allowing the singular, particular, unique, and unprecedented back into the culture. The far-flung efforts and productions of leaping consciousness, "the overwhelming profusion of phenomena," occur endlessly and everywhere without pause, continuously birthing the "real"; all of creation, ever leaping, never complete, eternally pouring into existence through the *lived poiesis* of the mandorla:

> The creation of the world is not an accomplished work, completed within a certain span of time (say, seven days), but a process continuing throughout the course of history refashioning the universe without cease, and pressing it on, every moment afresh. Like the human body, the cosmos is in part built up anew, every night, every day; by a process of unending regeneration it remains alive. But the manner of its growth is by abrupt occurrences, crises, surprising events and mortifying accidents. Everything is forever going wrong; and yet, that is precisely the circumstance by which the miraculous development comes to pass. The great entirety jolts from crisis to crisis; that is the precarious, hair-raising manner of self-transport by which it moves.[20]

Gnomonica

The Tree of Joyful Difficulty

"JOLTING FORWARD" to the next crisis, the task now at hand is to take up Jerome Rothenberg's proposition: that post-modern poetics has rediscovered, or has retained, certain shamanic intentions—specifically represented in Rilke's *Angel;* Lorca's *Duendé;** and Rimbaud's *Voyant:** intentions reaching back to "the animal-body-rootedness of 'primitive' poetry: recognition of a physical basis for the poem within a [person's] body—or as an act of body and mind together, breath and/or spirit . . . the poet as shaman, or primitive shaman as poet & seer."[1] The *Angel, Voyant,* and *Duendé* are the three faces of Blake's "poetic genius"— known herein as the not-I, the *daimon,* the Wounded Healer, the paraclete—the Genius of Deformity met suddenly in the precipitous fall of the shaman's death—leaving the herd like a stricken deer: "all this seems thrust upon him—a unifying vision that brings with it the power of song and image, seen in his own terms as power to heal-the-soul and all disease viewed as disorder-of-the-soul, as disconnection & rigidity."[2]

A preemptory effort must be made, at this point, to dispel any notion that the present course will constitute an advocacy of pop-shamanism; it does not. The model of shamanism employed here is due, mainly, to the shamanic expansion of reality to a triune cosmos, which permits the leap from zone to zone. More to the point, in the shamanic crisis—where the normative-imposed identity is shattered and the undomesticated implicate identity asserts itself—we find a primary model of this expansion: the "breakthrough in plane," as the departure which enables society's misfit to negotiate an imposed and arbitrary structure of the "real."

Additionally, it is important, before proceeding, to briefly attempt the remedy of a common misunderstanding: many scholars and experts on shamanism (including at times Eliade), have described the shamanic modality as "an escape from the human condition," that is, escape from Time, or temporality, or Death. This conception is entirely mistaken: the "escape" is actually a liberation from the psycho-social constraints of the reality/sanity consensus—i.e., the imposed limits of structure and status. In this view the truly shamanic impulse is to break with structure's reification of "time" and thus assume the original human condition: to enter *into* time as one caught-up and carried along in the tempo of a dance. The prior view, espousing shamanism as transcendence, is a hold over, a constraint, of the post-agrarian world, and the Judeo-Christian-Islamic-Cartesian legacy (Berman's non-participating consciousness). To restate: the view taken here is that the shamanic leap includes and accepts death as essential to life; it is a total engagement and participation *in* the world, *in* the flesh, and *in* Time.

The *Angel, Voyant,* and *Duendé* present three styles of approach to the centering power of the uncivilized edge. Moving away from the eviscerated civil center toward the sacred center, variously imagined as the World Tree,* the sacred mountain, the lodge-pole, the hearth, etc. Of its many symbolic incarnations we may take the "gnomon" as most apt to our inquiry. For it is by means of the gnomon's shadow that the measure of time and space is taken. If the gnomon stands for the center then *gnomonica**—all that pertains to the gnomon—will stand for the shadow, the edge, liminality, and all margent phenomena.

IN RILKE'S *Angel,* Rimbaud's *Voyant,* and Lorca's *Duendé,* we find a surprising correspondence to Eliade's "three cosmic zones"—heaven, earth, and underworld. In each case the poet uses a dominant symbol, a *coincidentia oppositorum,* axially partaking of the extremes—beginning with the *Duendé* of Federico García Lorca:

> I have heard an old guitar teacher say that "the *duendé* is not in the singer's throat, the *duendé* rises inside from the very soles of one's feet." That is to say, it is not a question of ability or aptitude but a matter of possessing an authentic living style; that is to say of blood, of culture most ancient, of creation in act.[3]

Rising up through the soles of the feet the *Duendé* is an "earth-force"— the fertile Black River of the underworld, the ichor* of the ancestors; the Water-of-Death.

In this way the *Duendé* works as the "rootedness" of the Shaman Tree,* the bottom-up informance of the *axis mundi.* "*Duendé* involves a kind of elation when death is present in the room, it is associated with dark sounds, and when a poet has *duendé* inside him, he brushes past death with each step, and in that presence associates faster. . . . Lorca says: *it rejects all the sweet geometry one has learned . . . it breaks with all styles.*"[4] (Recalling Thompson) "the mystics, crazies, and noisemakers . . . will be performing the *new unconscious geometry* that no one can yet see"; Lorca, rejecting all "*learned* geometry," invokes the "*unconscious* geometry" of *Duendé* and its radical gnosis.

It should be remembered also, that in greater Spain, and parts of South America, *El Duendé* is the Trickster of traditional folklore. Clarissa Pinkola Estés says: "*El Duendé* is the goblin wind or force behind a person's actions and creative life [and it] is also used to describe the ability to 'think' in poetic images."[5] The biomythic resonance of *Duendé* is incursive—a pre-reflective reflex, a visceral-experience of the animal-body—thus, it is invisible until it is performed: instinctively embodied, enacted, and given voice in a "ritual display."

I say that one must be a seer, make oneself a seer. . . . The poet makes himself a seer by a long prodigious, and rational disordering of *all* the senses. . . . This is an unspeakable torture during which . . . he becomes the great patient [sick man], the great criminal, the great accursed—and the great learned one [savant]!—among men. For he arrives at the *unknown!* Because he has cultivated his own soul.[6]

IN THE EXTRA-ORDINARY vision of Arthur Rimbaud, "Heaven and Earth are in contact and combine their influences." Partaking at once of the above and the below, the *Voyant's* trance induces a "disordering of the senses," a *synesthesia** that fosters the often startling associations of metaphor. A plurality that connotes the inclusivity of wisdom—the *Voyant* is the transgressor whose wild associations may be described, in Gardner's words, as the "genius figure, the individual whose abilities extend across various domains, and who, indeed, is marked by the capacity to find connections between language and music, dance and social communion, the spatial and the personal realms."[7] Alive in the axial-moment, in the crossed and conflated, the mad and ecstatic co-interpenetrations of self and Other:

> Rimbaud epitomized transgression. He was a maverick who made metaphors of his "alienation": "*Je est un autre* . . . I is another . . . I had to give up my life in order to be!" . . . Rimbaud vividly depicts the dizzy plunge from grace. . . . [he] lunges with a deranged delight . . . the fool on the precipice, moving ever closer to the edge. Delighting in demonizing himself. A French Prospero, using his magic to send a tidal wave crashing down on Western certitude.[8]

"I is another," " I am not I," the visionary eye of the "not-eye." Here is the heretic voice of a raving seer; Rimbaud, stands amongst his contemporaries, and still amongst the "good citizens" of today, as the *Cynocephalus*—conjuring and performing all which the Iron Gate stands to preserve us from, to keep out, repress, and deny.

The *Voyant* actualizes a total engagement, through the body, in and with the living world, not as transcendence but as merger, participation, and being. The *Voyant* stands in the middle-world, in the present, as the Tree's trunk: the extremes of past and future, primality and rationality, oscillating in the living presence of the Shaman Tree. The two-way flow of "presence" is the Red River of Blood, the confluence of life and death, rife and lambent* as "Passion's red thread" pulsing through the world.

Rimbaud's *Voyant* is the genius of the leap who consummates the "Marriage of Heaven and Hell." Making the mad dive, plunging from middle-earth down to the rootedness of Lorca's *Duendé,* and flying up again, blossoming through the impossible corridor, to the inspiration of Rilke's Angel.

When we win it's with small things,
and the triumph itself makes us small.
What is extraordinary and eternal
does not want to be bent by us.
I mean the Angel who appeared
to the wrestlers of the Old Testament:
when the wrestlers' sinews
grew long like metal strings,
he felt them under his fingers
like deep chords of music.
Whoever was beaten by this Angel
(who often simply declined the fight)
went away proud and strengthened
and great from that harsh hand,
that kneaded him as if to change his shape.
Winning does not tempt that man.
This is how he grows: by being defeated, decisively,
by constantly greater beings.[9]

RAINER MARIA RILKE's Angel teaches growth by failure, ascent by descent, wisdom by lunacy; this is the initiatory "wrestling"—*as if to change his shape*—that takes place when bright Gilgamesh is first met by his dark and elder brother, Enkidu.

The capacity to be defeated yet remain unconquered—via the performance of identity—is the essence of Trickster Wisdom. To remain unconquered is the specialty of the Trickster: by accident or intent, to find the blessing in the curse; as in the Coyote-like words of Nikki Giovanni: "I'm so hip, even my errors are correct."[10]

Rilke's paraclete is at once healing and harsh—this Angel *has duende,* and Rilke would not willingly forego the tutelage of either extreme: "I fear in myself only those contradictions with a tendency toward reconciliation. It must be a very narrow spot in my life if the idea should occur to them to shake hands, from one side to the other. My contradictions shall hear of each other only rarely and in rumors."[11] Thus recalling Guggenbühl-Craig's dictum: "a person without contradictory myths cannot be trusted." Perhaps this determination to hold such vast tensions explains why *Orpheus* became so important to Rilke; Orpheus—in whom the unresolved contradictions of culture and wilderness, of heaven and underworld, are met, embodied, yet never reconciled.

If, as Highwater says, "culture is a way of looking,"[12] then perhaps wildness affords humankind a way of *listening*—"listening like deer in the forest. As if their lives depended on it."[13] Surely this describes the ferocity of Rilke's listening—as if his life depended on it. From that rare moment on the high cliffs of Duino, in the storm above the sea, when that angelic voice first spoke—"it seemed to him as though in the roar of the wind a voice had called out to him: 'If I cried out, who would hear me up there among the angelic orders?'"[14]—better, then, to listen than join the clamor to be heard. The art of "listening" moves one from the outer ear to the inner—now the *Voyant,* the seer, becomes the clairaudient, listening "through the strings," in the "task of transformation," awakening "all the images imprisoned within you."[15]

Rilke's is not the naïve approach, it is not a lighthearted ascension: here, as in the situation of "Jack and the Beanstalk,"[16] having dared to ascend the axis, one does not encounter a world of happy elves and singing dolphins, rather one faces huge primitive energies both perilous and formidable—unlike Jack however, Rilke climbs the Shaman Tree knowing full well the terrible price he must pay:

> Rilke reached the conclusion that love for another human being was inimical to seeing and to being a poet. Love clouded the "mirror" by which the artist saw and reflected the world. Like Cézanne, he separated from his wife and gradually reduced his friendships to letter writing. I think Rilke's sacrifice of love and companionship for his work was rather extreme, and his reasons for eschewal of human relationships may have been an excuse for an inability to sustain them.[17]

Shall we follow Mark Levy in this estimation and find the poet slightly flawed, deficient, and making excuses? Rubbish. Of course it is extreme! The extremity of the sacrifice is proportionate to the generosity of the creation. Here, explicitly, is Gardner's Faustian bargain: "What pervades these unusual arrangements is the conviction that unless the bargain has been compulsively adhered to, the talent may be compromised or even irretrievably lost." Can we not, in this light, realize what Rilke *paid* for the gift he gave us? Rilke traded the consolation of human relationship for divine inspiration; and, whether we deem it "inability" or "necessity," he was bound, as by metal strings, to the stringent terms of that transaction. We should remember that the sacrificed part has been *made sacred* (Odin's missing eye has the deeper sight). The missing parts of us, the liminal parts, should be reverenced—they are the portals to sacrality. Ascent to the Angel reaches the blossoming branch tips of the Shaman Tree. "Blossoming" is the White River of milk and honey, of tears and breath, the Water-of-Life, and sometimes "what winter gives"—snow, bitterness, and ashes.

RILKE'S ANGEL, Rimbaud's *Voyant,* and Lorca's *Duendé* require, in exchange for their intimate revelations, a kind of brutal self-disclosure, "an act of body and mind together," a sacrifice, a shedding of skins and masks—postponing the marriage of the lovable bright-brother—taking up the difficulty of dissolving the impenetrable membrane and thus revealing the hidden and vulnerable nobility of the long-lost dark brother. If endowed with both cunning and grace—wearing seven skirts—the "leaper" may come away, as did Jack, with the genius of a singing golden harp: that precious instrument enabling the expressive per-formance and in-formance of a wild, undomesticated identity:

> *Winning does not tempt that man.*
> *This is how he grows: by being defeated, decisively,*
> *by constantly greater beings.*

The Lyre
Where the Callus Meets the String

THE FIRST ACT of the Trickster Hermes—using the shell of a tortoise "accidentally" stumbled over at the threshold of his cave—is to create the world's first *lyre*. At the mouth of the cave, where the innerworld and the outerworld meet, there, in the synesthesia of liminality—at the spatiotemporal limit—the unforeseen presents itself and the mythopoeic imagination is born.

Rootedness, presence, and blossoming, each seeking the departure of the axis in its own style. Weaving the many tonalities in which these energies sing, one may devise a resonant and expressive instrument. Once we strike the lines of association, across the nexus of trifurcated spheres—connecting above to below in cosmos, society, psyche, and body—then a harp of many tensions is strung; we have, at last, acquired the means of primal expressivity, the golden harp of the mythopoeic imagination, upon which the unbounded phenomena of creation may come to play.

It can now be stated that the recapitulation of this dramatic gesture—creating the primary instrument of expressive display, discipline, and paxis*—is the first and essential "act" (correct-mistake) of Trickster Wisdom and the leaping consciousness. For it is by means of this "music" that the Other Within negotiates a Hermetic sanctuary within the disconfirming world of Apollonian order:

Hermes . . . makes a kind of peace with Apollo. . . . Taking out his lyre and playing a beautiful melody, he begins "to soften that stern, far-shooting archer," and before long, "bright Apollo laugh[s] for joy as the sweet throb of that marvelous instrument stole into his heart, and a gentle longing seized his soul." Hermes sings Apollo a theogony, "the story of the gods . . . how each came to be . . . and how each came to have what is now theirs." I suspect we are meant to imagine this as a theogony of Hermes' own design, reshaping of old stories. . . . In addition, I suspect that this new Hermetic theogony includes both Hermes and Apollo in its cast and as such amounts to simultaneous self-promotion and flattery. At the end Apollo is helplessly enchanted, whereupon Hermes gives him the lyre. In return Apollo "placed his shinning whip in Hermes' hand, ordaining him Keeper of the Herds."

[Hermes] is admitted to the Pantheon, he is an acknowledged son of Zeus.[1]

In this Hyde reveals the revolutionary intelligence, the mythopoeic genius and graceful cunning, which can persuade the gods to adopt Hermes, to tolerate his transgressions, and "confirm" upon him a new and unparalleled status.

The songs of the leaping consciousness bring the cultural vitality of the shadowy (lunar) edge—Hermes, Coyote, Enkidu—as a gift to the luminous (solar) center—Apollo, Bear, Gilgamesh. These associative tensions are not linear but harmonic, and must be understood, in the final analysis, as neither-this-nor-that but something wholly Other. The friction between the kinetic-orectic-forest and the cognitive-normative-village produces the harmonic overtones of association thus expanding duality to triality; the "Third thing," which is "no-thing," the invisible, impossible, unthinkable leap—the overtone, the *interval,* the crossroads, the seat of the soul, the mandorla, the abyss: in this dance *my position is that I have no position.*

We have, in the West, many images that glorify the notion of creativity as being a triumph over adversity. We speak of "the shit that fertilizes roses," or the grain of sand in the oyster that leads to the generation of a pearl. This is the stuff of *Reader's Digest* stories and Ann Landers columns. And these images do capture a truth, though they mask a larger one. The truth they capture is that creative work can and often does emerge out of conflict; the truth they mask is that other psychodynamic patterns of the creative process are possible, and that historically the conflict model may represent an aberration.[2]

At first sight one might feel that the above quotation discredits the entire proposition of Trickster Wisdom and the leaping consciousness. Berman is, obviously, correct to suspect this sentimentalized version of "fruitful asynchrony"; and he may also be correct that creative genius does not always require adversity, "that other psychodynamic patterns of the creative process are possible" (although Gardner might disagree).

There is, however, another yet larger and more insidious truth masked by the puerile depiction of the "pearl" and the "rose": it allows the reader to gain a heavenly distance from the struggle, to say "Oh how courageous, and brave, and inspiring those poor unfortunate people are," and, with this distance-gained, to dismiss the entire melodrama as having nothing to do with one's "real life." Thus, having successfully unloaded a whole complex of unconscious fears onto the convenient and nobly-suffering Other, one feels buoyant, light-hearted, free—ironically, a sophisticated dismissal of such sentimentality can have the same distancing result: the actual suffering subject is obliterated.

Yet the betrayed and conflicted condition is ultimately the condition of everyone. The liminoid massman is unable, or refuses to *make sacred the missing parts,* and is, henceforth, compelled to hide the fault—even from him or herself. Hiding the "defect" is, in a manner of speaking, to hide one's "limp." What happens when people hide their limp? Bly answers clearly: "somebody has to limp it." In other words, we assign *our* defect to an Other. So it will not do to simply go out with goodwill helping or admiring those who limp on our behalf—the starving children, the homeless, the severe behavior youth at risk—we have to show our own defect first; not only show it but *live it* and express it, perform it in a dance:

> *Doing what you want . . .*
> *Is that like limping?*
> *. . . in bird masks, with pig noses, dancing,*
> *teeth like a dog's, sometimes*
> *dancing on one bad leg!*
> *They do what they want, the dog's teeth say that.*[3]

The limp is wyrd, and *showing* the limp means that one sets aside the desperate wish for approval, and that somehow one has managed to tap into the authentic or natural "desire." In other words, "doing what you want" and "dancing on one bad leg" are dependent on each other; the wound's desire cries for healing, wholeness, the promised-life, and desire's wound deforms us and makes us wyrd, revealing our style, dance, vision, genius. Marked by the wound and wounded for bearing the mark; *you cannot do what you want without showing the limp:*

Many people are degraded by the loss of connection to their own life energy in their own body. . . . If their natural desires were met by a constant "No," they gradually disconnected from their own "I desire" in the survival chakra in order to please. They pretend, even as children, to be reaching out from their own desire. Their place of desire is false; their desiring is not coming from *natural* instincts; therefore, those instincts cannot be satisfied. Because their bodies are not expressing desires that come from natural instincts, they fall into unnatural desires, driven desires that overwhelm them with stupor and manifest as addictions. They crave food that brings them no nurturance, drink that brings them no spirit, sex that brings no union.[4]

Are all desires to socialization (to function as part of a larger whole) driven by the compulsion to survive by pleasing others? Does the genotype take a "permanent" back seat to social conditioning? Or is there a portion of village desire that fits this (Marion Woodman's) idea of natural desire?

The answer, in true trickster fashion, is "yes-*and*-no." The village-desire and the forest-desire can be seen as "a dual tendency," on one hand, "to preserve and assert . . . individuality," and on the other "to function as an integrated part of [a] larger whole"[5]; these twin desires are biologically and mythologically innate to all life, from the smallest particle onward in complexity, and hence both desires qualify as "natural." We can say that natural desire arises in a bottom-up implicate way, while the unnatural desires arise in reaction to the constant "No" of top-down civilization: the arbitrary border-line, the fence, the wall—the archetypal imposition—where the self-assertive drive is utterly thwarted. Speculations (and wishful thinking) aside, the fact is: the immovable one-sidedness of the Iron Gate has been with us for at least ten thousand years and it is not likely to go away; therefore one had best "recognize the fact." Although it is certain that people *could* invigorate a village life which fosters a saturnalian or even an adoptive mythos, it must be conceded that there will always be those individuals who will be *too* strange for the village. The tyranny of idealism demands a conformity which discourages and often kills the natural desires; now those same desires return from death as unnatural assassins, abominations, seeking in vengeance to annihilate the entire normative world.

If this sounds cynical, it is: recall the Cynic who "did not disparage—much less abstain from—food, drink, and sex," thus embodying *Subversive Virtue*: "In reducing the . . . requirements of life to natural essentials, the Cynic also reduced his dependence . . . on the organization and structure of society itself."[6] And recall as well that the word "Cynic" is etymologically linked to the *Cynocephali* (dog-headed-people) who "do what they want, the dog's teeth say that."

When the *little black snake of natural desire* is thrown out the window by *the midwife of structure,* it must return to us as a huge devouring dragon. Even should one interpret the monstrous dragon to be the ferocious and insatiable appetite of addiction, it would be a grievous mistake not to recognize the fact that this overwhelming and seemingly "unnatural desire" is come to destroy all that bars us from destiny and authenticity of soul. If we recall the story, it must be realized that nothing from inside the kingdom will satisfy this Beast; the answer to the unnatural, undomesticated appetite lies in the wilderness, outside the collective, in the deep wisdom of the uncivilized crone and the forest girl with seven skirts, as well as in the scathing ministration of the steel-bristled brush. "Grief and Night toughen us, / Until people capable of sacrifice once more rock / in the iron cradle, *desire people,* like the ancients . . ." in this, Hölderlin's wisdom, is surely what Blake meant when he said: "He who desires but acts not breeds pestilence."[7]

Breaking-through the compass of civil society's oppressive conformity, whether by free-will or by compulsion, one will need the dog's teeth, for to break with the normative is to place oneself outside the window in the wild and the dark, where the sentimental *Reader's Digest* stories don't help us anymore. Here, the very mark of our exclusion (the limp) is the signature of our gift and our unique style. This "doing what you want" is the disciplined work, the "joyful difficulty" of poiesis, art, myth, and ritual—*not desiring not wanting anything that can ever be achieved.*

In the end we find that Trickster Wisdom begins in the split-consciousness, or disequilibrium, of being outsider *and* insider at the same time. Trickster's ambivalence nurtures the adoptive ability to hold our contradictions in the widest constellation of identity, and the performance of that identity, through *the lyre of the leaping consciousness,* allows us to survive the tragicomedy of civilized life.

And so it is up to each of us to recognize the fact: that the victories of the excluded are won on our behalf, that those precious wisdoms, eked out in suffering and ignominy, are gifts to the good of all; while at the same time, we must know what occurs: that the societal powers which shock us into such wisdom also strip us of community, of freedom and dignity; they are Evil and must be resisted.

Trickster Wisdom grows by defeat; our greatest enemies will be our greatest teachers. The vision of doom is stolen knowledge, illicit, contraband. As much as we witness and attest the separate and incompatible experiences of insider and outsider we are each of us both; and to believe we are one or the other is simple ignorance. In the paradox of the leaping consciousness we must learn to be grateful for that which we must ardently oppose. At this crossroads the initiand faces Baba Yaga's question: "Did you come here by compulsion, or by your own free-will?" If one answers one-sidedly with the arrogant New-Age, "my life is perfect, everything is as I ordained it to be," then one must deny the truth that there are powers beyond human control; and if one answers (again one-sidedly) with the victim abdicator's, "my life has been ruined by forces and enemies that leave me no choice and no option," then one denies the equal truth that each of us is responsible for our acts and our lives.

The radical task of the Other Within is to gain that no-*single*-position— the impossible locus of Shiva's dance: the Thunderbolt destruction-*and*-creation of the universe, the poetic task "to throw down and restore."[8] And Rilke says of this task, that it "is not desiring not wanting anything that can ever be achieved." Providential nature and the paraclete itself cannot reach us until we accept and commit to the "impossible," reaching beyond the categorically *possible,* otherwise it will simply be the same-old worn-out song-and-dance—as Lao Tzu said: "All greatness is improbable. What's probable is tedious and petty."[9] Impossibly, in the wound "where two roads intersect inside us," in the sole gap where we are split, where we are broken, where something is *missing*—on the blood-soaked earth of this dilemma the initiand must make a little dancing-ground, a woodland hut, a crucible, a cradle of sacred space, a refuge from unbelief, a final place to stand firm against the tides.

WHERE THE CALLUS *meets the string*—where the protective hardness (contentiousness) cultivated in "suffering" meets the disarming generosity (compassion) of "art"—all our vagabond and outcast must be returned—back from the prisons, ghettos, gutters, hospitals, nursing homes—into the wedding-dance, into the wide mandorla of the human heart. Of itself such goodwill is useless; without "people capable of sacrifice" possessing the cunning *and* the grace to make sacred our missing parts; to exonerate the exiled and anathema in every corner of humanity's incomplete and unfinished soul.

At bottom, each of us must stand in the depths of this impossible contradiction, set aside the feeling that we are owed anything, stand alone, in the sacred "no-place," torn between the demands of forest and village, take up the lyre, pluck the strings, and let the deep-chords roll, let the smoke of sacrifice rise, send forth a voice; and begin at last to weave our own artful *and* seditious telling of the tale. . . . What, one may well ask, does all this mean in *my* all-too-human life? That I must make this impossible leap through the strings of the convoluted instrument of held-tensions and creative expression? Surely, this advice is all well and good for the Trickster, he's a god! But what can we do? For us this task is out of the question, it is clearly impossible . . .

> *A god can do it. But tell me, how can a man*
> *follow his narrow road through the strings?*
> *A man is split. And where two roads intersect*
> *inside us, no one has built the Singer's Temple.*[10]*

CODA

Masquerade

Sensing the deep images lurking in life's history, and then understanding the history with imagination, is the function of the descent. . . . It is not that "my life is hell," but rather that "hell (hell's imaginal function) is my life."

DAVID L. MILLER, *HELLS & HOLY GHOSTS: A THEOPOETICS OF CHRISTIAN BELIEF*[1]

HOWEVER MUCH RESISTED and denied, the above words are real and true for all of us, and yet more immediately real and deeply true for the Other Within. David Miller's grasp of the *descensus ad inferos* is singular—"hell is my life," there is no exemption.

Knowing this, one must strive to keep a life-long rootedness, the "under-the-worldly point of view"; else all our knowledge—orientations, identities, motivations, and expectations—no matter how lofty, will be vapid and shallow. Yet such "knowing" comes with a price: "gone to Hell, you look like Hell" (that is to say, you look like Death incarnate) and are met and judged accordingly.

Every insider carries an infernal Otherness buried deep within, and it is that hidden abyss, denied and handed-off, which creates society's Other Within. Desperately wishing to remain a "real member of the flock" the insider projects this interior darkness onto (and even into) some convenient outsider. It should not be overlooked, however, that both insider and outsider carry—with whatever style—their own *intra-personal* Otherness. Hence it is only via the *descensus ad inferos*—the drop down into one's own private Hell—that a true *communitas* can be achieved; for only in hell's imaginal function is identity in its likeness-and-difference of self-and-other fully realized.

Perceived as Other, whether of heaven or hell, there is something evocative in one's countenance or bearing that invites the imposition (as far off-the-mark as it may feel): "The monster has been credited everywhere with the powers of a god or the diabolical forces of evil."[2] The idea that the degradations of the imposed identity arrive coupled with certain evocative and influential powers should not, by now, be entirely unfamiliar: "Deformity makes its victim the benign or malign intercessor between the known and the unknown, the dark and the bright side of nature, this world and the beyond."[3] Again: a visitation from the cynocephalic (dog-headed) deity confronts the human soul at the cusp of life and death. Just so, the deformed and abominable dog-man threatens the "structure-bound" with the corruption of Hell. Angelized-*and*-demonized the doubled identity of the Other Within remains categorically outside (before-*and*-beyond) the daylight, ordinary, civilized world.

When the normative self-world-view is threatened by the uncivilized wilderness of weeds and vermin, the insider comes to believe that the "inside" is the one-and-only, divinely revealed, sane reality. To the contrary, as Patchen once said: "The size of the world is determined by the size of your dwelling: the smaller your house the larger your world."[4] In other words, the limit of the structure we dwell in may prevent a genuine meeting with the wider-world as it really *is*. Structure's Big-House (*prison*) reaches its apex in the epistemic, ontic, and ideological limit of Alexander's Iron Gate—upon this monument, Cassirer speaks of the same structural limit from another vantage:

We have to look upon the great master works of human culture in a much humbler way. They are not eternal nor unassailable. Our science, our poetry, our art, [our government], and our religion are only the upper layer of a much older stratum that reaches down to a greater depth. We must always be prepared for violent concussions that may shake our cultural world and our social order to its very foundations. . . . The world of human culture may be described in the words of the Babylonian legend [Marduk's destruction of Tiamat]. It could not arise until the darkness of myth was fought and overcome. But the mythical monsters were not entirely destroyed. They were used for the creation of a new universe. The powers of myth were checked and subdued by superior forces. As long as these forces, intellectual, ethical, and artistic, are in full strength, myth is tamed and subdued. But once they begin to lose their strength chaos is come again. Mythical thought then starts to rise anew and to pervade the whole of man's cultural and social life.[5]

Apparently "Cassirer's . . . faith in the future led him to place his hope in the eventual defeat and transmutation of mythical thinking, and the progressive triumph of reason in history,"[6] yet, although he held the state "superior," ironically, Cassirer's conception of myth, as destructuring and de-formative, is decidedly correct—and flies in the face of the preponderant (Durkheimian) insistence on myth as "social cohesion." Outside the Big-House refugees clamber to get back inside the structure, while a few turn away from the wall to pursue the kaleidoscopic depths.

In this archetypal split, of myth from civilization, Marduk will stand (along with Gilgamesh and Beowulf) for the civilizing order of "history," the "explicate order," the so-called "superior forces"; whereas Tiamat must stand below in the "implicate order" along with all the other "outcast and vagabond," with Grendel, and Enkidu. Still, "the mythical monsters were not entirely destroyed," as Hölderlin saw: "The divine energies / Are still alive, but isolated above us, in the archetypal world. / They keep on going there, and, apparently, don't bother if Humans live or not."[7]

Above-*and*-below, these archegestic goings-on are today termed "interiority" and "unconscious"; unfortunately, thus reduced, psychology has so objectified this mysterious reality as to render itself impotent in the understanding of, or dealing with, the "violent concussions that shake our . . . order to its very foundations." Such shocking incursions, eruptions, explosions, and expulsions, of the hidden and denied Mythic-Reality, manifest in a chaotic array of (so-called "inexplicable") acts of senseless violence and destruction which assail society on every side.

The point here, to be made irrefutably clear, is that the Others Within—female, foreign, indigenous, crippled, homosexual, androgynous, old, young, homeless, criminal—the Dog-people and the Rat-people—are all inferior and therefore malformed and "deformed," and therefore covert harbingers of anarchy, chaos, Hell, and Death. No one will admit this: one says, "there's nothing wrong with me, I have rights!" and the answer comes, "Yes, of course, just leave your application and we'll get back to you" (when Hell freezes over). At bottom, this is what occurs, this is the fact. The question then becomes: does anyone take conscious responsibility to don pride's cloak of shame as mediator of the primordial abyss?

Having departed the prevailing "self-world view" and plunged into the scatological refuse pile—"the rag and bone shop of the heart"—one joins with all else that has been discarded and dropped, out of mind and out of sight: the wild dance of liminality, anti-structure, chaos, void, *prima materia,* undifferentiated flux, kaleidoscopic consciousness; the "ultimate and unknowable reality" which Bohm has called "Undivided Wholeness in Flowing Movement"—or more simply the "implicate order." Tumbling in the muck of "hell's imaginal function" one may take part in the Trickster's mythic and multivalent intelligence which flips the former one-sided reality/sanity structure on its head, upside down and bottom-up. As N. J. Girardot concludes: "The return to the chaos condition . . . mythically reveals man as more than conventionally human. Myth, not history, tells the true story of human identity."[8]

William Blake clearly understood the necessity of making this reversal, from conventionality into mythicality, as attested in "The Marriage of Heaven and Hell" where he describes "walking among the fires of Hell, delighted with the enjoyments of Genius, which to Angels look like torment and insanity"; and long before Blake, there is Lao Tzu: "*Heaven and earth begin in the unnamed. . . .*" Unnamed and unspeakable—the void of pre-existence, where dwell the monstrous myths—a deeper reality which is before-*and*-beyond (as well as betwixt-*and*-between) "the ten thousand things." Hence, the totality of the "real" cannot be apprehended by ordinary ways of knowing. In this forgotten and forbidden wisdom the only road to knowing the ultimate ground of creation is through the Trickster's modality: *implication*—a performative, phatic,* resonant, and gestic idiom of discernment, which is older, deeper, and more elementary than the literal indicative designations of our linguistically constructed world:

> Thus the trickster ironically symbolizes the symbolic reality of man, that "freak," as Pascal calls him, who is the "glory and refuse of the universe." Freakily, the trickster can image man's openness to the sacred by lust, gluttony, lying, and flatulence. . . . His satire affirms the doubleness of the real and denies every one-dimensional image of it. If he struggles with the High God and causes pain and death to enter the world, spoiling primordial bliss, his quarrel is not with the divine order as such, but with a false human image of the sacred, one that cannot encompass suffering, disorder, and the ultimate mess of death. If death is allowed to remain an anomaly lying outside all the taxonomies that make up life, then, immobilized by death's unyielding solidity, life will become stasis.[9]

In this, Robert Pelton is unsparingly definite: given the fragility of this "false human image" the structure-bound insider is "immobilized," terrified of losing *control*.

Sinking in horror from the *hawk,* through the *rider* into the con- sciousness of the *horse,* recall now Highwater's proverbial "insider"—the

Emperor: "The insider in us dreads the impetuousness of the horse, for the mythic horse represents the boundless possibilities of nature. And so the fainthearted Emperor insists on retaining control of the beast."[10] Given such paranoia every deviation, every Otherness, every "anomaly lying outside all the taxonomies that make up [this so-called] life," is seen, literally, as a *death threat*!—and thus the Emperor and his court, "immobilized by death's unyielding solidity," desperately fight for "control." Membership in this "spirit narrowed" way of life comes at a dear price, assayed precisely by Morris Berman:

> In order to win membership in the human race, we are asked to pay a "small" price: everything. We are asked to give up our basic, and most trustworthy, way of knowing the world in favor of a phony charade of polite agreement. This is a colossal mutilation, and it accounts for much of the rage and pain that all of us carry and that erupts periodically in orgies of war and barbarism.[11]

INTOLERANCE *WITHOUT* breeds intolerance *within*. Social castigation, on the one hand, and the shame of self-contempt on the other, make the ambivalent battleground of the Other Within. Here is the unremitting struggle, not to redeem or transform one's self-image in "the mirror of malicious eyes," but to reclaim and integrate all our negative and anomalous faces: the undomesticated, stupid, ugly, deformed, malignant—each arising to its singular orbit in the constellation of "what we consider we are."

In this effort the Mythic Trickster leads the way by modeling a supra-ambivalent ability to leap back and forth from civilization, over the ramparts of Alexander's Wall, down into wilderness and back again, thus embodying and expressing the leaping consciousness that mediates and is in-touch with all extremes. Traveling down the Trickster's path, the following "cluster of manifest trickster traits," cogently prepared by William Hynes, may be confirming: "1) the fundamentally ambiguous and anomalous personality of the trickster. Flowing from this are such other features as 2) deceiver/trick-player, 3) shaper-shifter, 4) situation-inverter, 5) messenger/imitator of the gods, and 6) sacred/lewd bricoleur."[12] For the Other Within all of these traits are strategic skills; more than mere coping strategies, they are skills for *thriving* within the no-place, the civilizing split of spirit from flesh: *and the Trickster is born in the breach.*

It has been suggested, by a few of the foremost thinkers on myth, that the figure of the Trickster is synonymous with the myth-making capacity itself—here, it can well be said that myth-making (mythopoesis) is the heart of Trickster Wisdom:

> Those who know the trickster understand that if the system of life embraces change and death, it is because its boundaries are ceaselessly enlarged by him—the image of a mind subtle enough and a heart playful enough to seize and affirm all that is negative and anomalous. That affirmation discloses the holiness of what is, as all of it, man's own anomalous being especially, becomes a vessel of the mysterious dynamism that continues always to make being *be*. In reaching into nothing the trickster touches the ultimate pollution [of chaos] that threatens every [explicate] something, and in discovering that nothing's power only thrusts him back into what is present, he transforms every potential avenue of corruption into a passageway of rebirth.[13]

"Reaching into nothing" we grasp the touchstone, the firmament, of utter liminality—the absolute no-thing-ness which is the *wellspring* of Mythic Reality. Most of us come to this "nothing" not by intention but by the "violent concussions" of devastation, robbery, and betrayal. Plummeting down the "avenues of corruption" back to the *no-place* and the low-life of the denied, forsaken, and dispossessed—immersed in the underworld, the unconscious, the body, the arche-cortex—psyche's Other Within, like the Trickster, must possess "a mind subtle enough and a heart playful enough to seize and affirm all that is negative and anomalous."

Cassirer stated: "Our science, our poetry, our art, and our religion are only the upper layer of a much older stratum that reaches down to a greater depth." And at that mythic depth lies all that we have "given up" in exchange for "membership"—in Berman's terms: "our basic, and most trustworthy, way of knowing the world." Myth forms "the very foundations of peoples' self-understandings, of their geography, history, and worth."[14] While the upper layer, the daylight-world, is "a phony charade of polite agreement."

The Other Within by virtue of exclusion from the courteous "charade" comes in-touch with the bottomless wisdom of that "greater depth." In this circumstance one may begin to awaken the denied, repressed, and forgotten *ways of knowing*. The pathways which constellate such wisdom are scattered and marginated in the remnants of "other people's myths" which have escaped the dismembering machine of Church and Empire. To our poverty, the legacies of some culture groups will not survive—as Gardner notes: "once these groups have disappeared, we may not even be able to envision that they could have been capable of the actions, skills, or traits that they in fact exhibited."[15]

There will be more, much more, to say of these lost "actions, skills, and traits"; the point now is that "they were not entirely destroyed," they are still down there, in the mythic realm, waiting to recombine and arise with the living body of myth, with Tiamat and Grendel. It follows, then, that one of the best ways available (and sometimes the only way) of entering such lost ways of knowing is through myths and stories—as John Emigh attests: "The story is a scaffolding used to show essentialized images of human capabilities and epistemologies—of different ways of knowing and of being in the world."[16]

THE TERRIBLY DIFFICULT task of coming to accept, integrate, and utilize the story of the mask-like imposed identity, formed in "the mirror of malicious eyes," and still somehow manage to affirm, cultivate, and maintain the implicate identity, is something akin to the task of a traditional performer wearing a mask. In both cases the mask occupies and displays an axial or transitional space between the actor and a deity or spirit. Thus the affective power of the imposed identity is that it functions exactly as the sacred mask: it invokes, in the mind of the beholder (as well as the wearer), the archegestic leap.

Within every rigid social structure the implicate identity is invisible; only the imposed identity is recognized. It is as if, unbeknownst to us, the Trickster Hermes has crowned us with his magical "helmet of invisibility"; yet instead of realizing the gift—invisibility in and of the soul—one is stricken with feelings of isolation, grief, and betrayal. This circumstance is, to say the least, uncomfortable—perhaps, for some, unendurable. Nevertheless, if the asynchronies and betrayals of life are to be truly faced and lived, infantile protestation against one's rotten lot in life will accomplish very little. Graceful acceptance will help; realization with cunning will be even better—deferral is dis-appointed destiny; assigning blame merely abdication.

However repugnant it may be, if one hopes to survive as the Other Within, it will be vital to accept and exercise the poetic-power in the deep ambivalence of the mask; and the act of grasping the "efficacy"— of the imposed or false identity—must be approached and executed with reverence:

> The mask is . . . approached through a process involving an exploration of its potential life, first by regarding it . . . and then grounding its life—its movement, its voice, its spirit—in the specific body of a specific actor. In the process, the actor addresses the mask and eventually puts it on, sequentially closing the gaps from "it" to "he" or "she" to "you" to "I" as different centers of energy that sustain and shape voice and movement are found and are tested. The bond between mask and actor is finally checked in a mirror, adjustments made, and the masked persona is then deployed to . . . tell stories . . . from his or her very specific vantage point. At each stage of the exercise, the problem is to find a meeting ground between the range of memories and possibilities experienced as the

actor's self—the locus of "I"—and that which begins outside the self—as "his" and "hers" as "it" and "you," as another person's story, another face, another way of talking and being.[17]

The "problem" of finding the "meeting ground" is the problem of holding the *interval*—while maintaining "the locus of 'I'"—and this without getting torn and reduced to a half-self, or losing one's sense-of-self entirely. In the trialogue of (universal) "it", (local) "you", and (personal) "I," the implicate identity is born in the breach—ever unfolding, ever blossoming, ever borne out of the *wound*—hence the term is an oxymoron: *implicate identity* is identity before-*and*-beyond identification; to be clear the implicate identity cannot be directly known, yet it can be implicated.

The implicate is Other; that is, it cannot be found in the explicate, known, and apparent world; it is deeply interior, rooted in the *Mundus Inferorum.* Therefore to implicitly display or perform this unknowable identity, one must recall Corbin's saying: "what the soul really sees, it is alone in seeing"—it is invisible. If one's Otherness is to move beyond the intra-personal realm, it must be moved outside the self—embodied, enacted, performed, danced, sung—and actualized *within* the exterior inter-personal realm. To put it bluntly, in order to communicate the personal/universal "unknown" one has to forego membership and *become* "unknown"—namely, the Other Within. In an attempt to understand the sense (or nonsense) of how this works, let the Winnebago Trickster lead the way:

Once Trickster was wandering around as usual when he heard a noise like a celebration. By and by he discovered the joyous sound was coming from inside the bleached-white skull of a dead elk with many branching antlers. A mass of flies was flying in through the neck-hole and making a great sound as they rushed in and out. Trickster tried to stick his head inside, but the hole was too small. "How can I join this celebration?" he asked, and the flies replied,

"Say the magic words: *neck become large*!" "Alright, neck, become large!" he commanded and then he put his head inside the skull, whereupon all the flies vanished, and the opening became small again, closing around his neck and leaving him completely stuck. Trickster shouted "neck become large!" again, and again, but nothing happened. He tried with all his might to pull the skull off, but finally realized that nothing could be done, so he went to the river and walked along the edge, until he came to a village of human beings. He decided to wait through the night in that very spot.

At this juncture, as Trickster walks along the mirror of the water's edge, one can imagine a strange reflection catching his eye—an image which illuminates the following events:

In the morning a woman came to get water, suddenly she saw Trickster—stretched out on the riverbank in full view, wrapped in a raccoon-skin blanket, and crowned with the white skull and spreading antlers—she started to run; but the "terrible being" spoke to her: "do not be afraid, come back and I will bless you." She turned and approached as near as she dared. Trickster said, "Now, go home and get all the customary offerings. Then if you strike the top of my head with an axe, you will be able to use what you find inside to make medicine. I am a water-spirit; I have come to give my blessing to your village."

The woman fled back home and told the story. Quickly the people prepared the offerings and a fine axe. They followed her back to the great water-spirit, terrible to look upon. The offerings were placed before him. Then a certain man advanced with the axe. He struck the skull, split it open, and behold! There was Trickster laughing at them. He laughed uproariously! The people groaned and said, "Oh no, it's only Trickster!" But he replied, "Since you've made these offerings they will not be lost. Whatever you produce from this skull, its purpose will be accomplished." Then, the Trickster

departed to continue his wandering way. The people made medi-
cines from the skull and found to their surprise and delight that
they were indeed healing and potent.[18]

When the Trickster said to the woman: "you will be able to use what
you find inside to make *medicine*," did he indicate the inner lining of
the elk-skull or himself? Or was he referring to the leaping mind-of-
trickster, the fertile emptiness *between* the inner and outer shape?

The invisible medicine of the mask is the interval of the leap, it is
neither the deity nor the performer, it is "neither this nor that," it is
"spirit *and* flesh"—the mandorla, a crossroads-thing, the Third Thing
which is no-thing; impossibly, it participates across all categories,
transgressing all boundaries, expressing chaos within cosmos, and the
forest within the village.

The mask is initiatory and confirmatory at the same time. Initiation
occurs *intra*-personally in isolation, in the forest, whereas confirmation
occurs *inter*-personally, in community, in the village. If one recalls that
the life-sequence of initiatory passages delineates the various stations of
socio-structural status, with an abysmal death between each station, then
all initiatory crises must be accepted as inevitable and unavoidable, with
liminality as fundamental to life. And with this acceptance comes the
further realization that what is desperately missing, in the modern world,
is the soulful confirmation of the newly initiated condition—i.e., the
confirmatory capacities of living myth—and this especially for the Other
Within, as it is our very Otherness which most longs for confirmation.

The Trickster allows his appetite for communal celebration to direct
him, he places his head (consciousness) into the hierophanous skull—
taking on the shamanic status of "bones" which endure beyond death—
but not merely his discarnate consciousness, his flesh and blood are
extended into the Otherworld. Thus his every gesture, his whole style
is imbued with a captivating and evocative "presence." Just as the sacred
may be beneficent *and* dangerous, healing *and* wounding, so the imposed
identity may be pleasant *and* horrid. In either case the piercing of the

imposed identity—the axial shattering of the mask—is the essential narcissine task: consciously separating the inner from the outer identity.

Trickster's manner toward the woman by the river is grounded in a
sure anticipatory imagination of her likely perceptions. He knows stories
about "water-spirits," and their "blessings"; and he does not deny the
woman's reaction, he accepts and uses it as the basis of communication
and rapport. As previously noted: the Trickster would certainly
never fail to take advantage of the opportunity presented in a case of
mistaken identity; whether superior or inferior, the "mistake" would be
exploited. The point is that we must *know* the imposition is mistaken,
and only then *accept* the correctness of the mistake—for, in this case,
it is the ignorant pretense of knowledge that displaces and overwhelms
the heart. Maturity demands that the Other Within be well versed in
the archegestic properties and effects of giants, trolls, dwarves, devils,
elves, dragons, hags, faery queens, princes, and princesses—whatever
monstrosity or apparition may correspond to the imposed identity.

To grasp the significance of the mask, it must be recalled that the
mask itself *is* a story. It is crucial to objectify the imposed identity as
"the masked persona," which "is then deployed to tell stories," and most
importantly, stories told subjectively, *personally,* from a "very specific vantage point"—from the deeper standpoint of identity prior to identification. As in the story of trickster: the implicate identity (which is neither
water-spirit nor Trickster) is revealed in the Thunderbolt-axe shattering
the intervallic mask—the axial leap between inner and outer identity. The
imposed identity/mask radiates the Sacred/Profane-Otherness of liminality which, to the structure-bound, represents a manifestation of lethal
chaos. The performance of liminality by the Other Within provides a
disclosure of the hidden yet implicate Mythic Reality, which is—as it has
always been—the wisdom and "medicine" necessary for the renewal and
revitalization of our individual and cultural lives.

REVISITING THE MYTH of Narcissus, in the context of this *masquerade,* yields a very different interpretation than the usual. There was

something archegestic in Narcissus's beautiful countenance which caused those around him to fall helplessly and hopelessly in love—but could it be that this perception and reaction was not congruent with his inner life? Could it be that Narcissus rejected all his suitors, not out of "pride," but out of despair? We all know the feeling of being identified by those who want what they imagine we have—money, sex, power, understanding, beauty—and yet such a person is not the least bit interested in the condition of our soul. If this is the case then the actual downfall of Narcissus is not to be found in the callous breaking of one too many hearts, rather it is that in the end he began to believe and was seduced by the imposed image—"the mask of beauty"—reflected in the mirror of adoring eyes. Here we find a Narcissus, inundated with a potent and overwhelming projection, "until at last he thinks that shape must be his shape."

There is, perhaps, another possible ending implicit with Narcissus's gaze into the mirror of the water's edge: "There I stooped to drink at a pool, and I saw myself in the chill water. I saw that I was hairy and tufty and bristled . . . stripped . . . withered and wrinkled . . . naked . . . and on my fingers and toes there were great curving claws, so that I looked like nothing that was known, like nothing that was animal or divine."[19] Rather than falling in love with himself, perhaps in seeing-through, there in the breach emerged and unfolded this unknowable and unimagined "shape," confronting in dreadful recognition: the daimon, the paraclete, the Other implicate identity. Upon this aporia—steeped in the one-sided sense-of-self, unprepared to sustain the non-identity between the "I" and the "not-I"—many a soul is overcome, driven even to suicide: "Darkly mirrored in the cosmic processes of nature, man's true face, mottled like a wizened and warty gourd, shines back as the faceless ancestor of all men".[20]

> *Yes, his face really is so terrible*
> *you cannot turn away. And only*
> *that thin sheet of glass between you,*

clouding with his breath.
Behind him: the dark scribbles of trees
in the orchard, where you walked alone
just an hour ago, after the storm had passed,
watching water drip from the gnarled branches,
stepping carefully over the sodden fruit.
At any moment he could put his fist
right through that window. And on your side:
you could grab hold of this
letter opener, or even now try
very slowly to slide the revolver
out of the drawer of the desk in front of you.
But none of this will happen. And not because
you feel sorry for him, or detect
in his scarred face some helplessness
that shows in your own as compassion.
You will never know what he wanted,
what he might have done, since
this thing, of its own accord, turns away.
And because yours is a life in which
such a monster cannot figure for long,
you compose yourself, and return
to your letter about the storm, how it bent
the apple trees so low they dragged
on the ground, ruining the harvest.[21]

The Drum

For the Serpent & the Bird

GREATNESS, AS IN Alexander "the Great," achieves its immortality by building personal history into a monument. Greatness, unlike genius, is superiority accomplished by decree of structure, by acclamation, renown, reputation, and approval—all of which, however, are substitutes for initiatory transformation, and ceremonial confirmation:

> For greatness is only the drayhorse that coaxes
> The built cart out; and reason is where we go.
> But genius is an enormous littleness, a trickling
> Of heart that covers alike the hare and the hunter.[1]

Patchen's opposition—the top-down "built cart" of *greatness* against the "enormous littleness" of bottom-up *genius*—is perfectly fitted to the contradictions and the vast distance between the imposed and the implicate shape of life.

With genius as counter-myth to greatness, we depart decisively from Gardner's theory of creativity which holds acclamation within the creative "domain" as a primary measure of genius: "Creativity," he says, "is inherently a communal or cultural judgement"[2]; thus, rendering a structure-bound view, constrained always to shadow the towering greatness of History's "Big-Man." To the contrary, "cultural judgement" and "renown" are superfluous for the Other Within—as for Robert

159

Graves: "No public honors, no consensus of other poets, no album of press-cuttings, nor even the passage of time can give me, or anyone else, more than the courtesy title of poet. The one sure reward for whatever labours we may have undergone is our continued love of the Muse"[3]—genius, then, the guiding source of creativity, is *confirmed* alone and in the soul.

Having thus far explored the necessity, value, and innovations of descent, it remains to establish the imperative of staying paradoxically descended even in ascent—remaining faithful to genius even in greatness; as Bly says, "the higher the spirit goes the more deeply the soul sinks down"[4]—we need the gnomon *and* its dark shadow. This dynamic is the paradox of "verticality" and is dramatically illustrated in the polarity of the mythic pair Gilgamesh and Enkidu.

In the scholarship of this Mesopotamian Epic, Thomas Van Nortwick, speaking of the Gilgamesh figure, has written: "the heroic perspective was a reflection of the preoccupation with renown as a hedge against death, and led to an easy defiance of the reality of death."[5]

The Trickster introduces death, but the jestless Emperor demands eternal life. Such a life of greatness—lived as a monument to immortality—is the imposed order of history, the eternal and fixed explicate-order of structure, the so-called "superior forces" of civilization.

The counter-myth to such a life is the wild genius of Enkidu—again turning to Bly: "Another instance of vertical thought is the idea that a 'spiritual twin'* was born with you. At birth the two of you separated, and perhaps you might not see your spiritual twin again in this life, although you would always long for her or him."[6] Regarding the Wild Man Enkidu as "the second self"—i.e., spiritual twin, daimon, paraclete, the "not-I"—Van Nortwick tells us: "the second self has the effect . . . of opening up for our consideration the gap between what we see in the sometimes narrow vision of conscious life and the different vista afforded by including truths from the darkness inside us."[7]

Enkidu, "the faceless ancestor of all men," like Cowper's Wounded Healer, opens that "different vista"—the counter-balance to greatness, the *descensus ad inferos*. The Wild Man, therefore, exemplifies the deep wisdom most crucial to the Other Within: "hell's imaginal function"; the implicate shape of life; those "deep images lurking in life's history"; "understanding . . . with imagination"—Enkidu embodies the "function of the descent."

There is a particularly applicable episode in which Gilgamesh accompanied by Enkidu received two implements from the goddess Inanna. These items are variously translated as a "stick and hoop" (used to play a hockey-like game), or as "drum and beater"; in either interpretation they can be said to represent the lost instruments of *play* and *creative expression*.

The *huluppu*-tree* from which the drum and beater were made had three inhabitants: the Zu-bird in the crown; the goddess Lilith in the trunk; and the snake "who knows no charm" in the roots (bird, mammal, reptile); a tripartite image which recalls the Nordic *Yggdrasill:** the divine ash tree with an eagle on top, a squirrel on the trunk, and the primordial würm gnawing at the roots (again bird, mammal, reptile). Hence, the image is the World Tree or *axis mundi* which intersects the zones of the shamanic triune cosmos. And this recalls again "the hawk, the rider, and the horse," which stand here for the divisions of a tripartite consciousness and the triune brain. The fact that Inanna wished to be rid of the tree's tenants, so as to make the horizontal Throne of privilege, and Bed of royal birthright from its wood, indicates that the valor of triality was already waning in favor of civilization's exploitative one-sidedness. Loss of triality is further suggested by the fact that the bright aspect of the "triple goddess," Inanna, wishes to rid herself of her own dark aspect, personified as Lilith. Inanna's determination to cut down the primordial tree is tantamount to Marduk's ritual dismemberment of Tiamat; the cosmogonic* act which brings about the new civilized order (an order that "could not arise until the darkness of myth was fought and overcome"). Nevertheless, one cannot dismiss the shamanic significance of this particular drum and beater—especially in connection with the theme of initiatory descent—for as the story goes on, suddenly a chasm opens in the earth, the drum and beater are lost in the depths of the netherworld, whereupon Gilgamesh laments:

> *O my drum, O my beater,*
> *My drum with irresistible heart,*
> *My beater with dance-rhythm unrivaled . . .*[8]

Considering Eliade's view that "the pre-eminently shamanic technique is the passage from one cosmic region to another—from earth to sky or from earth to the underworld,"[9] one can surmise that when the drum and beater fall into the abyss they are returned to the original pre-civilized source of shamanic power. Clearly the drum (*pukku*) being made from the root, and the beater (*mikku*) being made from the crown of the World Tree, derivatively carry the chaotic serpent and the cosmic bird forward into the new order. It should come as no surprise then that when the drum falls, of all present, only the half-civilized Enkidu is willing to descend to the underworld and attempt to retrieve the lost instruments of play and creative expression—whereupon he proclaims:

> *I will bring up now the drum from the underworld,*
> *land of the dead;*
> *I will bring up the beater from the mouth of darkness.*

The Emperor Gilgamesh, the proverbial "insider," and architect of civilized order, accepts the Wild Man's offer of descending to the underworld; but warns him with the following advice:

> *Do not put on a clean garment . . .*
> *Do not smooth your skin with sweet-smelling oil from*
> *   the bowl . . .*
> *Do not throw the throwing-stick in the underworld . . .*
> *Do not carry a staff of power in your hands . . .*
> *Do not put sandals on your feet.*

Make no bellow in the place of the
cry-out-of-the-earth.
Kiss not your beloved wife,
nor strike the wife you hated;
kiss not your beloved child,
nor strike the child you hated.[10]

It seems that the ascending heroic twin (Gilgamesh-consciousness) has strong advice for the descending anonymous twin (Enkidu-consciousness). Gilgamesh indicates that, in order to pass through the underworld unscathed, one ought to resume the original, tufty and bristled, uncivilized and wild condition; insisting that one should lay aside the refined emblems and accoutrements of the civil persona. This recommended procedure is identified herein as the false divestiture—a pose portrayed incisively by Deldon Anne McNeely in her work on the Trickster:

The look is naturally contrived—hair treated so that it looks as if it had never been touched by a comb, clothing made to look beaten and torn. Oversized clothes in layers gives us the charm of clowns, or homeless people who must wear all they own. Comfort defines propriety; yet we torture ourselves (tousled perms, tight jeans, etc.) to appear comfortable. One way to understand the current love of grunge is to recognize it as part of the a-heroic mystique.[11]

The emphasis on the look of grunge and comfort stands for the rejection of the stuffed-shirt formality of elevationism. One cannot, however, simply assume the "appearance" of descendedness—for that is mere renunciation.

The true divestiture takes place *in* the actual descent; as we know, particularly, from another Sumerian myth, "The Descent of Inanna." In preparation to enter the great below Inanna Queen of Heaven is elaborately adorned in the vestments and regalia of her exalted estate; and as she goes down, at each of seven gates, she is ritually divested of one more item—*the seven decrees, the crown of the plain, the rod of lapis lazuli, the stones about her neck, a gold ring, a breastplate, all her garments of ladyship*[12]—until finally naked, Inanna enters the deepest deep. Hence, as proposed from the outset, in the case of the Other Within, such emblems of status are not renounced but are initiatorily stripped away; and thus stripped, one is prepared and enabled to sustain the "under-the-worldly point of view" and to reclaim the lost instruments of *poiesis*.

Wisely then, Enkidu declines the misdirection; contrary to Gilgamesh's counsel, he performs all according to the "first exemplary model" of the goddess Inanna; "Winning does not tempt [him]. / This is how he grows: by being defeated, decisively."[13] Enkidu succeeds by failure: making a deep and permanent descent—whereupon a bereaved Gilgamesh cries out:

> *"Father Enlil, on the day the drum was beaten for me*
> *in the underworld,*
> *and the beater was struck where the earth cries out,*
> *Enkidu, who went down to bring them up,*
> *was trapped by the underworld."*

Along with the Wild Man, the axial drum is now hidden from the daylight world, and, much to our poverty, with it went our natural desires for: entrainment to the rhythms of the earth; wholehearted participation in the round-dance of life and death; the sacrality of sex and gender; and all the rites of passage. This condition is corroborated in Grimms' "Iron John," where the Wild Man is located in the darkest forest, hidden underwater in a pond—repressed, as Bly says, at the bottom of the psychic pool.

Retaining the descended reality means that one should not strive to conjure him *up*, rather one should join Lilith, Tiamat, Grendel, and Enkidu in the depths. The implication is that the great Eagle above stays in-touch with the genius of the Serpent below in the underworld by virtue of the squirrelly leap. In Van Nortwick's view, when Gilgamesh accepts the Wild Man as a part of himself, he reintegrates the second self:

> Gilgamesh has now accepted, on a deeper level, the presence of the wilderness inside himself. The loss of Enkidu has, then, made a difference in the way Gilgamesh sees the world: death, once something to be defied, then to be denied, has become a part of life; Enkidu, lost forever, is at the same time found again.[14]

The vertical axis between the ascendant and the descendant breaks through one-sidedness and actualizes the leaping consciousness. With the axial corridor intact one could say that Enkidu will anchor Gilgamesh to the sphere of earthly life, while Gilgamesh buoys Enkidu up into the sphere of human culture—the leaping voice of the axial drum thus speaks the extremes, from crown to root of Shaman Tree—as in Bringhurst: *If I speak for the serpent, the serpent may speak for the bird.*

The modern problem is that verticality has been abandoned in favor of the socially elevated life. Choosing one-sidedness enables both mass-society and the liminoid individual to avoid consciously feeling the amputations and fragmentations of modernity; however, avoiding that phantom-pain and maintaining buoyancy consumes more and more of our personal and cultural resources—leaving the massman vulnerable and ready to attack any sign of authentic depth. The effort to resist the seductive elevations of greatness and to regain and remain one's descendedness, within the ordinary daylight world, requires vigilance and remembrance—it means consciously *staying down*. Affirming this point McNeely appropriately cites the life of playwright Václav Havel who spent five years in a communist-run prison, before the revolution, and his accession to the office of president:

> Czechoslovakia's velvet revolution evolved under the leadership of Václav Havel, who refused to live in the palace. After becoming president he continued to reside in his working class digs in

downtown Prague. Although to his constituents he was a hero, Havel did not define himself as superior to the common man; he preferred to *be* the common man. Havel lives out a relationship to authority that seems to include respect for the hermetic as well as the heroic.[15]

Resisting the seductive delusion of the Big-Man in the Big-House an initiated and mature "verticality" will depend on keeping the "under-the-worldly point of view," which is the root of "wisdom"—the vision of doom, or doomed vision—a designation that has just the right sound of darkness.

AS THE STORY of Iron John begins, the people of the kingdom are unaware of the Wild Man. The only clue they have to his presence is that any hunters who enter the forest inexplicably never return (it's possible that those who descend into the chaos of wilderness are altered to such an extent that they become unidentifiable, invisible to the taxonomic ledger of the massman). It is significant that in the story the only person who is able to contact the Wild Man is a "hunter" and a "stranger" and hence a doubly liminal figure.

Like the shaman, the hunter mediates wilderness to civilization. As in the story, so in history and throughout the world: in the hunt, the vision quest, the initiatory vigil, *the hunter goes alone*—beyond civilization, into the primeval forest, into the dark, into the underworld; and yet the family, the whole village is carried along in the heart. This is what John Lash calls "the hunting bond"[16]—the filial bond of the solitary hunter. Perhaps it is only in such solitude that one comes to understand what human beings really are, as Bly once remarked, "it was first in solitude that I really felt affection for the human community."[17]

The insider/outsider ambivalence of the hunter *plays* across categorical and normative boundaries; and play within a "system"—a social and/or psychic structure—functions as an alimentary organ for the ingestion of the *prima materia,* the food of cultural and soulful vitality. With the hunter, as with the Trickster, the impenetrable boundary becomes a permeable membrane: "membranes act in a selectively permeable way, allowing nourishment in, keeping poisons out."[18] This, then, is the bond: although alone the hunter acts on behalf of the collective to go beyond its structure to gather the needed *medicine*—food for the body and food for the soul:

> The hunter is open to something there are no words for—the music of pattern: relationships of relationship in states of change. Altogether, they make up a polyphony, with each voice, each being, singing its own song or story . . . to hear this shifting music more keenly, the hunter cannot afford to be aware of it consciously. He carries the whole music of the forest in his soul. He cannot break it down for objective analysis or filter it through fixed frameworks of conscious purpose without losing the feel of it altogether. And usually, the less he has to say about what he feels, the better.[19]

Staying "open to something there are no words for" requires that "something" remain unnamed—as D. H. Lawrence said: "If people say they've got feelings, you may be pretty sure they haven't got them."[20] As with the modern substitute-reality of the ideal body, all the popular fascination with "feelings" and "honesty" is, most often, merely lip service and sentimentality. The excruciation of the *descensus ad inferos* is the only route to genuine feeling.

The hunter, to be successful in the hunt, must abandon the ordinary, structural categories of perception and descend from the mind of the rider into the mind of the "horse" and "dragon." This descent, an epistemic and ontic departure, understood in the words of biomusicologist Nils Wallin, delineates "a fundamental distinction between two types of perception: discrimination and identification, or, in different terms, discernment and designation."[21] Employing this distinction, "designation" may be placed on the side of dogmatic structure's endless classifications (beginning with heaven and earth and on to "the ten thousand things"); whereas "discernment" is nameless, pre- and para-lingual, before-*and*-beyond designation—beyond our linguistically constructed world—discernment is "the music of pattern."

"To hear this shifting music more keenly, the hunter cannot afford to be aware of it consciously." Maintaining descendedness, in this respect, is to submit to the "private storm," the visceral, proprioceptive,* and stereognostic intelligences,* and to enjoin the hyper-vigilance of the animal-body. In this submission we *discern* without the limitation of designation—as Rilke implores:

> If only we would let ourselves be dominated
> as things do by some immense storm,
> we would become strong too, and not need names.[22]

Dropping the reins, our tight-fisted rationality must come to trust the shaggy little horse of limbic discernment: what Wallin refers to as "emotional syntax." In this, Wallin takes us down to the genotype, the arche-cortex, the dragonish horse: "the syntax and morphology of emotion" is a sensibility "with the explicit task to constantly interpret and counterbalance" internal and external stimuli. In other words Wallin says "it is a kind of semiotic operator" (meaning an *intelligence*) which works "in the service of purposive behavior":

> According to these proposals, the syntax of emotional display in higher mammals and some bird-species would, in an evolutionary perspective, be regarded as a primordial qualification for the syntax of the human emotional repertoire, and the syntax of animal sound gestures as the main source for the syntax of early forms of music.[23]

In poetry the archegestic image breaks through and de-forms language to reach and reclaim the deep syntax of emotional display and tonality. Returning us to "the music of pattern"—as Kane proclaims, "in the beginning was, not the word, but the music. By music I mean a nonverbal discourse that protects its integrity from human possession and control."[24]

The visceral relationship of the initiand to this wordless animal-intelligence is laid out in a vast body of mythic and esoteric lore, stretching all the way back to the paleolithic and the painted cave-temples of Chauvet, Altamira, and Lascaux: animal-deities, animal-ancestors, animal-guides, animal-helpers, theriomorphic* guardians. The heritage of animal intelligence plays an integral part in bringing the initiand to the depths of wisdom. The civilized preference for the spiritual flight of objective-conceptual-thought with its distaste for the descended suffering of mythic-imaginal-gnosis has something to do with what Miguel de Unamuno called "affective stupidity":

> There are, in fact, people who appear to think only with the brain, or with whatever may be the specific thinking organ; while others think with all the body and all the soul, with the blood, with the marrow of the bones, with the heart, with the lungs, with the belly, with the life. And the people who think only with the brain develop into definition-mongers; they become the professionals of thought . . . [expounding in] vague verbiage which satisfies only those who suffer from affective stupidity, and who, for the rest, may be persons of a certain cerebral distinction. For it is possible to possess great talent, or what we call great talent, and yet to be stupid as regards the feelings and even morally imbecile. There have been instances.[25]

The ignorance which separates human intelligence from animal emotion is born of the same avoidance which holds the spirit far from flesh—thought from act, and the *said* from the *sung*. The grave error in denial of this fundamental and sophisticated emotional way of knowing presents the same problem as identified again and again throughout this work: that the denied material does not go away but becomes autonomous and returns to exert a vengeful influence. The uninitiated hyper-rational mentality is invariably accompanied by an unconscious, free-ranging and intentional emotional-hunger which is capable of perpetrating the most heinous affective blunders and injuries: "there have been instances."

IN THE RUSSIAN STORY "Maria Morevna" the initiatory journey of Prince Ivan begins with his facilitation of a triple *hieros gamos*: a ritual sequence of yearly marriages, having each of his three sisters wed, in turn, to three shape-shifting animal-deities—the Hawk, the Eagle, and the Raven. Having thus dramatically married his soul to the animal world he departs the boundaries of his kingdom and soon meets the Warrior Queen, Maria Morevna, who poses the ritual question: "Have you come of your own free will, or do you come by compulsion?" That this initiand has not yet reached the deeper stages of the journey is evident in the one-sided answer he provides: "A brave warrior would go nowhere by compulsion." The Warrior Queen, however, accepts this and takes Ivan as her husband.

After a time Maria becomes bored with the domestic palace-life and as she departs, to wage another war campaign, she warns Ivan that there is one room, only one in the whole palace, which he is forbidden to enter; a locked and chained door that must *never* be opened. This moment presents what has been referred to herein as a "trickster-situation." Ivan is now well in-touch with trickster energies, as evidenced by his total lack of hesitation; the moment Maria is gone he proceeds directly to the cellars, opens the door and there, chained to the wall, finds Koshchei the Deathless, who pleads in a dry voice for "water!" Ivan complies with this request three times which gives Koshchei the strength to break free, then intercept and abduct Maria. Ivan attempts three times to rescue his wife but each time as they escape Koshchei overtakes them—due to his magnificent Horse of Power:*

Koshchei was out hunting; at night-fall he returned home, and his good steed stumbled under him, "Why do you stumble hungry jade?" he cried, "Or do you sense some mishap?" The steed answered:

"Prince Ivan was here and has carried off Maria Morevna," "And can we overtake them?" To which the horse replied: "We could sow barley, wait till it grows, reap and thresh it, brew beer, drink ourselves drunk, sleep our fill—and even then we would catch them."[26]

This half of the story ends the third time the lovers are captured, with Ivan being chopped-up, by Koshchei, into tiny pieces, placed in a cask, the cask bound with iron bands, and then sunk into the deepest part of the sea. In this shamanic or Dionysian ritual-dismemberment, it is only by virtue of the pre-established theogamic* alliance with the animal-deities that the initiand is miraculously enabled to survive—the Eagle fetches the cask from the bottom of the sea; the Hawk fetches a vial of the Water-of-Life; and finally, the Raven fetches a vial of the Water-of-Death. The avian Divinities then break-open the cask; the Water-of-Death reconstitutes the body; and the Water-of-Life resuscitates Ivan:

Restored to life, Ivan stole back to the queen and said: "Find out from Koshchei the Deathless where he got his powerful steed." Maria Morevna seized an opportune moment and asked the question. Koshchei replied: "Beyond thrice nine lands, in the thrice tenth kingdom, beyond a river of fire, lives Baba Yaga; she has many splendid mares; I served as her herdsman for three days without letting one stray, and as a reward she gave me a colt." "How did you cross the river of fire?" "I have a handkerchief and if I wave it three times to the right, a bridge springs up and the fire cannot reach it."

Maria stole the handkerchief, gave it to Ivan and told him everything she had learned. Ivan departed and traveled, in a long arduous journey, to the thrice tenth kingdom, crossed the river of fire and proceeded through the wilderness to find Baba Yaga. After wandering a long time without food or water he happened upon a strange bird from beyond the sea, with her young. Ivan said: "I shall eat one of your little chicks." "Do not eat him, Prince Ivan," begged the bird. "Forego your appetite and one day I shall be useful to you."

"Let it be so," said Ivan. So he went on and soon saw a beehive. "I shall take some honey," he said, but the queen bee replied: "Do not touch my honey, Prince Ivan; forego your appetite, and some day I shall be useful to you." "Let it be so," said Ivan, and he went on. Soon he met a lioness and her cub. "Let me at least eat this little lion, I am so hungry that I am sick," he said. "Do not touch him, Prince Ivan," the lioness begged. "Please, forego your appetite and some day I shall be useful to you." "Well then, let it be so," said Ivan. He plodded on, and on, till at last he spied a little hut standing on a single chicken's leg. Around the hut were twelve stakes on which were set eleven decapitated human heads; the twelfth stake stood conspicuously bare. Out of the hut flew Baba Yaga; "Good day, grandmother," said the prince. "Good day, Prince Ivan! Why have you come—of your own free will or by compulsion?" "I have come to earn a mighty steed."

With this answer it is clear that a change has come over the prince—no longer so eager to boast, he has gained some grace and some cunning under the harsh tutelage of Koshchei the Deathless. It is also worth noting that he has learned something about sacrifice, and the foregoing of appetite, as evinced in the wilderness encounters with the bird, bee, and lioness. Nonetheless, it remains to be seen whether or not he is able to fulfill the initiatory task: earning a Horse of Power.

It should also be considered at this juncture that Ivan is now well beyond the merely psychological realm and is deeply into the Otherworld of the Mythic Reality. What Bly says of the Wild Man is equally if not more true of Baba Yaga: "We need to understand the [mythic figure] is not 'inside' us. The story suggests that [She] is actually a being who can exist and thrive for centuries outside the human psyche"[27]; thus, echoing Hölderlin: "the divine energies . . . apparently, don't bother if humans live or not." This information is particularly helpful to keep in mind when facing Baba Yaga—who would just as soon cut off your head and eat the rest of you for dinner—in Her words: "One need serve only three days for me. If you can tend my mares, I will give you a mighty steed; and if you cannot, don't hold it against me—but your head will go on the last stake." The consequence of initiatory failure—losing your head—is here reversed: the image of the head separated from the body, and suspended on the post, may stand for the psychological condition of consciousness or spirit divorced from, and vaunted above, the actual earthly flesh:

Baba Yaga gave Ivan meat and drink and ordered him to work. But he had no sooner driven the mares out when they raised their tails, scattered over the meadows, and vanished from sight. Hopelessly defeated Ivan, sat on a stone, wept and fell asleep. The sun was setting when the bird from beyond the sea flew down. "Arise, Prince Ivan! The mares have come home." The prince returned to the house, and found Baba Yaga scolding her mares: "Why did you come home?" But the horses replied. "How could we help coming home? birds swarmed up from every corner of the world and almost pecked our eyes out!" "Well then don't run into the meadows, tomorrow scatter through deep forests."

In the morning Baba Yaga said to Ivan: "Mind you, prince, if you lose even one mare, your head will go on that stake." Ivan drove the mares out; they raised their tails at once and scattered into the deep forests. Again Ivan sat on his stone, wept and wept, and finally fell asleep. The sun was setting when the lioness arrived. "Arise, Prince Ivan! The mares are gathered together." Ivan returned to the house and found Baba Yaga scolding her mares even more severely: "Why did you return home?" "How could we help going home when wild beasts came from every corner of the world and almost tore us to pieces!" "Well, tomorrow you are to run into the blue sea."

In the morning he drove the mares out; straightway they raised their tails and ran into the blue sea, standing in the water up to their noses. For a third time Ivan sat on his stone, wept, and fell asleep. The sun was setting when the bee flew up to him and said: "Arise, prince! All the mares are gathered. But when you return home, do not show yourself to Baba Yaga; go and hide behind stables. There you will find a mangy colt wallowing on a dung heap; steal him, and depart on the stroke of midnight." Ivan did as the queen bee advised. Baba Yaga scolded her mares and cried: "Why did you return?" "How could we help returning? An innumerable swarm of bees came from every corner of the world and fell to stinging our soft noses till the blood ran all down our necks!"

On the stroke of midnight Prince Ivan stole the mangy colt and galloped to the river of fire, waved his handkerchief to the right three times, crossed the magical bridge and looking back waved his handkerchief to the left side—but only twice, leaving only a remnant of the bridge. Next morning Baba Yaga awoke and found her mangy colt was gone. She rushed off in pursuit, galloping in an iron mortar and urging it on with a pestle. At the river of fire she looked and thought: "The bridge is good." She began crossing but as soon as she reached the middle the bridge broke; Baba Yaga fell and disappeared into the flames. Ivan fed his colt in the green meadows and soon it became a marvelous steed. He rode swiftly then to Maria Morevna who ran out to greet him and together they rode away. Koshchei the Deathless was returning home when his horse stumbled under him. "Why do you stumble, hungry jade?" he cried. "Do you sense a mishap?" "Yes; Prince Ivan was here and has carried off Maria Morevna, and this time we cannot overtake them for he has acquired a mighty steed better than myself." "No!" screamed Koshchei, "I won't endure it! I will catch him!" After a long hard ride, just as he caught up with Prince Ivan, the Horse collapsed and died. But Koshchei jumped to the ground, and tried to cut Ivan down with his saber. At that moment Ivan's steed swung a hoof with all his strength and struck Koshchei, smashing his head. Thereupon Ivan made a great fire, burned Koshchei the Deathless, and his horse; scattering the ashes to the winds.

Although Koshchei terrorizes and puts Ivan through Hell, he actually embodies the repressed and forgotten wisdom without which both Maria and Ivan could never become mature adults.

Everything that happens in this second half of the story depends first and foremost on the scavenger Raven and the Water-of-Death; as Pelton told us: "If death is allowed to remain an anomaly lying outside all the taxonomies that make up life, then, immobilized by death's unyielding solidity, life will become stasis."[28] In gaining the Horse of Power and dispatching Koshchei, Ivan accepts the Deathless genius within himself. For Ivan, as for Gilgamesh: "death, once something to be defied, then to be denied, has become a part of life."[29]

With animal shape-shifters, animal-helpers, and the dismembering-resurrection motif, this story clearly has shamanic origins. Moreover, according to Pyotr Simonov, "Koshchei the Deathless . . . is either Baba Yaga's son or nephew. He possesses the power of flight, is able to hang from a single hair, and can endure fire without being burned. The epithet 'Deathless' refers to his cycle of dying and rising."[30] While "flight," special powers (siddhis*), and "enduring fire" (tapas*), are also clearly shamanic, the "cycle of dying and rising" could suggest an agrarian mythos. However, the name Koshchei is derived from the word kost, meaning "bone," further indicating the lineage of shamanic hunter-gather myth.

Koshchei the Deathless initiates us in *this* world which leads inevitably to the Mythic Baba Yaga who initiates us in the *Other*— sending us back again to this world and to the integration of Deathlessness: the spiritual twin, the second-self, the "not-I," daimon, genius, paraclete. In this regard the story suggests that Prince Ivan is the bright solar civilized persona, who meets his dark brother chained and locked away in the last place one would look—in the cellars of the *beloved*. More than this, the story says that the "bright" side of us must be initiated at the hands of the dark side. The idea that Koshchei is the "son" of Baba Yaga, recalls the Celtic tale where the initiand Gwion is swallowed and gestated in the womb of the Hag, Cerridwen, to be reborn as her child Taliesin. Just as Gwion's passage displaces Cerridwen's son Afagddu, Ivan's successful passage will displace Koshchei; the two stories are further connected by the "ritual chase"; where the initiand flees in mortal terror from the enraged Hag. Perhaps, then, surviving the initiation, by assimilating the steed and powers of Koshchei, is to become the ritual progeny of the Great Mother.

The figure of Koshchei is particularly tricky—he is closer to the human world than Baba Yaga, and yet he is quite dangerous to us because when denied he embodies what Marion Woodman has called a person's "unnatural desire": "desires that overwhelm . . . with stupor and manifest as addictions."[31] The story tells us that if we set Koshchei free we will suffer. But if the fear of suffering compels us to deny the forbidden room, then life and marriage, the whole culture will stagnate in addiction, boredom, mediocrity, and false pride. With the deep-life locked safely in the cellar we hide from the wide-world, inside the Big-House of the Palace, "dying in the dishes."

The refusal to open the forbidden door allows the unfulfilled desire for "water" to possess the body and soul; and so one wastes the rest of their life trying to slake a haunting and inhuman thirst with substitute satisfactions. Our refusal to descend and look into the dark room drives the desire insane. It is strange to realize that even the "unnatural desire," in its own misguided and monstrous heart, wants to bring healing— even if it has to kill us to do so.

IT SEEMS THAT as far back as anyone can recollect there has always been a river of fire dividing the ordinary and the divine; a river, fordable only on pain of death—where mortality meets deathlessness in the permeability of the limen. The hierophanous exchange across the fiery *interval,* of myth, ritual, and art, reveals an image of how the mythological heals the psychological. The limen or threshold, as Sean Kane describes, is "the forest-edge, the sea-surface, the sky, the holes and caves in the earth, the transformation rituals, the boundary goddesses—these are all epistemological frames, markers of categories of knowledge, saying in effect: 'Beyond this point is a zone where ordinary human thinking cannot go. You must make a shift to another kind of thinking'"[32]—an-Other way of knowing that is "our basic, and most trustworthy, way of knowing the world."

The Mythic Horse of Power *is* the embodiment of this Other kind of thinking. The axial power of the horse, like the Wild Man's drum, is the power of *play* and *creative expression*—"'the drum,' said the Yakut shamans, 'is our horse.'"[33] Passing through the seven gates of hell is to suffer the descent to the unappealing little horse in the dung wallow, which is related to the shaggy horse in Con-Eda, who speaks to the rider as the Horse of Power in the Kirghiz epic poem, *Er-Töshtük:* "Your chest is broad, but your spirit is narrow. You are heedless. You do not see what I see, you do not know what I know."[34] Having gained the descendedness of this underworldly depth the time has come to *know what the horse knows.*

Of the Spirit & the Flesh

Long ago, in the before-time, they say the first shamans did not need to leave their bodies when they traveled to the other worlds; they flew to worlds, above and below, riding their double headed drums. And they say this power was lost when the gods decided that those first shamans had become too powerful. The gods then cut the shaman's drum in two (this is why the frame-drum used for shamanizing today has but a single head) and thus the shaman's power was halved; now they could only travel in spirit to the otherworld, leaving their vacant bodies behind, inert and entranced here in this world.[1]

JOSEPH CAMPBELL, ADAPTED FROM
THE BURIAT TALE "MORGAN-KARA"

THE SIGNIFICANCE of this splitting motif should by now be abundantly clear. The double-headed drum stands for the primordial body and consciousness of myth, sacrificially dismembered in order to inaugurate the "new spiritual reality" of the civilized world: thought is split from act, the said from the sung, object from subject, logic from magic, self from Other.

Caught between the antithetic perspectives of "history" and "story"—the ostensible denies the intrinsic—and we are *cut to the core*

178

between the privileging of spirit and castigation of the flesh: "For the mind of the flesh is death; but the mind of the Spirit is life and peace."[2] In this well-established biblical decree, it is not *spirit*, but the Otherness of mortal flesh which the gods fear and so prohibit.

It may be just fine for the lopsided "insider" to dismiss as irrelevant the lost half of the shaman's drum—the so-called "dead worlds" of myth—however, those of us on the receiving end of these lopped-off and denied energies had best pay attention—for the Other Within *is* a mythological creature, a *monstrum*: the sudden and terrible face at the window; a portent; a warning; a living sign of the perishing and corruptible flesh. In this, civilization's struggle to suppress the primordial serpent, "the dragon is losing," and yet:

> *As children, we knew ours*
> *Was a muddy greatness.*
> *We knew our part*
> *Lay with the dragon . . .*
> *[The] solar knight*
> *Grows victorious*
> *All over the world.*
> *And the dragon? He*
> *Is the great spirit*
> *The alchemists knew of.*
> *He is Joseph, sent down*
> *To the well. Grendel,*
> *What we have forgotten,*
> *Without whom is nothing.*[3]

Gilgamesh, now amnesic and mad with power, burns his dark brother at the stake; Prince Ivan, obedient to his bride, leaves his thirsty twin to rot in the palace dungeon. And the implicate heart of the Other Within withers in a mist of dragon-smoke, the smoldering *monstrum* of an ancient prophecy—Kammapa, Tiamat, P'an Ku, Ymir, Grendel,

Enkidu, Lilith, Leviathan, Behemoth, and Koshchei the Deathless—*slouching toward Bethlehem* to be born; not in the shopping-center of polis, but in the wild volcanic corridor of creation-*and*-destruction that even now abides unconquered in the depths.

So much herein has been aimed at this: if a person, dropped down into such lowliness, adversity, and madness, can imagine nothing more than the restoration of insiderhood, conceive of nothing other than attaining inclusion back in the highlife and Big-House of the "solar knight,"* then all is lost; *how many birds have died trapped in these granaries?* No revelation will occur, wisdom, the implicate identity, the original face—slips away: and "you will never know what he wanted, / what he might have done, since / this thing, of its own accord, turns away . . ."[4]

> *A shadow limps off among the trees.*
> *Already sentenced into wilderness,*
> *As if born wounded, he must stand*
> *Between man & what shines.*[5]

In the bright world of Gilgamesh, Beowulf, Alexander, and St. George, in the world of the "solar knight," despite all monumental efforts to block the gap, only that "thin sheet of glass" separates the "I" from the "not-I." To do the unthinkable, to break the glass and embrace the "muddy greatness" of the dragon, is to go the Trickster's cunning, limbic, and ludic* way—wearing the cloak of shame, descended in an elevated world. To enter this dance one needs *Imagination:* as much flesh as spirit; and *Mythos:* as much bios as logos. The leaping Waters of Life-and-Death re-member, reconstitute, and resuscitate the countless amputations of the fragmented imaginal body. Ambivalently, moving like the "hunter," through a living world "a polyphony, with each voice, each being, singing its own song or story"; imagination ranges beyond the best laid plans of structure, leaping in the warm-blooded, unbridled, and sinuousness stride of the dragonish "horse"—as theater-anthropologist Eugenio Barba explains:

Various fragments, various images, various thoughts are not connected due to a precise direction or according to the logic of a clear plan, but belong together because of "consanguinity."* . . . What does consanguinity mean in this context? That the various fragments, images, ideas, alive in the context in which we have brought them to life, reveal their own autonomy, establish new relationships, and connect together on the basis of a logic which does not obey the logic used when we imagined and sought after them. It is as if hidden blood-ties activate possibilities other than those which we think are useful and justified.[6]

The idea that the intelligence of myth and image are "useful and justified" is foreign to the Western mind; as Gardner points out, "some cultures do not even have a concept called intelligence, and others define intelligence in terms and traits Westerners might consider odd."[7] Yet Bly asserts: "a great image contains logic, that is thinking. One has to be intelligent to create an image and intelligent to under-stand it."[8] And the *Ufaina,* of the Northwest Amazon, say that "the ability to tell myths is necessary in order to learn how to 'think' and that the mythmaker himself is one who 'thinks well.'"[9]

The civilized aversion to the consanguineous vulgarity of the "odd" and primitive imagination is the Emperor's white-knuckled dread of mental disorder and the chaotic mind: "civilizations seek to suppress and control the 'primitive' mythological ambivalence of the chaos principle in individual and social life by claiming that the hierarchical ritual order of the ruling class is the original, one and only right/rite order."[10] When such civilized rule becomes too suppressive "psychic forces suddenly create Enkidu, 'the hairy man', as a companion for Gilgamesh, who is becoming too successful,"[11] and "mythical thought then starts to rise anew."

With this ever reenacted anthropogony* comes the healing of epistrophé to the *archai*—as Sumerologist Jeffrey H. Tigay observes: "Enkidu's creation was modeled on that of mankind in creation myths.

Mythical motifs about primitive man also supplied the model for the description of Enkidu's early life."[12] Given this connection, the sudden appearance of Enkidu presents a *renovatio:* the ritual recapitulation of an "archetypal gesture," the reiteration of a *dance,* a participation—across spatiotemporal boundaries—in and with a "first exemplary model," an act that restores and renovates creation. Thus, the dark figure of epistrophé arrives, as Koshchei the Deathless, to shatter the prevailing logic of the day. Now, born through the initiatory wound—if we are willing to drop the reins—issues the *renovatio* of a new imagination:

> The final point is not to slumber in the night of chaos: "Not to stay there, not to become beast or primeval matter but to start in a fresh direction, to discover new springs of development and action deep down in the roots of our being."[13]

THE NECESSITY of reaching back to the before-and-beyond-time, and down to the pre-existent and ever-present originary chaos is the Trickster's archegestic task of epistrophé and *renovatio;* a task which, in Pelton's words, will transform "every potential avenue of corruption into a passageway of rebirth."

Some, of course, will dismiss this as nostalgia and primitivism; they will say: "that was yesterday but this is today; all this gone-and-done, archaic, and primitive-past has nothing to do with the here-and-now." To the contrary—as one example of archegestic informance—consider the experience of players, in the Royal National Theatre of London, performing Robert Temple's *He Who Saw Everything* (Gilgamesh):

> A peculiar enchantment seems to have emanated from the archaic material, which worked powerfully upon the psyches of all involved, and many said it was the most amazing experience of their lives. In some strange way, immersing ourselves so deeply in aspects of thought and experience which were so many thousands of years old seemed to speak to a buried, elemental level of our psyches, and *it*

was the enactment and performance which brought this alive, like turning on an electric fire which had been inert for millennia.[14]

Hence, "the impulse of 'civilization' . . . to supersede & annihilate its past," is untenable and can only be sustained by a prodigious denial of the flesh—for in the body (bios) dwells the living presence of the past.

Again: the *archegestic image* incites a *biomythic reflex,* a "release" in which the "archetypal gesture" is spontaneously and atavistically embodied, enacted, ritualized, and performed. And again this can be understood in Rupert Sheldrake's terms as "morphic resonance" which "occurs between . . . rhythmic structures of activity on the basis of similarity, and through this resonance past patterns of activity influence the fields of subsequent similar systems." And most significantly: "this influence does not decline with distance in space or time."[15] In this sense the mythological-time of epistrophé defies linear historical-time reaching "new springs of development and action deep down in the roots of our being"—the archegestic in-formance of per-formance— igniting, through the hidden blood-ties, "an electric fire which had been inert for millennia":

> It can be said that the mystical return to an experience of primal unity implies a necessary cosmological interrelation of body and spirit, the reunion or marriage of *yin* and *yang,* the coexistence of the one and the two, nonbeing and being, the uncreated and the created . . . rooted metaphysically in the cosmogonic mystery of the third term or central gap—the "betwixt and between"—of chaos. This is a trinitarian formula of liminal order, the alchemical paradox of *mysterium coniunctionis.** The dynamic chaotic order, or chaosmos* . . . is the harmony of the creation time, the "concordant discord" of the beginnings.[16]

Spirit and flesh together make the imagination; it is not that Ouranos's thought/spirit should be deposed by the earthly flesh of Kronos, not that chaos utterly devour cosmos, but that "one-sidedness" be finally over-thrown and the painful "mystery of the third term or central gap"—the "soul gap" which is the wound—be openly admitted once and for all.

The "trinitarian formula of liminal order," brilliantly formulated by Girardot, begins with "*arché*—creation of the world, man, and culture," followed intermediately by "*peripéteia**—the 'dis-ease' of civilizational existence," and finally "*lysis**—an end that is a return to the beginning."[17]

"Arché" (of *archai,* archetype, and archegestic) is by now sufficiently familiar. "Peripeteia" is "a sudden change of fortune or reverse of circumstance." Borrowing Sheldrake's terms, it is the "two-way flow of influence: from fields to organisms and from organisms to fields"; the archegestic principle of peripéteia (i.e., the leaping consciousness) is the held tension, the "necessary cosmological interrelation," of spirit and flesh. Finally, "lysis," is "an insensible or gradual solution or termination of a disease or disorder without apparent phenomena"[18]; lysis, then, is the hidden and obscure *renovatio* intrinsic to epistrophé. The "trinitarian formula of liminal order" is the axial and mythic trialogue of contraries which inhere in the leaping consciousness.

Wishing to escape the disequilibrium and discomfort of "triality"— the dis-ease, and affliction of being split—the structure-bound insider attempts to inhabit various elevated, incorruptible, idealized, out-of-body, conceptualized, and virtual "substitute realities." In this weightless abscondence from flesh, the insidious fear and hatred of somatic mortality sends the intellect spinning off, out of gravity, uprooted from earth, leaving the dirty life of blood, tears, milk, sweat, semen, and shit far behind. The enraged and forgotten body, however, is still here, it cannot forget; and there is *no* soul apart from that body—the Red River of consanguinity will re-member:

> If you are in your body most of the time, the Void is not so threatening. If you are out of your body, on the other hand, you need a substitute for the feeling of being grounded. Much of what passes for "culture" and "personality" in our society tends to fall into this

substitute category, and is in fact the result of running from silence, and from genuine somatic experience.... The problem of hollowness, then, of a-Voidance,* is really one of secondary satisfactions, the attempt to find substitutes for a primary satisfaction of wholeness that somehow got lost, leaving a large gap in its place.[19]

A-voidance is "unbelief." Unbelief means flattening the imagination, stifling personal innovation, anesthetizing the wound with "secondary satisfactions," stuffing the void with "food that brings no nurturance, drink that brings no spirit, sex that brings no union."

The fear of initiatory suffering—which is, at bottom, the fear of death—compels us to deny that nagging little voice, the hollowness of the locked room in the cellar, the haunting and inhuman "thirst," which calls us to initiation. The "substitute life style" is employed to drown-out the summoning voices of myth. These substitute beliefs and behaviors are often described as "modern" myths, but myth is *not* whatever gets stuffed into the void. Although our devotion to such may be quite fervent and (behaviorally) ritualistic, the substitute life style is designed to stop the gap, whereas myth is the clear voice of the open abyss, the void: "What we have forgotten, / Without whom is nothing."

"THE CHUKCHEE SPEAK of those 'doomed to inspiration,' knowing how dangerous is the life-way of the shaman."[20] The vision of doom or being doomed to vision is the heterodox wisdom of Otherness which is the full fledged trialogue of horse, rider, and hawk—*epistrophé, renovatio, poiesis*—via the archegestic leaps of the "deep images lurking in life's history." As Rothenberg has worked so long to establish "The Deep Image is the Threatened Image," somatic, wounded, mortal, and vulnerable:

"The 'deep image' is the poetic image struggling with the darkness . . . the image rescued from the lie of the unthreatened." To apprehend a deep image, then, is to experience this sense of threat and struggle, to realize the extremity of creation and vision, and that this is the truth of things. The deep image renews creation and requires "heroes of the word," the "real poets" who refuse to be daunted by the "unfathomed darkness."[21]

The shaman-poet-hunter's great refusal "to be daunted by the 'unfathomed darkness'" is the first civil resistance; and, at once, it is a surrender to the true divestiture of losing all status and trusted tools—anchor, oar, and rudder—going down to the baptismal depths, swept-under in the wake of all which structure has thrown aside.

This "lie of the unthreatened," the Big-House of "the state," in Cassirer's ominous words, "could not arise until the darkness of myth was fought and overcome." The unthreatened is the perpetual delusion of monumental structure—the comfort and security of domestic and civil life. Invading, conquering, and colonizing, comes the monumental lie: warring against our minds, our hearts, our worlds—against creation itself. When half the heart is denied so begins the one-sided tyranny of "unbelief." Once the front is breached, however, and with the naïve longing to be safe in the Big-House at last laid to rest, suddenly disillusioned, a host of unforeseen realities come clear: THE ONLY WAR THAT MATTERS IS THE WAR AGAINST THE IMAGINATION / ALL OTHER WARS ARE SUBSUMED IN IT.[22] Yes, Diane di Prima is correct: there is only one war and it is our only wound—*all other wounds are subsumed in it*. The conventional trance of "normality" is blown away when one awakens to the suffering of this wound:

> The sick person is one who is plunged into a vortex of the most fundamental questions concerning life and death. The everyday routine of more or less uncritical acceptance of the meaning of life is sharply interrupted by serious illness, which has its own pointed way of turning all of us into metaphysicians and philosophers.[23]

The war against imagination is the war against initiatory sickness, interiority, and descendedness—the *descensus ad inferos,* the *Mundus*

Inferorum. To remain unconquered in such a war one needs deep roots—the ill-logic of the mortally wounded animal-body, the dark logic of *duendé,* the Water-of-Death. Else, uprooted, torn from the earth, "lacking the poetry" and lacking "the images and imaginings of the underworld, one takes one's torments literally and personally."[24] Taking the wound "literally and personally" is something the initiand, the victim/beneficiary, the Other Within, cannot afford to do.

Humans have understood this for millennia: the transpersonal breakthrough to hierophanic depth requires a traumatic lesion, a sharp interruption of one's "everyday routine uncritical acceptance"—a rupture achieved only by ordeal of corporeal affliction. This is the violation in which we are *in-formed* by *assault:* "plunged into a vortex of the most fundamental questions concerning life and death." The initiator, or ritual elder, guides the initiand to the sacred axis which links the personal wound to the originary wound. The initiator, as Bly says, does not give us *that* wound, "the scar stands for a wound that is already there."[25] In the Western world all such soulful wisdom is a casualty of war. Unbelief has mutilated and eviscerated the originary and holistic body of myth. Unbelief robs us of the sacred knowledge of liminality and of integrated Otherness—in Berman's words: "We have inherited a civilization in which the things that really matter in human life exist at the margin of our culture."[26]

Ours is not the first generation or era to endure the exiles and betrayals of unbelief—the Cynic "wanted to replace the debased standards of custom with the genuine standards of nature"; and likewise, as Girardot has amply shown, for the early Taoist: "'face' and 'name' are the fatally deceptive characteristics of a fallen human nature that accepts the values of human culture as ontologically definitive and norm-ative."[27] Yet, in the Confucian-insider's world the Taoist-outsider makes *a refuge from unbelief:* "a Taoist stands alone . . . dangerously or laughably outside the bounds of all ordinary standards. The true Taoist must accept the opprobrium* of being . . . *someone* who has 'lost face,'" who has "'humbled,' or 'shamed' . . . himself in the eyes of society."[28]

Re-membering "what matters": little by little in the space of "tolerated deviance," *a trickling of heart,* through the wound—the mask of deformity—furtively shifting from disguise to revelation. The wyrd one, "the 'man of Tao' is often pictured as . . . someone who is physically deformed (especially as a hunchback or as one-legged)."[29] *Dancing on one bad leg*—boldly limping his particular limp, dangerously-*and*-laughably performing a "doubled identity," the lone wandering Taoist exemplifies the proverbial outsider who is yet stranded within the Confucian establishment—"a civilization in which the things that really matter in human life exist at the margin"—no portrait of the Other Within could be more succinctly complete.

> *Dance when you're broken open.*
> *Dance, if you've torn the bandage off.*
> *Dance in the middle of the fighting.*
> *Dance in your blood.*
> *Dance, when you're perfectly free.*[30]

THIS IS THE TERRIBLE TRUTH: every ontic and epistemic "thing," or "creature," is threatened with the inevitable wounding rupture and disintegration of its existential boundaries: re-engulfed, re-enfolded in the dissolution of the explicate, the de-struction of structure, the de-formation of all forms into "no-thing-ness"; and this all-embracing, kaleidoscopic insight is actualized through "the faculty of *deforming*"— as envisioned by Gaston Bachelard:

> Imagination is always considered to be the faculty of *forming* images. But it is rather the faculty of *deforming* the images offered by perception, of freeing ourselves from the immediate images; it is especially the faculty of *changing* images.[31]

The "faculty of *deforming*" is the movement or action of *The Genius of Deformity,* the Mythic Trickster's soul-making play/work. If the "thing" we look at is an unfolded fixed explicate form in the ever enfolding-unfolding motion of the universe, then the deformation of the explicate form will allow the interiority of the "thing"—the *tremendum of the implicate*—to shine through. The "faculty of deforming" is *archegestic* in the sense that the "form" must be de-formed, broken open, in order to bring us in touch with the depths of the primal chaos/implicate—which is the first source of all fecundity—so that something unprecedented may emerge, unfold, be "born." From this vantage we can say that *archegestic* also means "to give birth"—in a *gestation* with all its deeply embodied labor, suffering, and joy.

The Genius of Deformity performs in the Trickster's extraordinary style: "the deformation of daily body technique . . . to create a condition of permanently unstable balance."[32] The deformed gesture conveys the logic of illness, the *ill-logic,* "the meaning of life sharply interrupted," the disequilibrium that injures the one-sided balance of ordinary-logic. When this catastrophe arrives and the rock-solid facts of life disintegrate in those "violent concussions"—sinking in quicksand, one suddenly re-members "what matters," and freed from the tyranny of normal ideals—"mythical thought then starts to rise anew and to pervade the whole of man's cultural and social life."[33]

"To apprehend a deep image is to experience this sense of threat and struggle, to realize the extremity of creation and vision"; here, like the Chukchee shaman, dis-illusioned, one is doomed to "realize" and, doomed thereby, to invoke the inspiration of the *axial moment*—in which the rootedness of the *Duendé,* the presence of the *Voyant,* and blossoming of the Angel coalesce in a spiral dance of the spirit *and* the flesh. Arcing through the interval of the leap—the Thunderbolt-axe opens identity to reveal the implicate depths:

> The first function of a living mythology, the properly religious function . . . is to waken and maintain in the individual an experience of awe, humility, and respect in recognition of that ultimate mystery, transcending names and forms.[34]

FINALLY, WHAT IS sought for is *not* a total theory of imagination, but the reconstitution and resuscitation of imagination as *a way of knowing*—in the Waters of Life-and-Death, of the spirit *and* the flesh, a way now matured by virtue of the initiatory wound, a mature imagination set forth as distinct from the connotations of abscondence, delusion, hallucination, and wishful-thinking—set forth distinctly, as in Avens's definition: "our whole power, the total functioning interplay of our capacities":

> It is crucial to realize—and here we enter Blake's territory—that the so called "spiritual states" of mysticism in which the senses are transcended, may not represent the desirable condition allotted to man. Quite the contrary, the "spiritual" state may signify, in Eliade's words, "a fall in comparison with the earlier situation, in which ecstasy was not necessary because no separation between body and soul was possible." This means that "for the primitive ideology present-day *mystical experience is inferior to the sensory experience of primordial man.*" Now, in this sense Blake is most emphatically not a mystic. There is nothing in him of the *via negativa,* the detachment from all phenomena in search of an unnamable God. He is not interested in suppressing sensory experience and losing himself in an undifferentiated Absolute or in a paradise which is unavailable to the bodily senses. Like the ancient shaman, Blake wants to transcend the human condition *in concreto,* in a sensual and natural manner.[35]

Like the ancient shamans, "*in concreto,*" following the wound's desire, through a multidisciplinary and multidimensional *Art,* the poet participates in the time before the shaman's drum was split, before the *huluppu*-tree was felled and hewn. Blake's *poiesis* is a living axial presence; "presence" as praxis, it is a simultaneous ascendedness and descendedness.

Life *and* death, eternal *and* mortal, spirit *and* flesh; "Imagination": *epistrophé, renovatio, poiesis.* The sacralities of Heaven and Hell are met

and married *in concreto,* in the *performance of identity.* The defect or
"limp," desire's wound, evincing its wyrdness, the doomed vision and
healing style, the singular gift of soul that each one bears—imagined,
danced, and sung-out—expressed from the void into the world—
"imagination is not the faculty of forming images of reality, but rather
'the faculty of forming images which go beyond reality, which sing
reality.'"[36]

> *Real singing is a different movement of air.*
> *Air moving around nothing. A breathing in a god.*
> *A wind.*[37]

The Singer
Throw Yourself Like Seed

ONE SURVIVES the underworld passage of hell, like Orpheus, by singing; but not ordinary song, only the *deep song* which wakens the soul: sung "in recognition of that ultimate mystery, transcending names and forms."[1] The first function of myth is to disclose a reality that sings. But what does it mean to sing the ultimate mystery, to "sing reality"? What is it that sings *in* the axial moment: the hierophany? the paraclete? A mystery, then, *the first experience*—of "awe, humility, and respect"—recaptured in the elegant words of Dylan Thomas:

> *these were the woods the river and sea*
> *Where a boy*
> *whispered the truth of his joy*
> *To the trees and the stones and the fish in the tide.*
> *And the mystery Sang alive.*[2]

As if remarking these very lines, Bly says, "the first experience . . . is interior. When the poet realizes for the first time . . . when he touches for the first time, something far inside him. It's connected with what the ancients called The Mysteries, and it's wrong to talk of it very much"[3]—wrong "because the massman will mock it right away." In the absence of any collective confirmation external events belie the depth of the soul's experience:

I have a feeling that my boat
has struck, down there in the depths,
against a great thing.
And nothing
happens! Nothing . . . Silence . . . Waves . . .

—Nothing happens? Or has everything happened,
and are we standing now, quietly, in the new life?[4]

So life goes on, as if nothing has happened, and the ordinary orderly-world doesn't seem to notice that anything about us has really changed—as in Jiménez: "Nothing happens? Or has everything happened"—now haunted by doubt and besieged by unbelief, Bly says, "there's the second necessary stage . . . which I would call something like cunning. And cunning involves the person rearranging his life in such a way that he can feel the first experience again." In the massman's world one guards the delicate grace of the "first experience" with devotion and cunning, rearranging one's life with Trickster Wisdom, to keep a "refuge from unbelief."

Many Native American cultures believe that a person receives a "song" from the deepest parts of their life. Out of the changes and chances, that make one distinctly who and what they are, comes a song which is theirs and theirs alone. The "deep song," in this sense, is Corbin's *"event of the soul"*—the whispered truth of some vast invisibility struck against in the unspeakable depths—"what the soul really sees, it is in each case alone in seeing."[5] The gift of such a "visionary song" is unique to the individual and yet it must be delivered, in one way or another, to the world. Here, then, is a third stage, the problem of non-delivery—as Bringhurst says: "Self expression is easy. Expressing what is / is a little more difficult."[6] Certainly, the inexpressibility of *what is,* such a deep and unprecedented vision, will be an uneasy burden—in the words of the Oglala Holy Man, Black Elk: "A man who has a vision is not able to use the power of it until after he has performed the vision on earth for the people to see."[7] That is to say, one is not fully in-formed by the vision until it is per-formed. The victim/beneficiary of the Thunderbolt, as Campbell says, "has had an experience of his own . . . which he seeks to communicate through signs . . . [with] the value and force of living myth"[8]—but how?

> How render back into light-world language the speech-defying pronouncements of the dark? How represent on a two-dimensional surface a three-dimensional form, or in a three-dimensional image a multi-dimensional meaning? How translate into terms of "yes" and "no" revelations that shatter into meaninglessness every attempt to define the pairs of opposites? How communicate to people who insist on the exclusive evidence of their senses the message of the all-generating void?[9]

Our message can have "the value and force of living myth," according to Campbell, only "for those . . . who receive and respond to it of themselves, with recognition, uncoerced."[10] The "Singer," of such efficacious song, according to indigenous wisdom, is "one who conducts ritual and is responsible for religious knowledge, including mythology."[11] In these, more fortunate, cultures the social group is ready and willing, "uncoerced," to receive, respond, and recognize—that is, to *adopt*—"the message of the all-generating void," as Schechner has it: "Performances made from vision-quests, drug-induced visions, or dreams are treated by many of the world's peoples with special respect precisely because they hinge two spheres of reality."[12]

Nevertheless, in monomaniacal cultures, like ours, such hierophanic visions are not confirmed, but rather are dismissed "precisely because they hinge" onto unauthorized "spheres of reality." Singing the soul's hinging event will, therefore, be quite risky—again, as Goethe warned, "Tell a wise person, or else keep silent, / Because the massman will mock it right away."[13] In the face of such uncertainty Black Elk's need, to "perform his vision on earth," is far from ensured; to the contrary, unable to "keep silent," life now becomes a "question": how to perform the reality of what the lone soul has seen?

If we take him as a sort of paradigm of what it means to be a man of vision, he *overturns our expectation* that the holy man arrives somewhere at the Truth, which is recognizable to him and to us. Instead Black Elk is deeply involved in *not knowing* and the risk that when he gives his vision away it will be ignored, misunderstood, or misused.[14]

Before the real significance of "giving the vision" can be appreciated, we must first break the constraint to see it as "heroic"—as cast in the glamour of the "Great Man." For the Other Within the giving of the "gift"—the endowment of the wound—is the blessing in the curse, the genius in the deformity; without the camouflage of infamy the gift would be diluted, desecrated, and ultimately destroyed.

With the absolute and heroic "Truth" thus overturned, once again, the Singer is "deeply involved in *not knowing*," as Lao Tzu says: "To know without knowing is best. / Not knowing without knowing it is sick."[15] When the know-it-all rider drops the reins, following the horse's nose (what the horse knows) *that* is "knowing" by "not-knowing," and suffering the submission with awareness, acting openly *in* the soul, performing the soul's event *in* the liminal void. "What we do with that radical uncertainty," in Michael Taussig's view, "is the measure not only of our ability to resist the appeal for closure, but also of our ability to prise open history's closure with the lever of its utterly terrible incompleteness."[16] To perform with not-knowing is to remain always in-touch with the implicate; in the incommunicable subjectivity of the soul's event such a performance will radiate the ever enfolding-unfolding informance of the implicate identity.

The worst possible thing, then, for human beings is the bandage of an "easy answer." That is to say, rendering the inscrutable vision into explicate literality, so as to please and appease the halfhearted, constitutes a hideous betrayal of the genius.

While the liminal life of the Other Within will, perforce, remain an open question, on the inside, in the Big-House, the liminoid massman demands the security of a final "closure": the unbreachable Iron Gates. The needed lesion arrives in the lived realization of *contradiction as reality*—permanent imbalance, radical uncertainty, not-knowing. To risk this life is "to live the questions," as Rilke advises, living with no fixed answers. More to the point, only by openly and unashamedly expressing one's own "terrible incompleteness" (*right there I'm sort of glued together*)—only by limping, singing, and dancing our wyrdness— will the "sole gap" of structure's closure ever be prised open. Those who speak from the "soul gap"—the *Beggar, Blind Man, Drunkard, Suicide, Widow, Idiot, Orphan, Dwarf, and Leper;* the Dog-people and the Rat-people; "the female, the proletariat, the foreign; the animal and vegetative; the unconscious and the unknown; the criminal and failure"[17]—all the vagabond and outcast, "have to sing; if they didn't sing, everyone / would walk past, as if they were fences or trees. . . ."[18] The only way to prise open the oppression of history's monumental "closure"—ignorance, denial, unbelief, and one-sidedness—will be in the uncovering of our own chronically entrenched (albeit unconscious) "self-loathings," the *private storm* of Otherness which plagues us, openly expressed, in the *miserere** of Miguel de Unamuno:

> I am convinced that we would solve many things if we all went out into the streets and uncovered our griefs, which perhaps would prove to be but one sole common grief. . . . The chiefest sanctity of a temple is that it is a place to which men go to weep in common. A *miserere* sung in common by a multitude tormented by destiny. . . . It is not enough to cure the plague; we must learn to weep for it. Yes, we must learn to weep! Perhaps that is the supreme wisdom.[19]

IN MYTHOLOGICAL TIME, when the wheel turns round again to the anniversary of an event, then *past, present, and future* intersect, forming a temporal axis. In mythological space, where boundaries cross and worlds are hinged, *heaven, earth, and hell* intersect, forming a spatial axis. In mythological consciousness, when-*and*-where the innerworld and the outerworld interpenetrate, in the spirit *and* the flesh, *instinct, intellect, and inspiration* intersect, forming a psychosomatic axis. And when the spatiotemporal and the psychosomatic align, and the nexus of axial connections coincide, when the golden harp is strung, only then is the Singer's Temple realized, in the abyss of the *miserere,* the "crisis of humankindness"—the time, tempo, and temple of *communitas.*

Such a profound and soulful coincidence of reality spheres, like the *first experience,* may last no more than a glimpsed instant—with devotion, practice, and the cunning to rearrange one's life, the axial-experience may be cultivated and sustained for hours, repeatedly throughout a lifetime. Needless to say, such a departure, viewed from the structure-bound and normative perspective, will look like the hellequin's infamous fall through a hole in the floor; thus, in the quest for temple, as maintained from the outset, those who are forced out of the Big-House have a certain excruciating advantage.

Walking the thorn-strewn way into such a sanctuary, then, is to pass through the jaws of hell, the all-swallowing mandorla, a multi-dimensional crossroads in space and time, body and mind. Admission to this multivalent zone requires "disillusionment": the shedding of any hoped-for return to the promised life. Gaining entry to the temple of the *miserere* will prove, therefore, to be costly, entailing grave risks, one of those "impossible tasks," an initiatory condition set for us by Baba Yaga: "Leave the herd *and* carry them with you."

Upon this aporia, "where two roads intersect / inside us, *no one has built the Singer's Temple.*" Standing here, at the crossroads of compulsion and freewill, one confronts the extremities of self and soul:

Hence the guardian figures that stand at either side of the entrances to holy places: lions, bulls, or fearsome warriors with uplifted weapons. . . . They are there to keep out the "spoil sports" . . . for whom the mask, the image, the consecrated host, tree, or animal cannot become God, but only a reference. Such heavy thinkers are to remain without. For the whole purpose of entering a sanctuary . . .

is that one should be overtaken by . . . "the other mind" . . . where one is "beside oneself," spellbound, set apart from one's logic of self-possession and overpowered by a force of "indissociation."[20]

I am not I . . . I am this one standing beside me . . . the impossible passageway into temple is through the no-place, the no-self, suspended between the mind of self and "the other mind" of the anti-self, the daimon, the paraclete, the spiritual twin.

And this comes as no dim dismissible inkling, but the detonation of a Thunderbolt! For the fragmented, ungrounded, and uprooted liminoid, this will be a waking nightmare of total chaos: the sudden confrontation of one's existential multiplicity, and the terrifying death of delusion. Of course, as Rilke says, "for a god that's easy," but we are not gods, we are mortal, and, surely, *that* is why we sing—to "live" in communion and exchange with the Otherworld—to make the living moment last because "Eternity is in love with the creations of time":[21]

[Of] death-in-life and life-in-death, it may be said that "immortality," far from being some sort of innate possession, is something that may arise within the cincture of time and mortality, a "something" we create out of a simultaneous acceptance of and rebellion against mortality. In other words, immortality, if the word is to have any meaning at all, must be a product of poiesis, that is, of soul-making. One can only, so to speak, poetisize [sic] oneself into "eternal life." And we must add that the product of this "making" is never finished or ever-lasting: like music or a Hamlet on the stage, it lasts only so long as it is being produced.[22]

Here, in the "simultaneous acceptance of and rebellion against mortality," Avens articulates that particular struggle which Unamuno has called *The Tragic Sense of Life.*

For Unamuno this is a conflict between vitality of feeling on one hand, and veracity of reason on the other, as he proclaims: "For my part I do not wish to make peace between my heart and my head, between my faith and my reason—I wish rather that there should be war between them."[23] In the "fruitful asynchrony" of this *coincidentia oppositorum,* like Blake's "intellectual war," or the wrestling tutelage of Rilke's angel, Unamuno finds the dynamic struggle between mortality and immortality to be creative and confirming: "it is the conflict itself, it is this self-same uncertainty, that unifies my action and makes me live and work."[24] To "live and work" in this radical uncertainty is the poiesis of soul-making—which "is never finished or ever-lasting," but like music "lasts only so long as it is being produced."

The problem with the temple experience, as conceived in the modern West, is the one-sided obsession with immortality, light, and ascent: like birds in the empty granary, in the monumental cathedrals of religion and commerce, with upturned faces, each worshiper *seeing the bands of light, flutters up the walls and falls back again and again*— but all this is halfhearted elevationism; for, as we know, in authentic verticality "the higher the spirit goes the more deeply the soul sinks down."[25] And the price paid to a-void "the message of the all-generating void," sinking into the *miserere* of *communitas,* is paid in civilization's never-ending labor of denial; only in this way, by closing the heart to half of life, can the massman pretend to be whole.

And yet the ancient longing to taste the Waters of Life *and* Death is still in us; the bittersweet music of mortal-eternity is at least as old as humankind. Consider the paleolithic cave-temples, when "the mystery Sang alive" thirty thousand, and more, years ago, where the locations of paintings have now been found to correspond with points of acoustic resonance: "It seems therefore clear that the paleolithic tribes who decorated these caves chose the places where they painted in relation with the sound value of these places, and it points to a ritual aspect—involving singing."[26] Singing to make the moment last. In musical terms "sustain" indicates "duration of tone," the lingering sweetness of the plucked string, or sung note, as the sonority decays and fades away into silence. The cry of mortal-eternity "lasts only so long as it is being produced," yet in the reverberant temple it lasts just a little longer—and in the fading echo one seems to hear a reply.

Affirming height, light, and life in denial of depth, dark, and death is the one-sided refusal to pass between the threatening guardians at the temple-gate, those dichotomous twins whose most ancient names are "Life" and "Death." No matter how we try we cannot pass one without meeting the other—there can be no ascent without descent. "Temple," therefore, presents the abyss, as "the sick person . . . plunged into a vortex . . . of questions," sacrality arrives in the vivid intimation of mortality; an axial-moment of which Rafael López-Pedraza testifies: "When some bulls die in the ring, in that moment of agony between the final sword thrust and death, time seems to stand still and a *temple* is created, a space which stirs our senses, because—why not say it?—there are bulls that die magnificently, as if giving a lesson in dying to everyone."[27] As far as our refined and elevated sensibilities are removed from appreciating the ritual death of the bull marks the very distance we have withdrawn from life and from the wisdom of the temple. Where the roads of life and death, spirit and flesh, intersect inside us, such a wholehearted sanctuary can never be finally "built," it cannot exist as literal architecture, rather, it is the indwelling and sustained resonance of *duendé,* a centering that surges in the blood, as López-Pedraza goes on:

> Temple is slowness, but that does not mean that it is uniquely and exclusively slow. I prefer to describe it as an enormously animated slowness, a slowed down state of being. . . . Temple is a slowness of movement that may appear in some bullfighting *suertes,** in singing or dancing flamenco and—why not say it?—in life itself: it pertains to its essence.[28]

In this "essence" life itself Sings, for "life itself, insofar as it is informed by imagination, is now poiesis—a work of art."[29] Yes, and—why not say it?—we desire this artful moment of eternity, this shimmering resonance, this "enormously animated slowness," *urgently,* because right-now we are alive!—and *serenely,* for, as sweet echoes fade, soon we are going to die.

The Singer's Temple is the human heart, decided and resolved to the "risk," the impossible task of the Trickster's masquerade. Like the heart of the hunter, to go alone, as the Wanderer, the outsider, and yet, carried within the breast, the whole communal choir of the *miserere* sings in confirmation of the lone soul.

THE GENIUS OF DEFORMITY has many voices, it sings to us "in the moment between the final sword thrust and death," between the callus and the string, through the wounds, the cracks and imperfections in ourselves and in the world.

The Celtic bard Taliesin's initiatory wound is the mark of three scalding drops from the cauldron—black, red, and white; past, present, and future. The Singer Orpheus carries his wound in his heart—broken for his twice-lost beloved who is trapped in the underworld, holding a part of the Singer descended forever. And, last but not least, there is *Kokopelli,* the Native American trickster—flute-playing, wandering-minstrel, sacred-messenger, divine-progenitor, and lover—he is the phallophoric* deformed-humpback who carries the people's dreams, songs, seeds, and medicine within the wound of his hunched shoulder:

> Like the wise fool in Shakespeare, his deformity belies his worth, and like the trickster heroes in many Native American cultures, his imperfection is inseparable from the benefits he brings. He represents both bane and boon, disability and healing, humor and high seriousness, and who he is cannot be distinguished from the dance he performs.[30]

With identity unfolding and implicit—"who he is cannot be distinguished from the dance [visionary gift] he performs." As with the humpback flute-player, so with the Other Within: the "imperfection is inseparable from the benefits"—the blessing inseparable from the curse.

Spirit *and* flesh, suffering *and* healing, unite as the inspirating flute and impregnating phallus are conflated in the generosity of the wound.

Such fecund and creative bounty, notwithstanding, suspicion and prejudice are always ready: "because Pueblo culture traditionally rejected unusual appearing individuals, such a deformed person, in order to be accepted, would have to present special attributes perceived as beneficial by the group."[31] Yet, as we know, very often these "attributes" are not seen as "special," but as specious and malignant, and therefore, the gift can be delivered only sideways through tolerated lunacy. Revelation and revilement, deformation and defamation, go hand in hand; shame *is* pride's cloak!

The fool's devotion to this task can be understood, in Hillman's phrase, as *loving the world anyway*: "Despite all my revulsions over its ugliness and injustice, and my bitterness over defeat at its hands, the world remains lovable anyway. But "anyway" also means any-which-way, any way at all, implying that there are many different openings out of self-enclosure and toward love of the world."[32] Prising open "self-enclosure," as well as "history's closure," moves us, in our many lunatic deviations and transgressions, "toward love of the world." Though naught that is visible, tangible, or even measurable can ever be achieved, and in defiance of all reason, the Singer *has* to sing. It is a "message" better sung than said; the real meaning lying more in the sound, the tonality, the "emotional syntax," than in any literal indicative explanation—as Campbell knew so well: "Though it is true that such living ideas become manifest only in terms and style of some specific historical moment, their force nevertheless lies not in what meets the eye but in what dilates the heart."[33] Widening the heart is, quite simply, a *mythopoeic praxis* (a matter of life and death); it is the heart's poiesis—*hieropoeic, cosmopoeic, sociopoeic, and psychopoeic*—and if not all of this and more, then, it is not Myth and it will not Sing.

"Real singing"—when the mystery Sings alive—may include, but is not limited to the voice, to literal human song: *real singing is a different movement of air*. Pouring out of that deep and generous wound, like Kokopelli, "throw yourself like seed"; for every act, every art, every gesture, however inconsequential, can have this fertile thread of eternity cunningly woven in—so that there is always devotion, always the nod to Mystery. Such a diaspora of self is the antithesis of the monumental life. For who can trace the fleeting genius of such anonymous abandon and generosity? If, finally, one understands that the "self" to be de-formed and scattered is not a "fixed" identity—an easy answer—that can ever be directly known, then the deep implication of Unamuno's saying is clear:

> *Throw yourself like seed as you walk . . .*
> *from your work you will be able one day to gather*
> *yourself.*[34]

The Cauldron
And Each Is the Work of All

You, the village; I, the stranger; this, the road:
And each is the work of all.
Then, not that man do more, or stop pity; but that he be
Wider in living.

Kenneth Patchen, "The Character of Love
Seen as a Search for the Lost"[1]

BETWEEN THE VILLAGE and the forest lies the long road of exile. In both the inner and outer worlds—for, surely, the individual is also a village—the road of exile is the distance and depth of denial dividing the village-hearth from the forest-hut of the "stranger": the wild one, who is the lost, unwanted, unwelcomed portion of self and soul. To be "wider in living," then, means widening the heart enough to make sacred our missing parts, for halfheartedness can never admit the defect—the lost leg, the lost eye, the wyrd incompleteness, the radical uncertainty—that is the doorway to the sacred.

Walking the road from "loss" to "sacrality" is the meaning of "sacrifice"; and this is more than mere semantics: it is the long-forgotten initiatory journey from the childish perspective of victimization to the fullness of a mature volitional exchange with the Otherworld—a "Faustian bargain." To make this sacrifice is not to be martyred to some great cause; nor does it mean that violence is justified and divinely ordained. Sacrifice, in the sense given here, means to make sacred, through the wound, in devotion to the trialogue of stranger, village, and road—personal, local, and universal.

The social relation of violence to the sacred has been well established in the work of René Girard, which, in its essence, is quite relevant to the predicament of the Other Within, where: "society is seeking to deflect upon a relatively indifferent victim, a 'sacrificeable' victim, the violence that would otherwise be vented on its own members, the people it most desires to protect."[2] What Girard has recognized, and brilliantly delineated, is the covert handing-off of the limp (liminoid a-voidance) where the, so-called, "indifferent victim" is so objectified as to have no subjective voice or view-point, rendering a sacrificial "object" infinitely manipulable and disposable.

Tensions build-up in society, repressed violence reaches dangerous levels causing the breakdown of "cultural distinctions" (return to chaos); a situation Girard terms a "sacrificial crisis," which is analogous to the "complexity catastrophe": where rigid intolerance requires ever increasing measures and controls against contamination, ultimately, reaching a *catastrophic level of complexity*—that is, the controls, and the controls of the controls (*ad infinitum*), go spinning "out-of-control."

In this view "social coexistence would be impossible if no surrogate victim existed, if violence persisted beyond a certain threshold and failed to be transmuted into culture."[3] This kind of (mobocratic) sacrifice is the device of structure, an hierarchic governor employed to maintain and uphold the "lie of the unthreatened"—the safe and comforting delusion of permanent structure—to this end, the liminoid-mob engages in "unanimous violence" (sacrifice); herein the expulsion or extermination of a scapegoat, or "surrogate victim," permits the collective purgation of all repressed, unfulfilled, and unacted desires.

No doubt, on a global scale, the institutionalized practice of surrogate-victimage has been the primary method and strategy of civilization's "conquest abroad and oppression at home."[4] Girard's analysis, of the unanimous function of violence, sets forth a clear blueprint of the social-mechanism of liminoid a-voidance. But where does this violence come from? Simplistically put, it comes from "resentment" which is due to a certain perceived "lack."

The mistake in all of this, however, is one of omission—the usual omission—where the victim's intra-personal voice, his or her actual individual sacrificial-experience, is not credited. What of the consciousness and sensibility of the victim/beneficiary? What if the perceived "lack" is transmuted from a source of resentment to a source of meaning? And if resentment is merely a defense against self-loathing, then what would happen if the self-loathing, at the root of violence, were interrupted in a *truly sacrificial act* of making sacred the missing parts by openly limping the limp and dancing the wyrd, generative, and agonizing dance of radical uncertainty?

It is easy to forget, as Highwater reminds us, that culture is made from the bottom up: "when individuals succeed in externalizing their personal experiences through the creation of images, sounds, phrases, structures, and movement, the result is culture. In this context culture is the collective aspect of individuated styles of expression. What sensibility is to the individual, culture is to the community—a distinctive voice."[5] Culture is the soul of society. The bottom-up influence on the social group of this "distinctive voice"—the *extraordinary person,* the deviant vision, the deep song—creates and recreates culture. And the process of the individual finding such a voice is the painful initiation into Otherness—the lack, the void, the defect.

The attempt to reclaim, and perhaps even heal, the heart of darkness which is Otherness, if undertaken in sentimental naïveté, will lead to an idealistic and utopian primitivism; while the same attempt undertaken in materialistic literality will lead to the supreme "unanimous violence" of genocide. Such misguided attempts at "placing" Otherness will ultimately fail, in Michael Taussig's view, by "either succumbing to its hallucinatory quality or losing that quality. Fascist poetics succeed where liberal rationalism self-destructs." Considering this profound "impasse"—i.e., the incapacity of both idealism and rationalism—as evinced in "History's" version of the enslavement, systematic torture, and mass-sacrifice of Indians, in Columbia's Putumayo river basin (early 1900s), Taussig provides us with a firm answer to the Girardian omission:

> What might point a way out of this impasse is precisely what is so painfully absent from the Putumayo accounts, namely the narrative mode of the Indians themselves. It is the ultimate anthropological conceit, anthropology in its highest, indeed redemptive, moment, rescuing the "voice" of the Indian from the obscurity of pain and time. From the represented shall come that which overturns the representation.[6]

Once there was a man who had no song. When the People gathered to sing and dance, he sat off alone, away from the fire, in the shadows; when people saw him they shook their heads and felt sorry. They called him "No-song." His was a pitiful circumstance: as everyone knows a person who lives in a good way will receive a sacred song; and a man without a song? Well, who could say.

Things went on this way till no one really gave it much thought; it seemed to simply be the way it is. No-song, for his part, busied himself with other tasks. As the seasons passed he spent so much of his time off alone in the wild that he became a good hunter. Once when he had taken an extraordinary amount of game, a strange idea occurred to him; he decided that he would make a stew—a huge amount of stew with all kinds of meat and corn.

Now, it happened that Coyote was wandering in that region of the world, and he began to catch a whiff of a savory aroma, as the fragrance grew it pulled Coyote away from his intended path, and soon enough he was peering into the circle of yellow light cast by No-song's cook-fire. The aroma of that abundant stew was so pungently delicious that Coyote stepped forward revealing himself in the firelight: "What will you take in exchange for this magnificent stew?"

No-song replied, "Well, Coyote, since you are the maker of songs, you can give me a song and I will give you all of this stew." Coyote scratched his ear and said, "It's possible; what kind of song would you want?" No-song knew exactly what kind of song he wanted—a song that would move the hearts of the People, a song to celebrate the great passages of life, a sacred song, a song of great power. After hearing this request Coyote thought it over, he smelled the stew, and at last he said: "I will give you such a song, but there is a condition: you must not sing at wrong times or in wrong places—if you do I will return and take the song away." The very suggestion offended No-song: "How could you think so poorly of me? I would never do such a thing." And so the bargain was struck.

At the next gathering all the villagers and the many guests were astonished when the recluse No-song strode confidently into the center of the dancing ground. And they were more than amazed when this one who had always had no voice suddenly sang the most beautiful and powerful song of all. "Wonderful," they said, "Sing it again!" they shouted—and indeed, as the evening drew on, he sang it many, many times. His lonely heart was filled with delight to be invited to other villages for feasts and festivals; and before the night was done he was given a new name: "Singing-wonderfully!" After that everyone who was anyone wanted Singing-wonderfully to consecrate their wedding, funeral, birthday, naming-day, with his wondrous voice. And how could he refuse? Now he had no time for hunting; always the honored guest wherever he went; he traveled from village to village and sang for every occasion; which, of course to those concerned, was a most important event. Time passed and soon enough Coyote came quietly in the dark of night and while the singer slept he took the song away.[7]

NO-SONG IS OBVIOUSLY a misfit, alienated and set apart, he is the Other dwelling within the tribe; and in this asynchrony, this margination, he contacts the implications of a separate and unprecedented identity.

In the forest, at the edge, he is inspired to eccentric behaviors; he makes a "stew of abundance"—this is the turning point (epistrophé)—his descent into wilderness has yielded a devotional praxis—the wyrdness of hunting. In this way his limp becomes generative, his lack becomes a source of meaning and bounty.

Symbolically, making soup or "stew" is an archetypal gesture, a reenactment of the return to prime. In his discussion, "soup, symbol, and salvation," Girardot shows that the ritual making of such a stew renders all the ingredients down to the primordial, undifferentiated, and abundant condition of "chaos." In Chinese the term *hun-tun*, meaning "chaos," is provocatively similar to the word *wonton;* hence, "the ritual eating, during the Chinese new year festival period, of a soup made of wonton skins filled with the mixed and minced flesh of plants and animals."[8]

This alchemical soup or stew is "cooked" in the ritual container—a cook-pot, crock, kettle, or "cauldron"—which is likened to the occult vessel, the alchemical retort, the mandorla-boat, the initiatory cauldron-womb-coracle, which both contains and navigates the abysmal waters; as Girardot confirms, "the gourd-drum-egg-cauldron-boat . . . can be identified both with the chaotic waters of the flood, and by extension, with the more cosmogonically relevant symbolism of the cosmic egg-gourd and primordial waters."[9] The initiatory return to chaos, via the cauldron, entails imbibing three drops of inspiration and wisdom arising from the "intoxicating cauldron, the Awen* of the cauldron of Cerridwen, containing probably a mash of barley, acorns, honey, bull's blood and such sacred herbs as ivy, hellebore and laurel."[10] The Celtic word *awen* is the inspirating breath and efficacious force of poetic power; as in "the Netsilik [Eskimo] word *anerca* [which] is used in fact to mean both *breath* and *poetry*."[11]

It takes a year and a day for Cerridwen to prepare the concoction; the ingredients must be meticulously gathered and added each according to its season and precise planetary hour. In regard to such care, Simon Ortiz offers sage advice for the making of the stew:

"Smelling and watching are important things, and you really shouldn't worry too much about it . . . but you should pay the utmost attention to everything, and that means the earth, clouds, sounds, the wind. All these go into the cooking."[12] Making the magical "stew of abundance" takes time, alertness, and precision, and it is this devotion and praxis which ultimately invokes the hierophanous presence of the paraclete-muse—this time manifest in the form of Coyote the Mythic-Trickster.

No-song is now prepared to make the return to the world and perform his vision on earth; but there is a condition—and here is the "Faustian bargain"—he is given just the kind of song that would amaze and move the people, yet he is required, on peril of forfeit, to refrain from singing in wrong times at wrong places. Once returned to "civil society" he performs the song for all to hear—and indeed they are astonished—before the night is done the people have given him a new name: Singing-wonderfully!

In this tremendous success is the story's deepest tragedy; for it is a fatal acclamation. How many have died in this white light? Here is the never-ending problem of losing the wildness of the whole divine night in favor of the bright civil center. Many important and revolutionary ideas, born at the cutting edge—*avant-garde*—have been killed, not by rejection, but simply by being made "fashionable." The whole problem of cooptation, assimilation, and appropriation is that the "shopping center" eviscerates and depotentiates whatever it claims. With the "refuge from unbelief" thus forsaken, the implicate heart cannot endure.

Part of taking the risk, that when I give my vision away it will be "ignored, misunderstood, or misused," is the other risk, that I myself will misunderstand, misuse, and abuse the vision. Despite the inform-ing depths and "different vistas" attained in the arduous and earnest descent of the soul, the human capacity to disregard and deny all which one has undergone is apparently infinite. How many times have I mar-veled at the horrific power of the egocentric identity, when utterly reduced to ashes, as it reassembles itself, molecule by molecule, a maca-bre automaton resuming all its former machinations, as if nothing had transpired. The immensity of this problem is that it can (and most often does) repeat itself over and over again.

Resisting the habitual and staying descended, in Lawrence's determination, means a "long, difficult repentance / realisation of life's mistake and the freeing oneself / from the endless repetition of the mistake / which mankind at large has chosen to sanctify."[13]

Without this vigilance the descendedness of No-song is forgotten: the rebel-leader eagerly moves into the presidential palace; Trickster refuses to call for the Thunderbolt-axe, believing himself to actually *be* the divine water-spirit. No-song makes the mistake of seeking salvation and redemption through the horizontal elevationism of the ever-improved structural status—the heroic mode of renown and monumental greatness. To the degree that we deny the potent capacity to backslide and forget, we will be bound to "the endless repetition of life's mistake," the tragicomedy of *la chappe d'Helle-quin,* but with no realization of the Rat's Way out.

Ultimately Coyote returns and takes back the gift of song. Singing-wonderfully, the bright public persona, dies; the paraclete betrays the no-longer-anomalous-individual by repossessing the song (thus returning the initiand to his original inferior condition). No-song finds himself once again falling back into the abyss of the original darkness, and the circle starts all over again (liminality, structure, liminality). Hence, one should consider: is it possible that in the hurtful destruction of the wonderful identity, perhaps, the paraclete-muse-daimon-Coyote, like The Hag O' the Mill, rescues the shaman-poet-hunter from abdication of the soul's vocation?

> For the daimon to have any chance, a hurtful cut is unavoidable. Your style of speaking or writing must confront the audience with the experience of the *non*-ego (i.e., the sense of "*not* you as you have been all along"); it must impose on the audience the narcissistic offense that you are *not* concerned with what *they* think and are *not* speaking to *them,* but to *their Other.*[14]

For the daimon, the paraclete, the not-I, to have any chance, as Wolfgang Giegerich declares, one dare not care "what *they* think." Not singing to *them* but to *their Other,* it is doubtful they will name you Singing-wonderfully.

If the message of the speaker, writer, singer, the message of the Other *to* the Other, is somehow miraculously received by the liminoid massman, with "the value and force of living myth," surely then the bright persona will take a "hurtful cut." But to do this one must have had that cut already, and more, one must have agreed to "wear it," to display and perform that awful and cutting stigma. The song must be performed *by* the "not-I," in the not-knowing and radical uncertainty of the widened and dilated heart. To perform the deep song of the implicate identity—the blessing of the curse, the fruit of asynchrony— one has to stay descended and remain in-touch with the abysmal void. Therefore *a hurtful cut is unavoidable*—in order that imagination be constantly rekindled and wrested away from the Wonderful life, from "the lie of the unthreatened"—the Singer remains fallen from grace, reduced to ashes, returned to the world as it is:

> *The ten thousand things arise together;*
> *in their arising is their return.*
> *Now they flower, and flowering*
> *sink homeward, returning to the root.*
>
> *The return to the root*
> *is peace.*
> *Peace: to accept what must be . . .*[15]

WHEN PRINCE IVAN was wandering in the wilderness, he had the understanding of animal-speech and so abstained from robbing the bees of their honey; and he spared the lives of the fledgling birds and the young lion. Unlike the Slavic hero, when the biblical Samson meets his young lion in the wild, he does not perceive any intelligible speech—

but hearing only the lion "roar against him" he kills it with his bare hands. And again, later on, when bees have nested in the lion's carcass, contrary to Ivan, Samson does not forego his appetite, but takes and eats the honey. We could say, then, that the initiand, Samson, in his heedlessness is ill-prepared to meet the Old Hag—he has not achieved the necessary descendedness, he must first undergo the rites of shamanic dismemberment and resurrection.

The story of "Samson"—meaning Of-the-Sun[16]—comes from an older mythic strata than the other stories in the Book of Judges.* Samson stands for fulfillment of destiny but his is more the doom of Enkidu than the promise of Gilgamesh. He was born to the wonderful identity of the "solar knight" so we know the betrayal has to come; he must be reduced to ashes, swallowed by the dragon, before anything important can happen.

In the cases of both Samson and Enkidu, the wild and instinctual energy they embody is mediated into society via the marginal figure of an independent woman—namely, the Semitic Deli'lah and the Mesopotamian harlot Shamhat—as noted by scholar Rivkah Harris: "It is the intermediary role of the prostitute in transforming Enkidu from one at home with nature and wild animals into a human being . . . which is crucial. . . . Relevant too is the fact that the prostitute in Mesopotamia, like the prostitute in ancient Israel, was a prime representative of urban life."[17] Here is the ritual power of the inferior: that is to say, emphatically, that the ambivalence assigned to the Other Within, as harlot, permits the active mediation of a deeper and wilder Otherness, which is the substance of cultural vitality and, perhaps, the subversive catalyst to a *renovatio*: "The image of Samson between the pillars bringing down the gigantic structure is an archetypal vision of crucifixion . . . this is an archetypal story performing the archetypal pattern of 'redemption through the primitive.' Samson brings down the superior civilization to make way for the next civilization."[18] As seen over and over the crisis of the epistrophé to the *archai* yields the Trickster Wisdom of "redemption through the primitive"—"new springs of development and action deep down in the roots of our being."[19]

Here, as Thompson shows, "the gigantic structure," the civilized constraint, is broken, yet more importantly, the pillars of Samson's ambitious solar-consciousness are toppled, to make way for a deeper and multivalent self-world view. Again citing Thompson, "the most dramatic image of the story is that of blind Samson bringing down the enormous building of the Philistines . . . the image of the savage oppressed and contained by an architectural form represent precisely the archetypal conflict of savagery versus civilization."[20] In the end, could the fall of Samson be reinterpreted as the personal transmutation of "loss" into "sacrifice," through the initiatory passage; the "hurtful cut," that outwardly blinds and enfeebles, yet opens the new life and "different vistas" of the paraclete?

Remember the African story of Lituolone? In the same way that the Philistines feared the Otherness of Samson, so with Lituolone: *people were not grateful to him, for they feared the power of one born only of a woman, one who had seen no childhood, one who had conquered the great formless monster Kammapa. So it was decided that Lituolone should be killed.* In this same manner it was determined that Samson should be enslaved, tortured, and put to death. And just as Lituolone, in fine trickster fashion, repeatedly eluded his assassins, so did Samson repeatedly mislead his betrayers, until at last, inexplicably, he revealed the secret of his power, thus allowing himself to be overcome. Perhaps Samson surrendered because, like Lituolone, he finally realized *that nothing would ameliorate this deep hatred for him, and he grew weary of countering these attempts to do him harm. So he offered himself without resistance, allowing himself to be killed.*

To be killed by the Thunderbolt of divine election, to be cast down into a life of permanent outsiderhood, is the life portrayed in so many ways throughout this book. Sooner or later, surely, it will come, the *katabasis,* the fall from grace, the hierophany of betrayal—and the question one must answer then: *Did you come here by compulsion or by free-will? By loss or sacrifice?*

Samson, grinding bread for widows and orphans,
Forgets he is wronged, and the answers
The Philistines wrangled out of him go back
Into the lion; the bitter and the sweet marry.
He himself wronged the lion. The burned wheat
Caresses the wind with its wifely tail; the jawbone
Runs in the long grass, and, having glimpsed heaven,
The fox's body saunters the tawny earth.[21]

The marriage of bitterness to sweetness sings in the plucked interval of the golden harp's axial string. Praise and lament are married in the mandorla-heart—spirit and flesh, the phallus and the flute, combine: "Joys impregnate. Sorrows bring forth."[22] Bly shows us a Samson in the new life. It is a wedding dance where life and death embrace one another—the lion forgives; the burned wheat forgives; the jawbone forgives; with no righteousness or piety, all our wrongs and wrongdoings sink back into the abiding and steadfast earth, "the cut worm forgives the plow":[23:]

After death the soul returns to drinking milk
And honey in its sparse home. Broken lintels
Rejoin the sunrise gates, and bees sing
In sour meat.

After all the persecutions, indignities, and betrayals, even after the horror of death, "what is living now?" As "bees sing" in the lion's hollow carcass, so sings *the unnamed:* the Bereaver, The Lord of Slaughter, the Genius of Deformity, demolishing and decomposing our oneness, our rigored self-enclosures, opening us, finally, to ourselves and to the living world *as it is*—"the catastrophe of the previously unforeseen [that] breaks the world progression forward."[24]

Living now means we make of our days, not a monument, but "a trickling of heart," in the anonymous and life-giving poiesis of the *creatio continua;* bringing forth, with gratitude, a kind of food—as in Vallejo's prayer: "I wish I could beat on all the doors and beg pardon from someone, and make bits of fresh bread for him here, in the oven of my heart!"[25]

> *Once more in the cradle Samson's*
> *Hair grows long and golden; Delilah's scissors*
> *Turn back into two tiny and playful swords . . .*

The battered hero, who has both wronged and been wronged, now blind and broken, rocked in the fatal crucible of Hölderlin's "iron cradle," torn open to the depths, and finally "capable of sacrifice," is reborn. "Once more in the cradle" all the torturous weapons and deceits of betrayal have become as "tiny and playful swords"—as in Lao Tzu: "Being full of power is like being a baby. Scorpions don't sting, tigers don't attack, eagles don't strike."[26]

"IN THE UNDERWORLD rivers flow backward to their sources."[27] It is a very old idea, that things in the Otherworld run counter to the directions of this one; the sun travels west to east, time runs from future to past—life goes from grave to cradle. . . . And so at last, in this halting and backward manner, we have come to an end which is also a beginning: *every human being, in the infinite variety of body and soul, comes into this world, so unique and so alike, with so much promise; each one prepared and appointed for the best . . .*

There is the childish fool who stands at the beginning, and then there is that Other fool, who, having passed through all the stations of the round, has returned to zero, returning to the root, the unnamed—the *chaosmos.*

Call it the implicate order, or holomovement; anti-structure; liminality; the mandorla; the collective unconscious; the crossroads; the seat of the soul; the void; the wound; the abyss; the sole/soul gap; undifferentiated chaos; *prima materia;* call it whatever you like! It isn't nice, it doesn't fit, it shouldn't be allowed, and it doesn't belong; it is Otherness—and the language of Otherness is myth.

The greatest oppression on earth is the suffering of meaningless wounds. The life of the Other Within—*nobility at odds with circumstance*—is madness, it is crazy, torturous, insane and inane, and the only help, the only medicine, is down here precisely where we have fallen: in the "meaning bestowing understanding" of the Mythic Reality.

Blake said: "If the fool would persist in his folly he would become wise."[28] On the long road of exile, between the forest and the village, the stranger, the shaman-poet-hunter, has only to follow in the reversible and backward footsteps of the Trickster: none other than the outlawed and repressed "myth-making function" itself: the mythopoeic intelligence. Epistrophé, peripeteia, the interval of the leaping consciousness, the profoundest heresy, the wisest trick, is to sing reality—this is the refuge from unbelief, the hidden lysis of the *masquerade:* "Grinding bread" for all that has been widowed and orphaned "the descent into hell is actually the ascent of soul." The bright star of the solar-knight has fallen from the sky . . . the shining one, on the path to the beloved, is devoured by the fierce dragon. . . . "And so long as you haven't experienced this: to die and so to grow, you are only a troubled guest on the dark earth."[29] Now the heart-bird, at last, breaks free, "The ten thousand things arise together; / in their arising is their return. . . ." *The flock rises. . . . The bird with one leg rises with them, but turns . . . and lands at his old place,* the no-place, the crucible—the "I" and the "not-I," sinking, entwined in the burning pyre of the mandorla-boat . . .

> *The sun, no longer haunted by sunset and shadows,*
> *Sinks down in the Eastern ocean and is born.*

Danny's Leap

By Martin Shaw

I THINK DANNY'S INFLUENCE is only just beginning. This beautiful, difficult book has a way of digging further and further into your being as the years go by. Deardorff was the greatest storyteller I ever saw, the most humane of men, the funniest of road companions. A tough guy, but gentle as a lamb. I never saw him complain once. He loved his wife, his daughters, his work. His cup runneth over.

Deardorff's inheritance is that he takes the established notion of comparative mythology and makes it associative. He breaks open laboured comparisons between cultures and beliefs and calls forth a wider frame: poetics, philosophy, music. He swoops between genres; a Taliesin moving between hawk, salmon, and grain of wheat. It's breathlessly exciting, what he is pointing towards.

If he'd called the book *Trickster Wisdom* he would have sold fifty times the amount of copies, but that wasn't his style. Too much of a hammer hitting a nail. Like Rilke, he preferred a language that circled around things. This is an ancient and magical technique, from the Bards of Ireland to Amazonia. It can be unwise to name magical things directly.

It seems there are no personal anecdotes. But look again and you realise the entire book is the story of his life. He raised his years into that rarefied, mythic register where "I" statements become "once upon a time." In a culture of compulsive disclosure, he had already distilled his intelligence and life experience into what you have just read. That's an act of terribly sophisticated alchemy.

As an oral storyteller, things could be different. In that hot seat, his language was simple and his teaching sometimes fierce, always brilliant. It was there that stories from his years tumbled out, street knowledge. People were crazy about Danny. You would always be playing second or third fiddle if you worked with him, and you wouldn't care. He just radiated something. There was no one in this whole wide world he couldn't look in the eye.

I met him and his beloved wife, Judith-Kate Friedman, at the Great Mother Conference back in 2006. He told stories that on a piece of paper would be about forty lines, but such was his skill he could navigate interior meanings, so they became epic in their impact and length. I was agog. There was no fluff, no ornamentation, just an elevator down to the very centre of the Underworld.

I introduced myself to him and he bellowed in (mock) exasperation, "Why haven't you got my fucking book?!" One trip to the conference store and my journey began. I was so impressed to have met someone who had written a book. It's a piece of art, really. It's scholarly but not academic, ambitious but not pretentious. There is a marked difference in its rhythm and how he actually spoke. It reads well out loud, but is another dimension again to his regular syntax. And that's part of what makes *The Other Within* so precious. It's a one-off, a castle hardily erected, and also the hawk that circles the castle. It was a tuned-up frequency he conjured. It's typical of Deardorff to have more than one tongue at his disposal.

We taught together for years, and I learnt from him. A generation younger, I felt lucky, in the same way he'd felt lucky to be in the orbit of Robert Bly, Marion Woodman, James Hillman, Gioia Timpanelli, and others. Though I miss him beyond measure, I am energised by the reality that his work is going to be absorbed by coming generations. His skill as a musician and his oral recordings as a teacher will continue to round out our appreciation of this extraordinary man. As I say, I think his influence is only just beginning.

And what would Danny want to tell us? I can make a few good guesses.

He would suggest we tell each other that we love each other frequently. He would want us to stop mowing our lawn and let the wild things back in. He would tell us to learn many poems and stories by heart and speak them to trees, rivers, mountains, and each other. He would tell us that if we don't know stories then how can we speak appropriately to the wider earth? Some of what Deardorff thought, we haven't caught up with yet. Though he dealt with ancient materials, that didn't mean they belonged in the past. They enable us sobering visions about quite where we may be heading.

Daniel Deardorff loved many everyday things, and could be incredibly direct if needed, but this book isn't that. We are back to the circling language again. This is his laboured crack at a kind of bardic tongue. With *The Other Within* I think we may get close to how thoughts actually roved through his mind, like wild geese overhead.

As a teacher sometimes you create a bridge, sometimes you make a leap. This was the moment to see just how incredible Danny's wingspan actually was.

This was Danny's leap.

MARTIN SHAW

Glossary

ad infinitum   Latin. Seemingly without limit; endlessly.

adoptive capacity   The ability of a social group or culture to adopt an individual without requiring him or her to adapt to the group's values, instead allowing the individual's uniqueness to shape the values of the group.

Alexander's Wall (Alexander's Iron Gate)   Legend says that Alexander the Great built a vast wall between two mountains at the edge of the world to keep the savage races, monsters, and the unknown out of civilization.

anthropogony   The origin of the human species.

aporia   An irresolvable internal contradiction or logical disjunction.

archai   Primary model; the primordial root source of a thing or idea.

archegestic   Of, or characterized by the gesture, image, resonance, or motion, that carries us toward the *archai*.

associative alacrity   See leaping consciousness.

a-voidance   The refusal to experience emptiness, one's interior void; see sole gap.

Awen   Welsh. Poetic inspiration; breath of poetic and magical power.

axis mundi   Latin. The Center of the world, where the three zones of the cosmos intersect—the heavens, the earth, and the underworld. The *axis mundi* is often represented in myth by the sacred tree that bridges the three worlds, also referred to in this book as the huluppu-tree, World Tree, Shaman Tree, and Yggdrasill.

biomythic   The innate neurological response to mythological stimuli, images, and experiences.

biophilia   Love of living things. Edward O. Wilson's term referring to humankind's innate affinity for all forms of life and the intricacies of nature.

Book of Judges   Theologically, a book in the biblical Old Testament (Hebrew bible).

both-and perspective   The perspective born of the ability to hold paradox, weighing opposites (black and white) with equal value.

bricoleur   French. One who engages in bricolage; a tinkerer, assembler, improviser who creates or fashions new, or newly useful, artistic works or practical tools from previous, often found, parts.

Center   See *axis mundi*.

chaosmos   The indivisibility of cosmos and chaos, which are inextricably bound together; the totality of reality.

Chymeric, chymera (chimera)   A mythic creature that combines more than one species

coincidentia oppositorum   Latin. The coincidence of opposites.

communitas   The sense of intimacy developed among persons who experience liminality together; the deep sense of connection that we experience when we are stripped down to nothing through crisis.

complexity catastrophe   When a system (like a society) becomes very complex it must create control-systems thus becoming more complex, now it may need systems to govern the control-systems, leading ultimately to a catastrophic collapse of the entire system.

consanguinity, consanguineous   Related by blood.

coracle   A small, rounded boat made from hides stretched over a wicker frame.

cosmogonic, cosmogony   The study of the origins of the universe.

cosmo-liminal locus   One's location in the universe outside of society; opposite of the social-structural locus, which is one's location and status within society.

creatio continua   Latin. The ongoing creation (for creation itself never stops being created).

crossroads of identity   The place where the imposed and the implicate identities coincide or collide.

Cynocephalic   From the Latin. Dog-headed.

daimon   See not-I.

descensus ad inferos   Latin. The descent inwards and into darkness, or hell, to gather wisdom and deepen the soul experience.

desideratum   Something lacked and wanted, considered necessary; a must-have.

duendé   A quality of emotion, authenticity, and passion in our expression; also a trickster in Spanish and Latin American mythology.

enantiodromia   The tendency of things to change into their opposites.

epistemology   The study of knowing.

epistrophé   Reversion through likeness, repetition (as in literary device), to lead something back to its origin, principle, or archetype.

fruitful asynchrony   Howard Gardner's idea that a certain amount of discord or asynchrony is required to activate and sustain the creative process.

gestic   Relating to bodily motion, especially dancing; pertaining to gestures, deeds, actions.

gnomonica   All things pertaining to the "gnomon"—the projecting piece on a sundial that shows the time by the position of its shadow. In this book, the definition is extended to include all things pertaining to the shadow itself.

hierophany   Literally, sacred manifestation (hiero: sacred; phany: manifestation).

hieros gamos   Latin. The sacred union that gave birth to creation.

holomovement   See implicate order.

Horse of Power   From Russian and Siberian mythology, a magical helper and counselor as well as a trusted steed, used here to represent deep instinctual intelligences.

huluppu-tree   See *axis mundi*.

ichor   From Greek mythology, the fluid that flows like blood in the veins of the gods.

implicate identity   Identity before and beyond identification; the deep identity that cannot be known or explained, but can be experienced through implication (i.e., glimpsed through ritual and the expressive arts); opposite of the imposed identity.

implicate order   From David Bohm's theory (also called the holomovement) which asserts that the totality of reality is unknowable but can be perceived by implication; the greater reality of creation, unexplainable, vast, in constant flux, and underlying everything; as opposed to the explicate order.

informance   Rather than gaining information prior to taking action, here one is informed by one's actions as they are being performed.

inter-personal   Relations between oneself and other people. (From Howard Gardner's theory of the multiple intelligences.)

intervallic   Pertaining to intervals (in time or space).

intra-personal   Relations and dynamics within oneself; interiority. (From Howard Gardner's theory of the multiple intelligences.)

kaleidoscopic consciousness   A multi-perspectival consciousness, which includes unconscious, instinct, inspiration, and gnosis as essential.

katabasis   The drop or journey downwards; the fall from grace.

la chappe d'Hellequin   The trap door in the stage through which the harlequin or fool disappears, out of site and into the underworld; the jaws of hell; the mouth of the dragon.

lambent   Of light or fire, glowing, gleaming or flickering with a soft radiance.

leaping consciousness   The ability to perform wider and wilder association, leaping great distances and still holding the thread of continuity; associative alacrity. "Leaping makes a jump from an object or idea soaked in unconscious substance to an object or idea soaked in conscious substance."— Robert Bly, from *Leaping Poetry*.

les extremes me touchent   French. "Extremes touch."

lexic   Pertaining to words, language, speech.

liminality   The primary, sacred condition, existing before and after structure and order; the condition of being between states or having no status; existing in the invisible or dark territory of the threshold as "other" or "outsider."

liminoid   In this volume, a condition that resembles liminality, but is lacking the essential connection to the sacred.

ludic   Spontaneous, risky, playful, mischievous.

lysis   An insensible or gradual solution or termination of a disease or disorder without apparent phenomena; opposite of crisis.

mandorla   The zone of two circles, an almond-shaped form used to represent the paradoxical union of two worlds; "neither-this-nor that," as well as "both this and that." Also referred to as *vesica pisci*.

miserere   Latin. An expression of lamentation or a cry for mercy.

mobocracy   Rule, domination, or political control by a mob.

morphic resonance   The field occurring between similar structures of activity, and influencing all subsequent related activities through stored or encoded informing pattern of activity.

mundus inferorum   Latin. The world interiority; the hidden reality beneath exterior appearances.

multivalent, multivalence   Of many meanings or values; evaluative plurality

multivocal   Of manifold meanings, definitions, values, or voices.

mysterium coniunctionis   Latin. Mystery of the conjunction; mystical paradoxes.

mythopoesis   Mythmaking; Participation in the on-going process of making myth, which is a trans-generational creation.

narcissine task   The fundamental problem faced by Narcissus: to apprehend oneself deeper than appearance and beyond presumption.

noetic   Pertaining to thinking or mental activity.

not-I   The Other Within; the implicate identity that, like the trickster, cannot be pinned down by explanation. "I am not I. I am this one, walking beside me, whom I do not see." —Juan Ramón Jiménez.

ontic, ontologically, ontology   Pertaining to Being; the study of Being; Existence

ontological gap   The gap between civilization and savagery, where we find the crossroads of identity; the gap, lacuna, split, or void within us, also referred to as sole gap.

opprobrium   Harsh criticism or censure.

orectic   Of or concerning desire or appetite.

paraclete   A divine or otherworldly mediator; one who intercedes on our behalf; comforter or advocate.

participation mystique   The experience of blurring psychological and/or subject-object boundaries between individuals and one another, their environment, and/or objects, resulting in a sense of primal or *a priori* oneness.

paxis   From the British. Used by schoolchildren to express immunity from "being caught" in games such as bulldog or "It."

peripeteia   A turning point; a sudden reversal of circumstance; an unprecedented leap of thought.

phallophoric   Bearing or carrying a sacred or ritual phallus.

phatic   Non-linguistic vocalizations uttered as cries or exclamations.

poiesis (poesis)   From the ancient Greek. The activity in which a person brings something into being that did not exist before; the process of making, formation, production, creation; the act of creativity, culture-making. (Also see mythopoesis.)

porosity   The quality or state of being porous; permeable as in a membrane; able to let substances in, out, or through. From the Greek poros, for "pore" or "passage."

praxis   Practice, as distinguished from theory.

prima materia   The alchemical primitive formless basic essence of all matter.

proprioception   The body's physical awareness of itself and its actions.

The Rat's Way   The dark, unaccepted, "other" route of descent; the way of deviance from or resistance to dogma and orthodoxy.

renovatio   Latin. Renewal, renovation, restoration.

rites of passage   Initiation; the change from one status to another, as in moving from adolescence to adulthood; this sacred passage consists of three stages: separation, liminality, and re-aggregation through ritual confirmation.

sacrality   Of or related to the sacred; the condition of being *in* the sacred.

sacred outsider   One who is necessary to the community, but not a member of the community; one who returns from the wilderness of death bearing the gift of the both-and perspective.

Saturnalia   A Roman festival in which the usual order of things is broken down and societal roles are reversed, turning slaves into masters and masters into slaves; unrestrained revelry.

Shaman Tree   See *axis mundi*.

siddhis   Sanskrit. Special or supernatural powers.

Solar Knight   The bright and shining knight, or quintessential insider, who represents order and ever-rising status; opposite of the Lunar Wild Man. Alexander, Beowulf, Gilgamesh, and St. George are examples of the Solar Knight.

sole gap (soul gap)   See ontological gap.

spatiotemporal   Pertaining to space and time together, inseparable.

spiritual twin   See not-I.

stereognostic intelligence (Stereognosis)   Ability to perceive the form of an object by using the sense of touch. See also proprioception.

Suertes   Spanish. In bullfighting, an action or pass performed by a bullfighter.

sui generis   Latin. Standing in a class by itself.

Symplegades (Cyanean rocks)   In Greek mythology, two cliffs that moved on their bases and crushed whatever sought to pass.

synesthesia   A neurological conflation of senses, i.e., hearing a smell, or seeing a sound.

tapas   Sanskrit. The build-up of one's own internal heat during meditation; also refers to the practice of enduring the pain of fire.

temple   Place and moment occupied by divine presence; coming to center (see *axis mundi*); the spatiotemporal intersection of life/death, heaven/earth, spirit/flesh.

theogamic   Related to theogamy, marriage to a god.

theriomorphic   A being (human or divine) in animal form.

vagina dentata   Latin. Vagina with teeth.

varilogical   Varied perspectives, connoting a flexibility of consciousness or mentality.

verticality   A consciousness connected to the *axis mundi,* denoting the ability to remain in rapport with the above and the below simultaneously.

vesica pisci   Latin. Fish-shaped vessel; see mandorla.

voyant   A visionary, a seer; one gifted with a heightened degree of insight and perception.

World Tree   See *axis mundi.*

wyrd   The unique path laid out for an individual by the weavers of destiny.

Yggdrasill   The divine ash tree of Nordic mythology, which has an eagle at the top, the primordial würm or serpent gnawing its roots, and a squirrel leaping up and down the trunk, carrying messages (insults) between the extremes. See *axis mundi.*

Notes

OVERTURE
Raven Whispers & Forbidden Doors

1. "Deformity," Oxford English Dictionary Second Edition on CD ROM (Oxford: Oxford University Press, 1999).

2. Heinrich Zimmer, *The King and the Corpse: Tales of the Soul's Conquest of Evil* (Princeton, N.J.: Bollingen, Princeton University Press, 1956), 94.

3. "Genius," Oxford English Dictionary Second Edition on CD ROM.

4. Roberts Avens, *Blake Swedenborg & the Neo-Platonic Tradition* (New York: Swedenborg Foundation), 8. "Far from being just one of our cognitive powers, valid in the field of art, scientific discovery and the like, it [imagination] is our whole power, the total functioning interplay of our capacities."

5. Gaston Bachelard, *On Poetic Imagination and Reverie,* trans. Colette Gaudin (Dallas, Tex.: Spring Publications, 1971), 19.

6. David Bohm, *Wholeness and the Implicate Order* (London: Routledge & Kegan Paul, 1980), 185–86.

7. Jerome Rothenberg, "Pre-Face (1967)," in *Technicians of the Sacred: A Range of Poetries from Africa, America, Asia, Europe & Oceania* (Berkeley: University of California Press, 1985), xxx.

8. Daniel Deardorff, *The Other Within: The Genius of Deformity in Myth, Culture, & Psyche* (Berkeley: North Atlantic, 2008), 139.

9. William Blake, "Milton Book: The Second" [Plate 32 {35}], in *The Complete Poetry and Prose of William Blake,* ed. David V. Erdman (Berkeley: University of California Press, 1982), 132.

10. Lao Tzu, *Tao Te Ching: A Book About The Way and the Power of The Way,* trans. Ursula K. Le Guin (Boston: Shambhala, 1997), 90.

11. Blake, "Proverbs of Hell," in "The Marriage of Heaven and Hell" in *Complete Poetry,* 36.

12. "I juggle therefore I am." Motto of The Flying Karamazov Brothers.

13. Lao Tzu, *Tao Te Ching,* 4.

14. William Blake, *The Marriage of Heaven and Hell,* ed. Geoffrey Keynes (Oxford: Oxford University Press, 1975), xvi [Plate 3].

15. Blake, "Milton Book: The Second" [Plate 32 {35}], in *Complete Poetry,* 132.

16. James A. Francis, *Subversive Virtue: Asceticism and Authority in the Second Century Pagan World* (University Park, Penn: Pennsylvania State University Press, 1995).

17. Blake, *The Marriage of Heaven and Hell,* xx.

18. Lao Tzu, *Tao Te Ching,* 60.

19. Robert Bly, *Iron John: A Book About Men* (Reading, Mass.: Addison-Wesley, 1990), 70.

20. Roque Dalton, "Matthew," in *Small Hours of the Night: Selected Poems of Roque Dalton,* ed. Hardie St. Martin, trans. Jonathan Cohen, James Graham, Ralph Nelson, Paul Pines, Hardie St. Marin, and David Unger (Willimantic, Conn.: Curbstone Press, 1996), 116.

PRELUDE
Songs of the Dog-Man

1. W. B. Yeats, "Dialogue of Self and Soul," in *The Rag and Bone Shop of the Heart: Poems for Men,* ed. Robert Bly, James Hillman, and Michael Meade (New York: HarperCollins, 1992), 505.

2. Mircea Eliade, *The Sacred and the Profane: The Nature of Religion* (San Diego, Calif.: Harcourt, Brace & Company, 1957), 11.

3. Eliade, *The Sacred and the Profane,* 21.

4. Morris Berman, *Coming to Our Senses: Body and Spirit in the Hidden History of the West* (New York: Simon and Schuster, 1989), 36.

5. "Deformity," in *The Penguin Dictionary of Symbols,* ed. Jean Chevalier, Alain Gheerbrant, trans. John Buchanan-Brown (London: Penguin Books, 1996), 282.

6. "Mutilation," in *The Penguin Dictionary of Symbols,* 689.

7. Rainer Maria Rilke, "The Voices," in *Selected Poems of Rainer Maria Rilke: A Translation from the German with Commentary by Robert Bly* (New York: Harper & Row, Perennial Library, 1981), 111.

8. Daniel Deardorff, "Bright-Mind, Strange Companions," *Mythosphere: A Journal of Myth, Image and Symbol* 2, no. 1 (2000).

9. Robert Johnson, "Crossroads," Genius, Web.

10. Friedrich Hölderlin, "Bread and Wine," in *The Rag and Bone Shop of the Heart: Poems for Men,* ed. Robert Bly, James Hillman, and Michael Meade (New York: HarperCollins, 1992), 12.

11. Robert Graves, *The White Goddess: A Historical Grammar of Poetic Myth* (New York: Farrar, Straus and Giroux, 1966), 91.

Scapegoat: A Stricken Deer

1. William Cowper, "I Was a Stricken Deer," in *The Soul Is Here for Its Own Joy: Sacred Poems from Many Cultures,* ed. Robert Bly (Hopewell, N.J.: The Ecco Press, 1995), 64.

2. Robert Bly, *Iron John: A Book About Men* (Reading, Mass.: Addison-Wesley, 1990), 70.

3. Roberts Avens, *Blake, Swedenborg & the Neo-Platonic Tradition* (New York: Swedenborg Foundation), 5.

4. Johann Wolfgang von Goethe, "The Holy Longing," in *The Rag and Bone Shop of the Heart: Poems for Men,* ed. Robert Bly, James Hillman, and Michael Meade (New York: HarperCollins, 1992), 382.

5. James MacKillop, "Lug Lámfhota," in *Dictionary of Celtic Mythology* (Oxford: Oxford University Press, 1998), 271.

6. David L. Miller, *Hells & Holy Ghosts: A Theopoetics of Christian Belief* (Nashville, Tenn.: Abingdon Press, 1989), 42–43.

7. Miguel De Unamuno, *The Tragic Sense of Life,* trans. J. E. Crawford Flitch (New York: Dover Publications, 1954), 45.

8. Miller, *Hells & Holy Ghosts,* 40.

9. Miller, *Hells & Holy Ghosts,* 43.

10. Victor W. Turner, *The Ritual Process: Structure and Anti-Structure* (Chicago: Aldine Publishing Company, 1969), 95.

11. Turner, *The Ritual Process,* 128–29.

12. Miller, *Hells & Holy Ghosts,* 34.

13. Miller, *Hells & Holy Ghosts,* 51.

14. Miller, *Hells & Holy Ghosts,* 60.

15. Novalis, *Novalis: Pollen and Fragments,* trans. Arthur Versluis (Grand Rapids, Mich.: Phanes Press, 1989), 27.

16. Turner, *The Ritual Process,* 116.

17. Robert Graves, *The White Goddess: A Historical Grammar of Poetic Myth* (New York: Farrar, Straus and Giroux, 1966), 21.

18. Richard Schechner, *Performance Theory* (New York: Routledge, 1977), 219.

19. Turner, *The Ritual Process,* 127–28.

20. Miller, *Hells & Holy Ghosts,* 98.

21. Juan Ramón Jiménez, "I am not I," in *The Rag and Bone Shop of the Heart: Poems for Men,* ed. Robert Bly, James Hillman, and Michael Meade (New York: HarperCollins, 1992), 367.

Aporia: Alexander's Iron Gate

1. David Gordon White, *Myths of the Dog-Man* (Chicago: University of Chicago Press, 1991), 55.

2. "Civil Society," in *A Dictionary of Cultural and Critical Theory,* ed. Michael Payne (Oxford: Blackwell, 1996), 102–3.

3. Michael Meade, private communication.

4. Stanley Diamond, *In Search of the Primitive: A Critique of Civilization* (New Brunswick, N.J.: Transaction Books, 1974), 1.

5. Clyde W. Ford, *The Hero with an African Face: Mythic Wisdom of Traditional Africa* (New York: Bantam, 1999), 11–12.

6. "Dog," in *The Penguin Dictionary of Symbols,* ed. Jean Chevalier, Alain Gheerbrant, trans. John Buchanan-Brown (London: Penguin Books, 1996), 302 [author's italics].

7. Robert Graves, *The White Goddess: A Historical Grammar of Poetic Myth* (New York: Farrar, Straus and Giroux, 1966), 151.

8. White, *Myths of the Dog-Man,* 14–15.

9. Malidoma Somé, private communication.

10. Clarissa Pinkola Estés, *Women Who Run with the Wolves* (New York: Ballantine Books, 1992), 123–24.

11. Yusef Komunyakaa, "Scapegoat," in *The Best American Poetry 1999,* ed. Robert Bly (New York: Scribner, 1999), 106. Also in Yusef Komunyakaa, *Talking Dirty to the Gods* (New York: Farrar, Straus and Giroux, 2000).

Wasters, Rhymers, Minstrels & Other Vagabonds

1. Robert Graves, *The White Goddess: A Historical Grammar of Poetic Myth* (New York: Farrar, Straus and Giroux, 1966), 146.

2. Arthur Koestler, quoted in Rupert Sheldrake, *The Presence of the Past: Morphic Resonance & the Habits of Nature* (Rochester, Vt.: Park Street Press, 1988), 95.

3. Jerome Rothenberg and Pierre Joris, eds., *Poems for the Millennium: The University of California Book of Modern & Postmodern Poetry,* vol. 2 (Berkeley: University of California Press, 1998), 4.

4. Henri J. M. Nouwen, *The Wounded Healer: Ministry in Contemporary Society* (New York: Image Books, 1979), 17.

5. James A. Francis, *Subversive Virtue: Asceticism and Authority in the Second Century Pagan World* (University Park, Pa.: Pennsylvania State University Press, 1995), xiii.

6. David Gordon White, *Myths of the Dog-Man* (Chicago: University of Chicago Press, 1991), 50.

7. Francis, *Subversive Virtue,* 65.

8. "Cynics," in *The Cambridge Dictionary of Philosophy* (Cambridge: Cambridge University Press, 1995), 175.

Fire on the Mountain

1. *The I Ching: or Book of Changes,* trans. Richard Wilhelm and Cary F. Baynes (New York: Princeton University Press, 1967), 216–17.

2. William Blake, "Proverbs of Hell" in "The Marriage of Heaven and Hell," in *The Complete Poetry and Prose of William Blake,* ed. David V. Erdman (Berkeley: University of California Press, 1982), 36.

3. Victor W. Turner, *The Ritual Process: Structure and Anti-Structure* (Chicago: Aldine Publishing Company, 1969), 99.

4. Henri J. M. Nouwen, *The Wounded Healer: Ministry in Contemporary Society* (New York: Image Books, 1979), 16–17.

5. William Stafford, "The Wanderer Awaiting Preferment," in *The Way It Is* (Saint Paul, Minn.: Graywolf Press, 1997), 101.

6. Rainer Maria Rilke, "The Man Watching," in *Selected Poems of Rainer Maria Rilke: A Translation from the German with Commentary by Robert Bly* (New York: Harper & Row, Perennial Library, 1981), 105.

7. William Cowper, "I Was a Stricken Deer," in Robert Bly, ed., *The Soul Is Here for Its Own Joy: Sacred Poems from Many Cultures* (Hopewell, N.J.: The Ecco Press, 1995), 64.

Mandorla: The Bird-Masked Dog-Toothed Dancers

1. Robert Bly, "My Father's Wedding 1924," in *The Rag and Bone Shop of the Heart: Poems for Men,* ed. Robert Bly, James Hillman, and Michael Meade (New York: HarperCollins, 1992), 133.

2. J. E. Cirlot, "Mandorla," in *A Dictionary of Symbols* (New York: Barnes & Noble, 1995), 203–4.

3. Robert Bly, "Warning to the Reader," in *Eating the Honey of Words: New and Selected Poems* (New York: HarperFlamingo, 1999), 104.

4. Jerome Rothenberg and Pierre Joris, eds., *Poems for the Millennium: The University of California Book of Modern & Postmodern Poetry,* vol. 2 (Berkeley: University of California Press, 1998), 1.

5. Rothenberg and Joris, *Poems for the Millennium,* 2:6.

6. Roberts Avens, *Blake Swedenborg & the Neo-Platonic Tradition* (New York: Swedenborg Foundation), 10.

7. David L. Miller, *Hells & Holy Ghosts: A Theopoetics of Christian Belief* (Nashville, Tenn.: Abingdon Press, 1989), 34.

8. Rothenberg and Joris, *Poems for the Millennium,* 2:8.

9. William Irwin Thompson, *The Time Falling Bodies Take to Light: Mythology, Sexuality & the Origins of Culture* (New York: St. Martin's Press, 1981), 8.

10. Roberts Avens, *Imaginal Body: Para-Jungian Reflections on Soul, Imagination and Death* (Washington, D.C.: University Press of America, 1982), 135.

11. Avens, *Imaginal Body,* 201.

12. Miller, *Hells & Holy Ghosts,* 75–76.

13. Clyde W. Ford, *The Hero with an African Face: Mythic Wisdom of Traditional Africa* (New York: Bantam, 1999), 36–37.

14. Joseph Campbell, *The Hero with a Thousand Faces* (Princeton, N.J.: Princeton University Press, 1968), 30.

The Bird with One Leg

1. Robert Bly, "A Godwit" in *What Have I Ever Lost By Dying: Collected Prose Poems* (New York: HarperCollins, 1992), 45.

2. "Darkening of the Light," in *The I Ching: or Book of Changes,* trans. Richard Wilhelm and Cary F. Baynes (New York: Princeton University Press, 1967), 140.

PART ONE
Trickster Wisdom

1. Caitlin Matthews and John Matthews, *Encyclopedia of Celtic Wisdom: A Celtic Shaman's Sourcebook* (Shaftesbury, Dorset, UK: Element Books, 1994), 168.

2. Robert Graves, *The White Goddess: A Historical Grammar of Poetic Myth,* (New York: Farrar, Straus and Giroux, 1966), 450–51, 455.

3. Paul Youngquist, *Madness & Blake's Myth* (University Park, Pa.: Pennsylvania State University Press, 1989), 25.

4. Blake, in Youngquist, *Madness & Blake's Myth,* 24.

5. Friedrich Hölderlin, "Bread and Wine," in *The Rag and Bone Shop of the Heart: Poems for Men,* ed. Robert Bly, James Hillman, and Michael Meade (New York: HarperCollins, 1992), 12.

6. William Irwin Thompson, *Imaginary Landscape: Making Worlds of Myth and Science* (New York: St. Martin's Press, 1989), 157.

7. Jamake Highwater, *The Mythology of Transgression: Homosexuality as Metaphor,* (New York: Oxford University Press, 1997), 9–10.

8. José Ortega y Gasset, in Joseph Campbell, *The Masks of God,* vol. 4, *Creative Mythology* (New York: Penguin Arkana, 1991), 390.

9. Lao Tzu, "78, Paradoxes," *Tao Te Ching: A Book About The Way and the Power of The Way,* trans. Ursula K. Le Guin (Boston: Shambhala, 1997), 98.

10. Robinson Jeffers, "Fire on the Hills," in *The Rag and Bone Shop of the Heart: Poems for Men,* ed. Robert Bly, James Hillman, and Michael Meade (New York: HarperCollins, 1992), 300.

The Crucible: In the Iron Cradle

1. Theodore Roethke, "In a Dark Time," in *The Rag and Bone Shop of the Heart: Poems for Men,* ed. Robert Bly, James Hillman, and Michael Meade (New York: HarperCollins, 1992), 22.

2. Richard Schechner, *The Future of Ritual: Writings on Culture and Performance* (London: Routledge, 1993), 237–38.

3. Howard Gardner, *Creating Minds: An Anatomy of Creativity* (New York: BasicBooks, HarperCollins, 1993), 381.

4. Gardner, *Creating Minds,* 44.

5. William Irwin Thompson, *Imaginary Landscape: Making Worlds of Myth and Science* (New York: St. Martin's Press, 1989), xx–xxi.

6. Sean Kane, *Wisdom of the Mythtellers* (Peterborough, Ontario: Broadview Press, 1994), 119.

7. Mircea Eliade, *Shamanism: Archaic Techniques of Ecstasy* (Chicago: University of Chicago Press, 1964), 259.

8. Mircea Eliade, *Cosmos and History: The Myth of the Eternal Return,* trans.

Willard R. Trask (New York: Harper Torchbooks, Harper & Brothers, 1954), 22.

9. Eliade, *Cosmos and History*, 28.

10. James Hillman, *The Dream and the Underworld* (New York: Harper & Row, 1979), 4.

11. James Hillman, *The Thought of the Heart & the Soul of the World* (Dallas, Tex.: Spring Publications 1981, 1982), 58–59.

12. Rupert Sheldrake, *The Presence of the Past: Morphic Resonance & the Habits of Nature* (Rochester, Vt.: Park Street Press, 1988), 109–110.

13. Mircea Eliade, *From the Stone Age to the Eleusinian Mysteries* (Chicago: University of Chicago Press, 1978), 285.

14. David Gordon White, *Myths of the Dog-Man* (Chicago: University of Chicago Press, 1991), 207.

15. Robert Bly, *The Sibling Society* (Reading, Mass.: Addison-Wesley, 1996), 213, [author's italics].

Kaleidoscope: The Ten Thousand Things

1. Oswald Spengler, *The Decline of the West,* vol. 1 (New York: Alfred A. Knopf, 1926), 120.

2. Jerome Rothenberg, *PRE-FACES & Other Writings* (New York: New Directions, 1981), 17.

3. "T'ai/Peace," in *The I Ching: or Book of Changes,* trans. Richard Wilhelm and Cary F. Baynes (New York: Princeton University Press, 1967), 48.

4. David Bohm, *Wholeness and the Implicate Order* (London: Routledge & Kegan Paul, 1980), 2.

5. Bohm, *Wholeness and the Implicate Order,* 22.

6. John Michel, *At the Center of the World: Polar Symbolism in Celtic, Norse and Other Ritualized Landscapes* (London: Thames and Hudson, 1994), 13.

7. Richard Schechner, *The Future of Ritual: Writings on Culture and Performance* (London: Routledge, 1993), 239–40.

8. James Hillman, *The Dream and the Underworld* (New York: Harper & Row, 1979), 14.

9. Bohm, *Wholeness and the Implicate Order,* 185–86.

10. Bohm, *Wholeness and the Implicate Order,* 11.

11. Kenneth Patchen, *The Journal of Albion Moonlight* (New York: Padell, 1941), 84.

12. William Blake, "Milton Book: The First," in *The Complete Poetry and Prose*

of William Blake, ed. David V. Erdman (Berkeley: University of California Press, 1982), 107.

13. Richard Leakey, *The Origin of Humankind* (New York: BasicBooks, 1994), 133.

14. Lao Tzu, "1 Taoing," *Tao Te Ching: A Book About The Way and the Power of The Way,* trans. Ursula K. Le Guin (Boston: Shambhala, 1997), 3.

15. Lao Tzu, "32 Sacred Power," *Tao Te Ching,* 43.

16. Schechner, *The Future of Ritual,* 237–38.

17. Anne Doueihi, "Inhabiting the Space Between Discourse and Story in Trickster Narratives," *Mythical Trickster Figures: Contours, Contexts, and Criticisms* (Tuscaloosa: University of Alabama Press, 1993), 198.

18. David Gordon White, *Myths of the Dog-Man* (Chicago: University of Chicago Press, 1991), 162, 167.

19. Joseph Campbell, *The Masks of God,* vol. 4, *Creative Mythology* (New York: Penguin Arkana, 1991), 5. All subsequent citations refer to this edition.

20. Campbell, *Masks of God,* 4:4.

21. Donna Lee Berg, *A Guide to the Oxford English Dictionary* (New York: Oxford University Press, 1993), 25.

22. Campbell, *Masks of God,* 4:674.

23. Campbell, *Masks of God,* 4:4.

24. Joseph Campbell, *Part 2: Mythologies of the Great Hunt, Historical Atlas of World Mythology,* vol. 1: *The Way of the Animal Powers,* (New York: Perennial Library, Harper & Row, 1988), 171.

25. Adolf Guggenbühl-Craig, *The Old Fool and the Corruption of Myth* (Dallas, Tex.: Spring Publications, 1991), 76.

26. Guggenbühl-Craig, *The Old Fool and the Corruption of Myth,* 54–55.

27. Blake, "Jerusalem: Chapter 1," *Complete Poetry,* 153.

28. Ernst Cassirer, *The Myth of the State* (New Haven: Yale University Press, 1946), 67.

29. White, *Myths of the Dog-Man,* 12.

30. White, *Myths of the Dog-Man,* 5.

31. D. H. Lawrence, "The Heart of Man," in *D. H. Lawrence: The Complete Poems,* ed. Vivian de Sola Pinto and F. Warren Roberts (New York: Penguin Books, 1964), 606.

32. Campbell, *Masks of God,* 4:674.

33. Robert Bly, *Leaping Poetry: An Idea with Poems and Translations* (Boston: A Seventies Press Book, Beacon Press, 1990), 5.

34. Wendy Doniger, *The Implied Spider: Politics & Theology in Myth* (New York: Columbia University Press, 1998), 80.

35. Mircea Eliade, *Autobiography: Journey East, Journey West, vol. 1: 1907–1937* (San Francisco: Harper & Row, 1981), 257.

36. Jerome Rothenberg and Pierre Joris, eds., *Poems for the Millennium: The University of California Book of Modern & Postmodern Poetry,* vol. 2 (Berkeley: University of California Press, 1998), 8.

37. James Stephens, "The Story of Tuan Mac Cairill," in *Irish Fairy Tales* (Ireland: Gill and Macmillan Ltd., 1979), 15.

Chymera: Mirror of the Beast

1. James Hillman, *The Thought of the Heart and the Soul of the World* (Dallas, Tex.: Spring Publications, 1981, 1982), 21.

2. Robert Bly, *Leaping Poetry: An Idea with Poems and Translations* (Boston: A Seventies Press Book, Beacon Press, 1990), 1.

3. Jamake Highwater, *The Mythology of Transgression: Homosexuality as Metaphor* (New York: Oxford University Press, 1997), 20.

4. Michael Meade, *Men and the Water of Life: Initiation and the Tempering of Men* (San Francisco: HarperSanFrancisco, 1993), 164.

5. Katharine Berry Judson, *Myths and Legends of the Pacific Northwest* (Lincoln: University of Nebraska Press/Bison Books, 1997), 119.

6. Bly, *Leaping Poetry,* 1.

7. Mircea Eliade, *The Sacred and the Profane: The Nature of Religion* (San Diego, Calif.: Harcourt Brace & Company, 1957), 48.

8. Robert Bly, "Craft Interview" in *Talking All Morning* (Ann Arbor: University of Michigan Press, 1980), 174–75.

9. Allan B. Chinen, "Adult Liberation & the Mature Trickster," in *Saga: Best New Writings on Mythology,* vol. 1, ed. Jonathan Young (Ashland, Ore.: White Cloud Press, 1996), 52–53.

10. Robert Bly, *The Sibling Society* (Reading, Mass.: Addison-Wesley, 1996), 21. Note: This is an abbreviated version taken from Bly's telling of the Swedish "Lind Würm."

11. Sean Kane, *Wisdom of the Mythtellers* (Peterborough, Ontario: Broadview Press, 1994), 103.

12. Victor Turner, *The Forest of Symbols: Aspects of Ndembu Ritual* (Ithaca, N.Y.: Cornell University Press, 1967), 107.

13. Morris Berman, *Coming to Our Senses: Body and Spirit in the Hidden History of the West* (New York: Simon and Schuster, 1989), 78.

14. Berman, *Coming to Our Senses,* 64.

15. William G. Doty, "Imagining the Future-Possible," in *Violence, Utopia, and the Kingdom of God: Fantasy and Ideology in the Bible* (London: Routledge, 1998), 109.

16. Lao Tzu, *Tao Te Ching: A Book About The Way and the Power of The Way* trans. Ursula K. Le Guin (Boston: Shambhala, 1997), 16.

17. William Stafford, "A Ritual to Read to Each Other," in *The Rag and Bone Shop of the Heart: Poems for Men,* ed. Robert Bly, James Hillman, and Michael Meade (New York: HarperCollins, 1992), 233.

18. Paul Radin, *The Trickster: A Study in American Indian Mythology* (New York: Shocken Books, 1956), 140.

19. James Taggart, *The Bear and His Sons: Masculinity in Spanish and Mexican Folktales* (Austin: University of Texas Press, 1997), 32.

20. Morris Berman, *The Reenchantment of the World* (Ithaca, N.Y.: Cornell University Press), 16.

21. Edward O. Wilson, *Biophilia* (Cambridge, Mass.: Harvard University Press, 1984).

22. Hillman, *The Thought of the Heart,* 21.

23. Lewis Hyde, *The Gift: Imagination and the Erotic Life of Property* (New York: Vintage Books, 1979), 136.

24. William Doty, *Mythography: The Study of Myths and Rituals* (Tuscaloosa: University of Alabama Press, 1986), 92.

25. Richard Schechner, *The Future of Ritual: Writings on Culture and Performance* (London: Routledge, 1993), 255.

26. Lewis Hyde, *Trickster Makes This World: Mischief, Myth, and Art* (New York: Farrar, Straus and Giroux, 1998), 13.

27. Colin Turnbull, "Liminality: A Synthesis of Subjective and Objective Experience," in *By Means of Performance: Intercultural Studies of Theatre and Ritual,* ed. Richard Schechner and Willa Appel (Cambridge: Cambridge University Press, 1990), 80.

28. David Bohm, *Wholeness and the Implicate Order* (London: Routledge & Kegan Paul, 1980), 156.

29. Robert Bly, "December 23, 1926," in *Selected Poems* (New York: Harper & Row, 1986), 118.

30. Antonio Machado, in Robert Bly, *The Sibling Society* (Reading, Mass.: Addison-Wesley, 1996), 212.

31. W. B. Yeats, "Crazy Jane Talks with the Bishop," in *The Rag and Bone Shop of the Heart: Poems for Men,* ed. Robert Bly, James Hillman, and Michael Meade (New York: HarperCollins, 1992), 221.

32. Robert Duncan, "Rites of Participation," in *Symposium of the Whole,* ed. Jerome Rothenberg and Diane Rothenberg (Berkeley: University of California Press, 1983), 328.

PART TWO
The Leaping Consciousness

1. Howard Gardner, *Frames of Mind: The Theory of Multiple Intelligences* (New York: BasicBooks, HarperCollins, 1983), 293.

2. Heinrich Zimmer, *The King and the Corpse: Tales of the Soul's Conquest of Evil* (Princeton, N.J.: Bollingen, Princeton University Press, 1956), 259.

3. Zimmer, *The King and the Corpse,* 262.

4. Howard Gardner, *Creating Minds: An Anatomy of Creativity* (New York: BasicBooks, HarperCollins, 1993), 7.

5. Valhjalmur Stefansson, in John Greenway, *Literature Among the Primitives* (Hatboro, Pa.: Folklore Associates, 1964), 187–88.

6. Mircea Eliade, *Cosmos and History: The Myth of the Eternal Return,* trans. Willard R. Trask (New York: Harper Torchbooks, Harper & Brothers, 1954), 42.

7. Eliade, *Cosmos and History,* 44.

8. Eliade, *Cosmos and History,* 44–45.

9. Kenneth Patchen, *The Journal of Albion Moonlight* (New York: Padell, 1941), 16.

10. Robert Bly, "Thoughts in the Cabin," in *Meditations on the Insatiable Soul* (New York: HarperPerennial, 1994), 22.

11. Richard Schechner, *The Future of Ritual: Writings on Culture and Performance* (London: Routledge, 1993), 94–97, 103.

12. Victor Turner, "Are There Universals of Performance in Myth, Ritual, and Drama?" in *By Means of Performance: Intercultural Studies of Theatre and Ritual,* ed. Richard Schechner and Willa Appel (Cambridge: Cambridge University Press, 1990), 9.

13. William Blake, "Auguries of Innocence," in *The Complete Poetry and Prose of William Blake,* ed. David V. Erdman (Berkeley: University of California Press, 1982), 492.

14. W. B. Yeats, "Dialogue of Self and Soul," in *The Rag and Bone Shop of the Heart: Poems for Men,* ed. Robert Bly, James Hillman, and Michael Meade (New York: HarperCollins, 1992), 505.

15. Jerome Rothenberg, in Sherman Paul, *In Search of the Primitive: Rereading David Antin, Jerome Rothenberg, and Gary Snyder* (Baton Rouge, La.: Louisiana State University Press, 1986), 88.

Dragon Smoke: The Marriage of Heaven and Hell

1. Robert Bly, *Leaping Poetry: An Idea with Poems and Translations* (Boston: A Seventies Press Book, Beacon Press, 1990), 1.

2. William V. Davis, *Understanding Robert Bly* (Columbia: University of South Carolina Press, 1988), 24–25.

3. Sean Kane, *Wisdom of the Mythtellers* (Peterborough, Ontario.: Broadview Press, 1994), 18–19.

4. Daniel Deardorff, *The Other Within: The Genius of Deformity in Myth, Culture, & Psyche* (Berkeley: North Atlantic, 2008), 19–20.

5. Morris Berman, *Coming to Our Senses: Body and Spirit in the Hidden History of the West* (New York: Simon and Schuster, 1989), 72.

6. Kane, *Wisdom of the Mythtellers,* 115.

7. Robert Bringhurst, "Nagarjuna," in *The Calling: Selected Poems 1970–1995* (Toronto: McClelland & Stewart, 1995), 119–20.

8. Marion Woodman in Robert Bly and Marion Woodman, *The Maiden King: The Reunion of Masculine and Feminine* (New York: Henry Holt and Company, 1998), 195.

9. Turner, *The Anthropology of Performance* (New York: PAJ Publications, 1988), 174–75.

10. Turner, *The Anthropology of Performance,* 160.

11. Turner, *The Anthropology of Performance,* 172.

12. William Blake, "The Marriage of Heaven and Hell," in *The Complete Poetry and Prose of William Blake,* ed. David V. Erdman (Berkeley: University of California Press, 1982), 36.

13. Robert Bly, *American Poetry: Wildness and Domesticity* (New York: Harper & Row, 1990), 62.

14. Bly, *Leaping Poetry,* 72.

15. Turner, *The Anthropology of Performance,* 160.

16. Robert Bly, "The Hawk, the Horse and the Rider," in *Choirs of the*

God: Revisioning Masculinity, ed. John Matthews (London: Mandala, HarperCollins, 1991), 23, 25, 27.

17. "Horse," in *The Penguin Dictionary of Symbols,* ed. Jean Chevalier, Alain Gheerbrant, trans. John Buchanan-Brown (London: Penguin Books, 1996), 517, 519.

18. "Horse," in *The Penguin Dictionary of Symbols,* 517.

19. Turner, *The Anthropology of Performance,* 168–69.

20. Heinrich Zimmer, *The King and the Corpse: Tales of the Soul's Conquest of Evil* (Princeton, N.J.: Bollingen, Princeton University Press, 1956), 251.

Gnomonica: The Tree of Joyful Difficulty

1. Jerome Rothenberg, "Pre-Face (1967)," in *Technicians of the Sacred: A Range of Poetries from Africa, America, Asia, Europe & Oceania* (Berkeley: University of California Press, 1985), xxx.

2. Jerome Rothenberg, "The Poetics of Shamanism (1968)," in *PRE-FACES & Other Writings* (New York: New Directions, 1981), 187.

3. Federico García Lorca, "The Havana Lectures," in *The Rag and Bone Shop of the Heart: Poems for Men,* ed. Robert Bly, James Hillman, and Michael Meade (New York: HarperCollins, 1992), 165.

4. Robert Bly, *Leaping Poetry: An Idea with Poems and Translations* (Boston: A Seventies Press Book, Beacon Press, 1990), 29. Bly is referencing Frederico Garcia Lorca's essay "Theory and Function of the Duende."

5. Clarissa Pinkola Estés, *Women Who Run with the Wolves* (New York: Balantine Books, 1992), 472n.

6. Jerome Rothenberg and Pierre Joris, eds., *Poems for the Millennium: The University of California Book of Modern & Postmodern Poetry,* vol. 1 (Berkeley: University of California Press, 1995), 1:43.

7. Howard Gardner, *Frames of Mind: The Theory of Multiple Intelligences* (New York: BasicBooks, HarperCollins, 1983), 291.

8. Jamake Highwater, *The Mythology of Transgression: Homosexuality as Metaphor* (New York: Oxford University Press, 1997), 38.

9. Rainer Maria Rilke, "The Man Watching," in *Selected Poems of Rainer Maria Rilke: A Translation from the German with Commentary by Robert Bly* (New York: Perennial Library, Harper & Row, 1981), 105.

10. Nikki Giovanni, "Ego Tripping," in *The Rag and Bone Shop of the Heart: Poems for Men,* ed. Robert Bly, James Hillman, and Michael Meade (New York: HarperCollins, 1992), 410.

11. Rainer Maria Rilke, *The Book of Images: A Bilingual Edition,* trans. Edward Snow (San Francisco: North Point Press, 1991), xv.

12. Highwater, *Mythology of Transgression,* 185.

13. Stephen Mitchell, introduction to *The Sonnets to Orpheus* by Rainer Maria Rilke, trans. Stephen Mitchell (Boston: Shambhala, 1993), xviii.

14. Wolfgang Leppmann, Russell M. Stockman, trans., Richard Exner, verse trans., *Rilke: A Life* (New York: Fromm International Publishing Corporation 1984), 288.

15. Rothenberg and Joris, *Poems for the Millennium,* 1:110.

16. Robert Bly, *The Sibling Society* (Reading, Mass.: Addison-Wesley, 1996).

17. Mark Levy, *Technicians of Ecstasy: Shamanism and the Modern Artist* (Norfolk, Conn.: Bramble Books, 1993), 29–30.

The Lyre: Where the Callus Meets the String

1. Lewis Hyde, *Trickster Makes This World: Mischief, Myth, and Art* (New York: Farrar, Straus and Giroux, 1998), 73.

2. Morris Berman, *Coming to Our Senses: Body and Spirit in the Hidden History of the West* (New York: Simon and Schuster, 1989), 325.

3. Robert Bly, "My Father's Wedding 1924," in *The Rag and Bone Shop of the Heart: Poems for Men,* ed. Robert Bly, James Hillman, and Michael Meade (New York: HarperCollins, 1992), 133.

4. Robert Bly and Marion Woodman, *The Maiden King: The Reunion of Masculine and Feminine* (New York: Henry Holt and Company, 1998), 130–31.

5. Arthur Koestler, quoted in Rupert Sheldrake, *The Presence of the Past: Morphic Resonance & the Habits of Nature* (Rochester, Vt.: Park Street Press, 1988), 95.

6. James A. Francis, *Subversive Virtue: Asceticism and Authority in the Second Century Pagan World* (University Park, Pa.: Pennsylvania State University Press, 1995), 65.

7. William Blake, "The Marriage of Heaven and Hell," in *The Complete Poetry and Prose of William Blake,* ed. David V. Erdman (Berkeley: University of California Press, 1982), 35.

8. Jerome Rothenberg and Pierre Joris, *Poems for the Millennium: The University of California Book of Modern & Postmodern Poetry,* vol. 2 (Berkeley: University of California Press, 1998), 6.

9. Lao Tzu, *Tao Te Ching: A Book About The Way and the Power of The Way* trans. Ursula K. Le Guin (Boston: Shambhala, 1997), 86.

10. Rainer Maria Rilke, "Sonnets to Orpheus, III," in *Selected Poems of Rainer Maria Rilke: A Translation from the German with Commentary by Robert Bly* (New York: Harper & Row, Perennial Library, 1981), 199.

CODA
Masquerade

1. David L. Miller, *Hells & Holy Ghosts: A Theopoetics of Christian Belief* (Nashville, Tenn.: Abingdon Press, 1989), 54.

2. Rudolf Wittkower, in Michael Taussig, *Shamanism, Colonialism, and the Wild Man: A Study in Terror and Healing* (Chicago: University of Chicago Press, 1987), 212.

3. "Deformity," in *The Penguin Dictionary of Symbols,* ed. Jean Chevalier, Alain Gheerbrant, trans. John Buchanan-Brown (London: Penguin Books, 1996), 282.

4. Kenneth Patchen, *The Journal of Albion Moonlight* (New York: Padell, 1941), 152.

5. Ernst Cassirer, *The Myth of the State* (New Haven, Conn.: Yale University Press, 1946), 297.

6. Ivan Strenski, *Four Theories of Myth in Twentieth-Century History: Cassirer, Eliade, Lévi-Strauss and Malinowski* (Iowa City: University of Iowa Press, 1987), 26.

7. Friedrich Hölderlin, "Bread and Wine," in *The Rag and Bone Shop of the Heart: Poems for Men,* ed. Robert Bly, James Hillman, and Michael Meade (New York: HarperCollins, 1992), 12.

8. N. J. Girardot, *Myth and Meaning in Early Taoism: The Theme of Chaos* (Berkeley: University of California Press, 1983), 165.

9. Robert D. Pelton, *The Trickster in West Africa: A Study of Mythic Irony and Sacred Delight* (Berkeley: University of California Press, 1980), 262–63.

10. Jamake Highwater, *The Mythology of Transgression: Homosexuality as Metaphor* (New York: Oxford University Press, 1997), 20.

11. Morris Berman, *Coming to Our Senses: Body and Spirit in the Hidden History of the West* (New York: Simon and Schuster, 1989), 37.

12. William J. Hynes, "Mapping the Characteristics of Mythic Tricksters:

A Heuristic Guide," in *Mythical Trickster Figures: Contours, Contexts, and Criticisms,* ed. William J. Hynes and William G. Doty (Tuscaloosa: University of Alabama Press, 1993), 34.

13. Pelton, *The Trickster in West Africa,* 281.

14. David Gordon White, *Myths of the Dog-Man* (Chicago: University of Chicago Press, 1991), 208.

15. Howard Gardner, *Frames of Mind: The Theory of Multiple Intelligences* (New York: BasicBooks, HarperCollins, 1983), 36.

16. John Emigh, *Masked Performance: The Play of Self and Other in Ritual and Theatre* (Philadelphia: University of Pennsylvania Press, 1996), 140.

17. Emigh, *Masked Performance,* 276.

18. Paul Radin, *The Trickster: A Study in American Indian Mythology* (New York: Shocken Books, 1956), 32–35.

19. James Stephens, "The Story of Tuan Mac Cairill," in *Irish Fairy Tales* (Ireland: Gill and Macmillan Ltd., 1979), 15.

20. Girardot, *Myth and Meaning in Early Taoism,* 253.

21. Lawrence Raab, "Sudden Appearance of a Monster at a Window," in *A Book of Luminous Things: An International Anthology of Poetry,* ed. Czeslaw Milosz (New York: Harcourt, 1996), 254.

The Drum: For the Serpent & the Bird

1. Kenneth Patchen, "The Character of Love Seen as a Search for the Lost," in *The Collected Poems of Kenneth Patchen* (New York: New Directions, 1968), 73.

2. Howard Gardner, *Creating Minds: An Anatomy of Creativity* (New York: BasicBooks, HarperCollins, 1993), 36.

3. Robert Graves, *Mammon and the Black Goddess* (London: Cassell, 1965), 143.

4. Robert Bly, *The Sibling Society* (Reading, Mass.: Addison-Wesley, 1996), 212.

5. Thomas Van Nortwick, "The Wild Man: The Epic of Gilgamesh," in *Gilgamesh: A Reader,* ed. John Maier (Wauconda, Ill.: Bolchazy-Carducci Publishers, 1997), 350.

6. Bly, *The Sibling Society,* 211.

7. Van Nortwick, *Gilgamesh: A Reader,* 353.

8. Adapted from Samuel Noah Kramer, *Sumerian Mythology: A Study of Spiritual and Literary Achievement in the Third Millennium B.C.* (Philadelphia: University of Pennsylvania Press, 1972).

9. Mircea Eliade, *Shamanism: Archaic Techniques of Ecstasy* (Chicago: University of Chicago Press, 1964), 259.

10. John Gardner and John Maier, *Gilgamesh: Translated from the Sîn-leqi-unninni Version* (New York: Vintage Books, 1985), 257, 253 [Tablet XII].

11. Deldon Anne McNeely, *Mercury Rising: Women, Evil and the Trickster Gods* (Woodstock, Conn.: Spring Publications, 1996), 34.

12. Kramer, *Sumerian Mythology,* 91.

13. Rainer Maria Rilke, "The Man Watching," in *Selected Poems of Rainer Maria Rilke: A Translation from the German with Commentary by Robert Bly* (New York: Harper & Row, Perennial Library, 1981), 105.

14. Van Nortwick, *Gilgamesh: A Reader,* 351.

15. McNeely, *Mercury Rising,* 18.

16. John Lash, *The Hero: Manhood and Power* (London: Thames and Hudson, 1995), 15.

17. Robert Bly, *Talking All Morning* (Ann Arbor: University of Michigan Press, 1980), 10.

18. Sean Kane, *Wisdom of the Mythtellers* (Peterborough, Ontario: Broadview Press, 1994), 103.

19. Kane, *Wisdom of the Mythtellers,* 115.

20. D. H. Lawrence, "To Women, as Far as I'm Concerned," in *The Rag and Bone Shop of the Heart: Poems for Men,* ed. Robert Bly, James Hillman, and Michael Meade (New York: HarperCollins, 1992), 338.

21. Nils L. Wallin, *Biomusicology: Neurophysiological, Neuropsychological, and Evolutionary Perspectives on the Origins and Purpose of Music* (Stuyvesant, N.Y.: Pendragon Press, 1991), 58.

22. Rainer Maria Rilke, "The Man Watching," *Selected Poems,* 105.

23. Wallin, *Biomusicology,* 58.

24. Kane, *Wisdom of the Mythtellers,* 118.

25. Miguel de Unamuno, *The Tragic Sense of Life* (New York: Dover, 1954), 14, 16.

26. Adapted from "Maria Morevna," Aleksandr Afens'ev, in *Russian Fairy Tales,* trans. Norbert Guterman (New York: Pantheon, 1945), 553.

27. Robert Bly, *Iron John: A Book About Men* (Reading, Mass.: Addison-Wesley, 1990), 36.

28. Robert D. Pelton, *The Trickster in West Africa: A Study of Mythic Irony and Sacred Delight* (Berkeley: University of California Press, 1980), 262–63.

29. Van Nortwick, *Gilgamesh: A Reader,* 351.

30. Pyotr Simonov, *Essential Russian Mythology: Stories that Change the World* (London: Thorsons, 1997), 17.

31. Robert Bly and Marion Woodman, *The Maiden King: The Reunion of Masculine and Feminine* (New York: Henry Holt and Company, 1998), 130–31.

32. Kane, *Wisdom of the Mythtellers,* 112–113.

33. Jerome Rothenberg, "The Poetics of Shamanism (1968)," in *PRE-FACES & Other Writings* (New York: New Directions, 1981), 187.

34. "Horse," in *The Penguin Dictionary of Symbols,* ed. Jean Chevalier, Alain Gheerbrant, trans. John Buchanan-Brown (London: Penguin Books, 1996), 517.

Of the Spirit & the Flesh

1. Adapted from the Buriat tale "Morgon-Kara," in Joseph Campbell, *The Hero with a Thousand Faces* (Princeton, N.J.: Princeton University Press, 1968), 199.

2. Romans 8:6.

3. Robert Bly, "St. George and the Dragon," in *Eating the Honey of Words: New and Selected Poems* (New York: HarperFlamingo, 1999), 202–3.

4. Lawrence Raab, "Sudden Appearance of a Monster at a Window," in *A Book of Luminous Things: An International Anthology of Poetry,* ed. Czeslaw Milosz (New York: Harcourt, 1996), 254.

5. Yusef Komunyakaa, "Scapegoat," in *The Best American Poetry 1999,* ed. Robert Bly (New York: Scribner, 1999), 106. Also in Komunyakaa, *Talking Dirty to the Gods* (New York: Farrar, Straus and Giroux, 2000).

6. Eugenio Barba, *A Dictionary of Theatre Anthropology: The Secret Art of the Performer* (London: Routledge, 1991), 59.

7. Howard Gardner, *Intelligence Reframed: Multiple Intelligences for the 21st Century* (New York: Basic Books, 1999), 19.

8. Robert Bly, *American Poetry: Wildness and Domesticity* (New York: Harper & Row, 1990), 276.

9. John Bierhorst, *The Mythology of South America* (New York: William Morrow, 1988), 54

10. N. J. Girardot, *Myth and Meaning in Early Taoism: The Theme of Chaos* (Berkeley: University of California Press, 1983), 40.

11. Robert Bly, *Leaping Poetry: An Idea with Poems and Translations* (Boston: A Seventies Press Book, Beacon Press, 1990), 1.

12. Jeffrey H. Tigay, "Summary: The Evolution of The Gilgamesh Epic," in *Gilgamesh: A Reader,* ed. John Maier (Wauconda, Ill.: Bolchazy-Carducci Publishers, 1997), 46.

13. Girardot, *Myth and Meaning in Early Taoism,* 303–4.

14. Robert Temple, "Introduction to He Who Saw Everything," in *Gilgamesh: A Reader,* ed. John Maier (Wauconda, Ill.: Bolchazy-Carducci Publishers, 1997), 319 [author's italics].

15. Rupert Sheldrake, *The Presence of the Past: Morphic Resonance & the Habits of Nature* (Rochester, Vt.: Park Street Press, 1988), 109–10.

16. Girardot, *Myth and Meaning in Early Taoism,* 43.

17. Girardot, *Myth and Meaning in Early Taoism,* 10.

18. "Lysis," Oxford English Dictionary Second Edition on CD ROM (Oxford: Oxford University Press, 1999).

19. Morris Berman, *Coming to Our Senses: Body and Spirit in the Hidden History of the West* (New York: Simon and Schuster, 1989), 20.

20. Joan Halifax, *Shaman: The Wounded Healer* (New York: Crossroad, 1982), 15.

21. Sherman Paul, *In Search of the Primitive: Rereading David Antin, Jerome Rothenberg, and Gary Snyder* (Baton Rouge, La.: Louisiana State University Press, 1986), 87.

22. Diane di Prima, "RANT," in *Poems for the Millennium,* ed. Jerome Rothenberg and Pierre Jorris, vol. 1 (Berkeley: University of California Press, 1998), 449–50.

23. Michael Taussig, *The Nervous System* (New York: Routledge, 1992), 87.

24. David L. Miller, *Hells & Holy Ghosts: A Theopoetics of Christian Belief* (Nashville, Tenn.: Abingdon Press, 1989), 98.

25. Robert Bly, *Iron John: A Book About Men* (Reading, Mass.: Addison-Wesley, 1990), 29.

26. Berman, *Coming to Our Senses,* 341–42.

27. Girardot, *Myth and Meaning in Early Taoism,* 258.

28. Girardot, *Myth and Meaning in Early Taoism,* 266.

29. Girardot, *Myth and Meaning in Early Taoism,* 269.

30. Jalāl ad-Dīn Mohammad Rumi, *The Essential Rumi,* trans. Coleman Barks (New York: HarperCollins, 1995), 281.

31. Gaston Bachelard, *On Poetic Imagination and Reverie,* trans. Colette Guadin (Dallas, Tex.: Spring Publications, 1971), 19.

32. Eugenio Barba, *A Dictionary of Theatre Anthropology: The Secret Art of the Performer* (London: Routledge, 1991), 34.

33. Ernst Cassirer, *The Myth of the State* (New Haven: Yale University Press, 1946), 297.

34. Joseph Campbell, *The Masks of God*, vol. 4, *Creative Mythology* (New York: Penguin Arkana, 1991), 609.

35. Roberts Avens, *Imaginal Body: Para-Jungian Reflections on Soul, Imagination and Death* (Washington, D.C.: University Press of America, 1982), 188–89.

36. Avens, *Imaginal Body*, 208–9.

37. Rainer Maria Rilke, "Sonnets to Orpheus, III," in *Selected Poems of Rainer Maria Rilke: A Translation from the German with Commentary by Robert Bly* (New York: Harper & Row, Perennial Library, 1981), 199.

The Singer: Throw Yourself Like Seed

1. Joseph Campbell, *The Masks of God,* vol. 4, *Creative Mythology* (New York: Penguin Arkana, 1991), 609.

2. Dylan Thomas, "Poem in October," *Collected Poems* (New York: New Directions, 1957), 115.

3. Robert Bly, "Craft Interview," in *Talking All Morning* (Ann Arbor: University of Michigan Press, 1980), 174–75.

4. Juan Ramón Jiménez, "Ocean," in *Lorca & Jiménez Selected Poems,* trans. Robert Bly (Boston: Beacon, 1973), 63.

5. Roberts Avens, *Blake Swedenborg & the Neo-Platonic Tradition* (New York: Swedenborg Foundation), 5.

6. Robert Bringhurst, "Xuedou Zhongxian," in *The Calling: Selected Poems 1970–1995* (Toronto: McClelland & Stewart, 1995), 132.

7. Black Elk as quoted in Joseph Campbell, *The Flight of the Wild Gander* (South Bend, Ind.: Regency / Gateway, 1979), 118.

8. Campbell, *Masks of God,* 4:4.

9. Joseph Campbell, *The Hero with a Thousand Faces* (Princeton, N.J.: Princeton University Press, 1968), 218.

10. Campbell, *Masks of God,* 4:4.

11. "Singer," in *The Dictionary of Native American Mythology,* ed. Sam D. Gill and Irene F. Sullivan (Santa Barbara, Calif.: ABC-CLIO, 1992), 274.

12. Richard Schechner, *Performance Theory* (New York: Routledge, 1977), 219.

13. Goethe, "The Holy Longing," in *The Rag and Bone Shop of the Heart: Poems for Men,* ed. Robert Bly, James Hillman, and Michael Meade (New York: HarperCollins, 1992), 382.

14. Roger Dunsmore, in Michael Taussig, *The Nervous System* (New York: Routledge, 1992), 161.

15. Lao Tzu, *Tao Te Ching: A Book About The Way and the Power of The Way,* trans. Ursula K. Le Guin (Boston: Shambhala, 1997), 91.

16. Taussig, *The Nervous System,* 161.

17. Robert Duncan, "Rites of Participation," in *Symposium of the Whole,* ed. Jerome Rothenberg and Diane Rothenberg (Berkeley: University of California Press, 1983), 328.

18. Rainer Maria Rilke, "Title Poem" [First poem in "The Voices"], *Selected Poems of Rainer Maria Rilke: A Translation from the German with Commentary by Robert Bly* (New York: Harper & Row, Perennial Library, 1981), 111.

19. Miguel De Unamuno, *The Tragic Sense of Life,* trans. J. E. Crawford Flitch (New York: Dover Publications, 1954), 17.

20. Joseph Campbell, *The Masks of God,* vol. 1, *Primitive Mythology* (New York: Penguin Arkana, 1968), 25.

21. William Blake, "The Marriage of Heaven and Hell," in *The Complete Poetry and Prose of William Blake,* ed. David V. Erdman (Berkeley: University of California Press, 1982), 36.

22. Roberts Avens, *Imaginal Body: Para-Jungian Reflections on Soul, Imagination and Death* (Washington, D.C.: University Press of America, 1982), 151.

23. Unamuno, *The Tragic Sense of Life,* 119.

24. Unamuno, *The Tragic Sense of Life,* 260.

25. Robert Bly, *The Sibling Society* (Reading, Mass.: Addison-Wesley, 1996), 212.

26. This quote comes from an abstract of a paper presented by Iegor Reznikoff at a symposium on music archaeology, unfortunately I can no longer locate the source. For more information see Chris Scarre, "Painting by Resonance," *Nature* 338 (1989): 382. For more recent information on Reznikoff's work see, Iegor Reznikoff, "On Primitive Elements of Musical Meaning," *Journal of Music and Meaning* 3 (Fall 2005).

27. Rafael López-Pedraza, "Reflections On The Duendé," in *Cultural Anxiety* (Einsiedeln, Switzerland: Daimon Verlag, 1990), 63 [italics in the original].

28. López-Pedraza, *Cultural Anxiety,* 65.

29. Avens, *Blake Swedenborg & the Neo-Platonic Tradition,* 10.

30. Stephen W. Hill and Robert B. Montoya, *Kokopelli Ceremonies* (Santa Fe, N.Mex.: Kiva Publishing, 1995), 16.

31. Hill and Montoya, *Kokopelli Ceremonies,* 24.

32. James Hillman, "Loving the World Anyway," in *The Rag and Bone Shop of the Heart: Poems for Men,* ed. Robert Bly, James Hillman, and Michael Meade (New York: HarperCollins, 1992), 473.

33. Joseph Campbell, *The Flight of the Wild Gander* (South Bend, Ind.: Regency / Gateway, 1979), 48–49.

34. Miguel de Unamuno, "Throw Yourself Like Seed," in *The Rag and Bone Shop of the Heart: Poems for Men,* ed. Robert Bly, James Hillman, and Michael Meade (New York: HarperCollins, 1992), 234.

The Cauldron: And Each Is the Work of All

1. Kenneth Patchen, "The Character of Love Seen as a Search for the Lost," in *The Collected Poems of Kenneth Patchen* (New York: New Directions, 1968), 73.

2. René Girard, *Violence and the Sacred* (Baltimore, Md.: Johns Hopkins University Press, 1977), 4.

3. Girard, *Violence and the Sacred,* 144.

4. Stanley Diamond, *In Search of the Primitive: A Critique of Civilization* (New Brunswick, N.J.: Transaction Books, 1974), 1.

5. Jamake Highwater, *The Mythology of Transgression: Homosexuality as Metaphor* (New York: Oxford University Press, 1997), 185.

6. Michael Taussig, *Shamanism, Colonialism, and the Wild Man: A Study in Terror and Healing* (Chicago: University of Chicago Press, 1987), 143–45.

7. Adapted from "Coyote-Giving," in Richard Erdoes and Alfonso Ortiz, eds., *American Indian Trickster Tales* (New York: Penguin, 1998).

8. N. J. Girardot, *Myth and Meaning in Early Taoism: The Theme of Chaos* (Berkeley: University of California Press, 1983), 238.

9. Girardot, *Myth and Meaning in Early Taoism,* 141.

10. Robert Graves, *The White Goddess: A Historical Grammar of Poetic Myth* (New York: Farrar, Straus and Giroux, 1966), 439–40.

11. Jerome Rothenberg, *Technicians of the Sacred: A Range of Poetries from Africa, America, Asia, Europe & Oceania* (Berkeley: University of California Press, 1985), 563.

12. Simon Ortiz, "How to Make a Good Chili Stew," in *Woven Stone* (Tucson: University of Arizona Press), 175.

13. D. H. Lawrence, "Healing," in *The Rag and Bone Shop of the Heart: Poems*

for Men, ed. Robert Bly, James Hillman, and Michael Meade (New York: HarperCollins, 1992), 113.

14. Wolfgang Giegerich, *The Soul's Logical Life: Towards a Rigorous Notion of Psychology* (Frankfurt: Peter Lang, 1998), 18.

15. Lao Tzu, *Tao Te Ching: A Book About The Way and the Power of The Way* trans. Ursula K. Le Guin (Boston: Shambhala, 1997), 22–23.

16. Graves, *The White Goddess,* 316.

17. Rivkah Harris, "Images of Women in the Gilgamesh Epic," in *Gilgamesh: A Reader,* ed. John Maier (Wauconda, Ill.: Bolchazy-Carducci Publishers, 1997), 82.

18. William Irwin Thompson, *Coming Into Being: Artifacts and Texts in the Evolution of Consciousness* (New York: St. Martin's Press, 1996), 211.

19. Girardot, *Myth and Meaning in Early Taoism,* 303–4.

20. William Irwin Thompson, *Coming Into Being,* 209–10.

21. Robert Bly, "The Sun Crosses Heaven from West to East Bringing Samson Back to the Womb," in *Meditations on the Insatiable Soul* (New York: HarperPerennial, 1994), 82. Also entitled "Time Runs Backward After Death," in *Collected Poems* (New York: W. W. Norton, 2018), 305. The poem is quoted in four parts throughout this chapter.

22. William Blake, "The Marriage of Heaven and Hell," in *The Complete Poetry and Prose of William Blake,* ed. David V. Erdman (Berkeley: University of California Press, 1982), 36.

23. Blake, *Complete Poetry,* 35.

24. Heinrich Zimmer, *The King and the Corpse: Tales of the Soul's Conquest of Evil* (Princeton, N.J.: Bollingen, Princeton University Press, 1956), 259.

25. César Vallejo, "Our Daily Bread," in *Neruda and Vallejo: Selected Poems,* trans. James Wright (Boston: Beacon, 1971), 199.

26. Lao Tzu, *Tao Te Ching,* 70.

27. Mircea Eliade, *Shamanism: Archaic Techniques of Ecstasy* (Chicago: University of Chicago Press, 1964), 205.

28. Blake, *Complete Poetry,* 36.

29. Goethe, "The Holy Longing," in *The Rag and Bone Shop of the Heart: Poems for Men,* ed. Robert Bly, James Hillman, and Michael Meade (New York: HarperCollins, 1992), 382.

Select Bibliography

Avens, Roberts. *Imaginal Body: Para-Jungian Reflections on Soul, Imagination and Death*. Washington, D.C.: University Press of America, 1982.

Barba, Eugenio, and Nicola Savarese. *A Dictionary of Theatre Anthropology: The Secret Art of the Performer*. London: Routledge, 1991.

Berman, Morris. *Coming to Our Senses: Body and Spirit in the Hidden History of the West*. New York: Simon and Schuster, 1989.

Blake, William. *The Complete Poetry and Prose of William Blake*. David V. Erdman, ed. Berkeley: University of California Press, 1982.

Bly, Robert. *American Poetry: Wildness and Domesticity*. New York: Harper & Row, 1990.

———. *Eating the Honey of Words: New and Selected Poems*. New York: Harper-Flamingo, 1999.

———. *Iron John: A Book About Men*. Reading, Mass.: Addison-Wesley, 1990.

———. *Leaping Poetry: An Idea with Poems and Translations*. Boston: A Seventies Press Book, Beacon Press, 1990.

———. *Neruda and Vallejo: Selected Poems*. Robert Bly, John Knoepfle, and James Wright, trans. Boston: Beacon, 1971.

———. *The Rag and Bone Shop of the Heart: Poems for Men*. Robert Bly, James Hillman, and Michael Meade, eds. New York: HarperCollins, 1992.

———. *The Sibling Society*. Reading, Mass.: Addison-Wesley, 1996.

———. *The Soul Is Here for Its Own Joy: Sacred Poems from Many Cultures*. Robert Bly, ed. Hopewell, N.J.: The Ecco Press, 1995.

Bly, Robert, and Marion Woodman. *The Maiden King: The Reunion of Masculine and Feminine*. New York: Henry Holt and Company, 1998.

Bohm, David. *Wholeness and the Implicate Order*. London: Routledge & Kegan Paul, 1980.

Bringhurst, Robert. *The Calling: Selected Poems 1970–1995*. Toronto: McClelland & Stewart, 1995.

Campbell, Joseph. *The Flight of the Wild Gander*. South Bend, Ind.: Regency / Gateway, 1979.

———. *The Masks of God, vol. I: Primitive Mythology* and *vol. IV: Creative Mythology*. New York: Penguin Arkana, 1991.

———. *Part 1: Mythologies of the Primitive Hunters and Gatherers Historical Atlas of World Mythology, vol. 1: The Way of the Animal Powers*. New York: Perennial Library, Harper & Row, 1988.

———. *Part 2: Mythologies of the Great Hunt Historical Atlas of World Mythology, vol. 1: The Way of the Animal Powers*. New York: Perennial Library, Harper & Row, 1988.

Chevalier, Jean, and Alain Gheerbrant. *The Penguin Dictionary of Symbols*. John Buchanan-Brown, trans. London: Penguin Books, 1996.

Cirlot, J. E. *A Dictionary of Symbols*. Jack Sage, trans. New York: Barnes & Noble, 1995.

Doty, William G. *Mythography: The Study of Myths and Rituals*. Tuscaloosa: University of Alabama Press, 1986.

Doty, William G., and William J. Hynes. *Mythical Trickster Figures: Contours, Contexts, and Criticisms*. Tuscaloosa: University of Alabama Press, 1993.

Eliade, Mircea. *Autobiography: Journey East, Journey West. Vol. 1: 1907–1937*. Mac Linscott Ricketts, trans. San Francisco: Harper & Row, 1981.

———. *Cosmos and History: The Myth of the Eternal Return*. Willard R. Trask, trans. New York: Harper Torchbooks, Harper & Brothers, 1954.

———. *From the Stone Age to the Eleusinian Mysteries, Vol. 1* in *A History of Religious Ideas*. Willard R. Trask, trans. Chicago: University of Chicago Press, 1978.

———. *The Sacred and the Profane: The Nature of Religion*. Willard R. Trask, trans. San Diego, Calif.: Harcourt, Brace & Company, 1957.

———. *Shamanism: Archaic Techniques of Ecstasy*. Willard R. Trask, trans. Chicago: University of Chicago Press, 1964.

Emigh, John. *Masked Performance: The Play of Self and Other in Ritual and Theatre*. Philadelphia: University of Pennsylvania Press, 1996.

Erdoes, Richard, and Alfonso Ortiz. *American Indian Trickster Tales*. New York: Penguin, 1998.

Ford, Clyde W. *The Hero with an African Face: Mythic Wisdom of Traditional Africa*. New York: Bantam, 1999.

Gardner, Howard. *Creating Minds: An Anatomy of Creativity Seen Through the Lives of Freud, Einstein, Picasso, Stravinsky, Eliot, Graham, and Gandhi*. New York: BasicBooks, HarperCollins, 1993.

————. *Frames of Mind: The Theory of Multiple Intelligences*. New York: BasicBooks, HarperCollins, 1983.

Gardner, John, and John Maier. *Gilgamesh: Translated from the Sîn-leqi-unninni Version*. New York: Vintage Books, 1985.

Giegerich, Wolfgang. *The Soul's Logical Life: Towards a Rigorous Notion of Psychology*. Frankfurt: Peter Lang, 1998.

Girardot, N. J. *Myth and Meaning in Early Taoism: The Theme of Chaos (hun-tun)*. Berkeley: University of California Press, 1983.

Graves, Robert. *The White Goddess: A Historical Grammar of Poetic Myth*. New York: Farrar, Straus and Giroux, 1966.

Guggenbühl-Craig, Adolf. *The Old Fool and the Corruption of Myth*. Dorothea Wilson, trans. Dallas, Tex.: Spring Publications, 1991.

Highwater, Jamake. *The Mythology of Transgression: Homosexuality as Metaphor*. New York: Oxford University Press, 1997.

Hillman, James. *The Dream and the Underworld*. New York: Harper & Row, 1979.

————. *The Thought of the Heart and the Soul of the World*. Dallas, Tex.: Spring Publications, 1981, 1982.

Hyde, Lewis. *Trickster Makes This World: Mischief, Myth, and Art*. New York: Farrar, Straus and Giroux, 1998.

Kane, Sean. *Wisdom of the Mythtellers*. Peterborough, Ontario: Broadview Press, 1994.

Lao Tzu. *Tao Te Ching: A Book About The Way and the Power of The Way*. Ursula K. Le Guin, trans. Boston: Shambhala, 1997.

Maier, John, ed., *Gilgamesh: A Reader*. Wauconda, Ill.: Bolchazy-Carducci Publishers, 1997.

Matthews, Caitlin, and John Matthews. *The Encyclopedia of Celtic Wisdom: The Celtic Shaman's Sourcebook*. Shaftesbury, Dorset, UK: Element Books, 1994.

McNeely, Deldon Anne. *Mercury Rising: Women, Evil and the Trickster Gods*. Woodstock, Conn.: Spring Publications, 1996.

Meade, Michael. *Men and the Water of Life: Initiation and the Tempering of Men*. San Francisco: HarperSanFrancisco, 1993.

Miller, David L. *Hells & Holy Ghosts: A Theopoetics of Christian Belief*. Nashville, Tenn.: Abingdon Press, 1989.

Milosz, Czeslaw, ed. *A Book of Luminous Things: An International Anthology of Poetry*. New York: Harcourt, 1996.

Nouwen, Henri, J. M. *The Wounded Healer: Ministry in Contemporary Society*. New York: Image Books, 1979.

Paul, Sherman. *In Search of the Primitive: Rereading David Antin, Jerome Rothenberg, and Gary Snyder*. Baton Rouge: Louisiana State University Press, 1986.

Patchen, Kenneth. *The Collected Poems of Kenneth Patchen*. New York: New Directions, 1968.

———. *The Journal of Albion Moonlight*. New York: Padell, 1941.

Pelton, Robert D. *The Trickster in West Africa: A Study of Mythic Irony and Sacred Delight*. Berkeley: University of California Press, 1980.

Radin, Paul. *The Trickster: A Study in American Indian Mythology*. New York: Shocken Books, 1956.

Rothenberg, Jerome. *PRE-FACES & Other Writings*. New York: New Directions, 1981.

———, and Diane Rothenberg, eds. *Symposium of the Whole*. Berkeley: University of California Press, 1983.

———, ed. *Technicians of the Sacred: A Range of Poetries from Africa, America, Asia, Europe & Oceania*. Berkeley: University of California Press, 1985.

———, and Pierre Joris, eds. *Poems for the Millennium: The University of California Book of Modern & Postmodern Poetry, Volume One: From Fin-de-Siecle to Negritude*. Berkeley: University of California Press, 1995.

———, and Pierre Joris, eds. *Poems for the Millennium: The University of California Book of Modern & Postmodern Poetry, Volume Two: From Postwar to Millennium*. Berkeley: University of California Press, 1998.

Schechner, Richard. *The Future of Ritual: Writings on Culture and Performance*. London: Routledge, 1993.

———. *Performance Theory*. New York: Routledge, 1977.

Schechner, Richard, and Willa Appel, ed. *By Means of Performance: Intercultural Studies of Theatre and Ritual*. Cambridge: Cambridge University Press, 1990.

Sheldrake, Rupert. *The Presence of the Past: Morphic Resonance & the Habits of Nature*. Rochester, Vt.: Park Street Press, 1988.

Stafford, William. *The Way It Is*. Saint Paul, Minn.: Graywolf Press, 1997.

Taussig, Michael. *The Nervous System*. New York: Routledge, 1992.

———. *Shamanism, Colonialism, and the Wild Man: A Study in Terror and Healing*. Chicago: University of Chicago Press, 1987.

Thompson, William Irwin. *Imaginary Landscape: Making Worlds of Myth and Science*. New York: St. Martin's Press, 1989.

Turner, Victor W. *The Anthropology of Performance*. Richard Schechner, ed. New York: PAJ Publications, 1987.

———. *The Ritual Process: Structure and Anti-Structure*. Chicago: Aldine Publishing Company, 1969.

Unamuno, Miguel de. *The Tragic Sense of Life*. J. E. Crawford Flitch, trans. New York: Dover Publications, 1954.

Wallin, Nils L. *Biomusicology: Neurophysiological, Neuropsychological, and Evolutionary Perspectives on the Origins and Purposes of Music*. Stuyvesant, N.Y.: Pendragon Press, 1991.

White, David Gordon. *Myths of the Dog-Man*. Chicago: University of Chicago Press, 1991.

Zimmer, Heinrich. *The King and the Corpse: Tales of the Soul's Conquest of Evil*. Joseph Campbell, ed. Princeton, N.J.: Princeton University Press, 1956.

Index

About the Authors and the Mythsinger Legacy Project

Daniel Deardorff (1952–2019) was a "singer" in the old sense of that word: a musician, a storyteller, and a maker of ritual. Spanning more than five decades, his career as a composer, performer, recording artist, and producer included ten years touring with renowned soft-rock band Seals and Crofts and producing award-winning albums for other artists. A polio survivor from infancy, Deardorff used a wheelchair for most of his sixty-seven years; this gave him a lived perspective that deeply informed his views on myth. At mid-life, when post-polio sequelae required change, Deardorff focused his work as an independent scholar of myth and became a prominent figure in the area of mythopoesis (myth-making) as well as one of the early contemporary teachers about "Otherness." He taught frequently with poet and mentor Robert Bly, mythologist Martin Shaw, and others. In his last years, Deardorff enjoyed a musical resurgence composing collections of songs rich in mythic imagery and previously untold life stories. Mythsingerlegacy.org is continuing his work, restoring myth to culture and community.

Robert Bly (1926–2021) was one of America's preeminent poets. In his numerous roles as groundbreaking poet, editor, translator, storyteller, and father of what he has called "the expressive men's movement," Bly remained one of the most influential American artists of the last half of the twentieth century and the first decades of the twenty-first.

Dr. Martin Shaw is the award-winning author of many books, his most recent include: *Smoke Hole, Courting the Wild Twin,* and *The Night Wages.* Reader in Poetics at Dartington Art School (UK), Shaw founded both the Oral Tradition and Mythic Life courses at Stanford University (US).

Robert Simmons is the author of *The Alchemy of Stones, The Book of Stones,* and *Stones of the New Consciousness* and co-founder of Heaven and Earth, a company offering gem and jewelry creations for healing, as well as spiritual and emotional development. A long-time friend and creative co-conspirator with Daniel Deardorff, he co-published the second edition of *The Other Within* and introduced Inner Traditions • Bear & Company to Deardorff's work.

Judith-Kate Friedman is an award-winning performing songwriter, producer, and multi-media artist. Her publications include musical recordings, poetry, radio broadcasts, documentary film, and scholarly writing about the cognitive and physical benefits of music-making. She and Daniel Deardorff met at the crossroads of art, activism, ritual, oral tradition, and social practice at Robert Bly's Great Mother Conference. They shared love and creative partnership for fourteen years.

About the Mythsinger Legacy Project

In his last decade Daniel Deardorff had a creative renaissance: He founded the Mythsinger Foundation to *restore the wisdom of myth to culture and community.* He led rites of passage camps for young men, created *Living Myth, Living World,* a five-year 100-day immersive course in myth and ritual, wrote essays and composed, performed, and produced three albums of yet-to-be released music, from his bedside digital studio. With life partner Judith-Kate Friedman, he began working on a documentary film about his life. His work is now being carried forward by the Mythsinger Legacy Project, a project of the Songwriting Works Educational Foundation (501c3 charitable organization). Learn more at mythsingerlegacy.org.

Credits